Engaging Students
Through Global Issues

W9-CUA-363

Facing the Future

Engaging Students through Global Issues:
Activity-Based Lessons and Action Projects

Engaging Students through Global Issues: Activity-Based Lessons and Action Projects

Developed by *Facing the Future: People and the Planet*

Copyright © 2006 *Facing the Future: People and the Planet*

In general, it is necessary to obtain advance, written permission to copy *Facing the Future* publications. However, since worksheets, tests, quizzes and other student handouts in *Facing the Future* publications are designed to be copied and distributed in class, it is not necessary for an individual educator to request permission from *Facing the Future* to make copies of these student handouts for use by his or her students in a school or other nonprofit educational organization.

Other than the exception outlined above for the non-commercial purposes of teachers and individual classrooms, USERS MAY NOT REPRODUCE, MODIFY, TRANSLATE, SELL OR DISTRIBUTE THE MATERIALS FOR ANY PURPOSE WITHOUT *FACING THE FUTURE'S* PRIOR WRITTEN AUTHORIZATION. To request written authorization, please contact *Facing the Future* at office@facingthefuture.org. Users must provide proper attribution and identifying information for *Facing the Future* as the author and developer of the materials, and may not delete or in any manner alter any copyright, trademark or other proprietary rights notices that have been placed on the materials.

ISBN 0-9711005-5-1
Printed on recycled paper

Some lessons in this book are updated from ones that appeared in *Facing the Future: People and the Planet Curriculum Guide*, developed by *Facing the Future: People and the Planet*, 2002

Facing the Future is a nonprofit, nonpartisan organization providing resources and community action opportunities on global issues and sustainability for teachers, students, and the public. For more information about *Facing the Future* and to order copies of this book, visit our website at www.facingthefuture.org or contact us at:

FACING THE FUTURE
811 First Avenue, Suite 454
Seattle, WA 98104
(206) 264-1503
Email: office@facingthefuture.org

www.facingthefuture.org

Acknowledgements

Lesson Developers & Writers

Gilda Wheeler, M.Ed.
Program Director, *Facing the Future*
Kim Rakow Bernier, M.P.A.
Outreach Director, *Facing the Future*
Josh Michael Isgur
M.P.A. Candidate, Evans School of Public Affairs,
University of Washington
Heidi Radenovic
Program Assistant, *Facing the Future*
Andra DeVoght, M.P.H.
Population Health, University of Washington
Wendy Church, Ph.D.
Executive Director, *Facing the Future*

Research and Editorial Assistants

Caitlin Dean, *Facing the Future* Intern
Adriane Nowland, *Facing the Future* Intern
Adam Sher, *Facing the Future* volunteer

Teacher, Student, & Expert Reviewers

Larry Steele and his students at
Franklin High School
Ben Wheeler and his students at Rainier Scholars
and at Explorer West Middle School
Abigail Banker and her students at
Rainier Scholars
Wendy Ewbank and her students at
Seattle Girls' School
Marie Marrs and her students at
Eagle Harbor High School
Lisa Becerra, Teacher, Washington Middle School
Dave Ketter, Teacher, Summit K-12
Laine Lenihan and her students at
Auburn Riverside High School
Amy Locke, Student, Franklin High School
Jacqueline Sherris, Ph.D, Director of
Reproductive Health Strategic Program, Program
for Appropriate Technology in Health
Sandra Pederson, M.Ed., Freelance Editor, Writer
&Training Materials Consultant
Mark Jordahl, Wilderness Awareness School

Copy Editors

Sandra Pederson
Cecilia Lund

Design and Layout

Amy Marchegiani, Graf X design

Facing the Future Advisory Council

Char Alkire
Science Teacher Supervisor,
University of Washington
Jim Bennett
Vice President,
Cinematch Engineering Netflix
John DeGraaf
Filmmaker and Author of "Affluenza:
The All-Consuming Epidemic"
Dee Dickinson
Founder and CEO,
New Horizons for Learning
Wendy Ewbank
Social Studies and Language Arts
Teacher, Seattle Girls' School
Scott Jamieson
Science Teacher, Lakeside School
Marie Marrs
Global Sustainability and Language Arts
Teacher, Eagle Harbor High School
Kate McPherson
Director, Project Service Leadership
Robin Pasquarella
CEO, Alliance for Education
Abby Ruskey
Executive Director, Environmental
Education Association of Washington
Dr. Debra Sullivan
Dean, Praxis Institute for
Early Childhood Education
Dr. Anand Yang
Director, Jackson School of International
Studies, University of Washington

We dedicate this book to Nancy Ketcham and her family, who consistently demonstrate their belief in the positive power of education, and to Alden Garrett, whose ongoing support and dedication have been invaluable to our work.

Table of Contents

Activity-Based Lessons

Introduction to Global Issues and Sustainability

A fun way to introduce your students to
global issues and sustainability vocabulary
words and concepts. Includes an
intermediate and advanced puzzle.
R, W, SS, ENV

Use this trivia game to test your students'
knowledge of global issues. Students
collaborate in teams to answer questions
about world population, economics, and
environmental issues. **M, SS, SC, ENV**

Students debate a controversial global
issue standing on opposite sides of the
room, organized by whether they agree or
disagree with a statement provided by the
teacher. This exercise is a great "hook" to
get students interested in further study of
global issues. **SS, SC, ENV**

Key to Learning

M = Appropriate for **Math**

R = Includes a **Reading** focus

W = Includes a **Writing** connection

T = Includes a **Technology** connection

SS = Appropriate for **Social Studies**

SC = Appropriate for **Science** (Life, Earth, or Physical)

ENV = Appropriate for **Environmental Science**

© 2006 FACING THE FUTURE: PEOPLE AND THE PLANET   www.facingthefuture.org

Quality of Life and Community Indicators

In this economics simulation, students graph changes in the personal incomes of different community residents and in the community's proportion of the Gross Domestic Product (GDP) following an oil spill. The lesson explores the effect of an environmental disaster on the GDP, and the accuracy of GDP as a measurement of a community's overall health. **M, R, T, SS, ENV**

Students develop indicators to measure quality of life and conduct a survey of peers and adults to obtain data for their indicators. They analyze the survey data using spreadsheet software and then compare their own performance as measured by the quality of life indicators against averages determined by the survey results.
M, W, T, SS, ENV

Media Literacy

In this media literacy activity, students use an "iceberg model" to analyze the global patterns and underlying structural causes that drive events in the news.
R, W, T, SS, ENV

Students work in groups to create and present mock television commercials for products linked to unsustainable or unhealthy behavior. Students first present the commercial as it would typically be seen on television, and then present it again incorporating the product's negative impacts. **W, SS, ENV**

Global Health

Students compare life expectancy (a common indicator of good health) among several countries and discuss possible explanations for the differences. They also examine the connection between per capita expenditures on health care and life expectancy. **M, W, T, SS, SC**

Students learn about the impact of today's most urgent global health issues (such as HIV/AIDS, malaria, and tuberculosis), and practical solutions to help address these issues. The activity concludes with a writing assignment in which students research and develop a proposal to address a particular global health issue. **R, W, T, SS, SC**

Governance

Students create a national energy policy via cooperation and negotiation among the 3 faces of governance: the State (Government), Civic Organizations, and the Private Sector. In groups representing each of these areas, students work to accomplish their individual policy goals while negotiating and forming coalitions with other groups to strengthen their overall energy policy. **R, W, T, SS, SC, ENV**

© 2006 FACING THE FUTURE: PEOPLE AND THE PLANET www.facingthefuture.org

About this Book

Engaging Students through Global Issues includes 40 inspiring lesson plans to help students understand complex global issues and sustainable solutions, and offers creative tools for them to take action in their local and global community. The book can be used as a core teaching component for a semester or year-long course, as a short unit on global issues, or as an engaging contextual framework within which core subjects are taught. Lessons are designed for a range of student levels, from advanced elementary to middle and high school classes. Many lessons are also appropriate for undergraduate college courses. Pages 19-20 include sample modules for middle and high school science and social studies classes.

Use this book for a short unit in:	**Use this book as a core teaching component for:**	**Use activities in this book as an engaging framework to teach core subjects and skills in:**
• Life Science • Physical Science • U.S. History • World History • Economics • Business/Finance • Math • Language Arts • Health/Nutrition	• Global Studies • Environmental Education • World Issues • Global Sustainability • Geography • Contemporary World Problems • Civics and Civic Engagement • Service Learning • ESL Social Studies/Science	• Social Studies • Science • Reading and writing comprehension • Math applications • Critical thinking and problem solving • Student collaboration

These interactive and engaging lessons address a range of learning styles and student populations and include both collaborative and individual activities.

All lessons have been reviewed and field tested by content experts, teachers, and students.

Each lesson plan includes everything you need from start to finish including materials, timing, step-by-step instructions, assessment for both intermediate and advanced students, action project ideas, resources for further information, and reproducible handouts. Lessons also include extension activities to explore issues further and to make writing, technology, math, and art connections. All lessons reference reading from *Facing the Future's* intermediate textbook, ***Global Issues and Sustainable Solutions: Population, Poverty, Consumption, Conflict and the Environment*** and advanced textbook, ***It's All Connected: A Comprehensive Guide to Global Issues and Sustainable Solutions***.

Facing the Future lessons are:
- Aligned with national and state learning standards
- Culturally appropriate
- Interdisciplinary: relevant to social studies, science, math, and language arts
- Geared toward multiple intelligences/learning styles

 © 2006 FACING THE FUTURE: PEOPLE AND THE PLANET www.facingthefuture.org

Facing the Future Resources for Educators

Facing the Future offers a comprehensive set of resources for educators and students for teaching global issues and sustainability. Our resources include student textbooks, activity-based lessons, an extensive website of teaching and learning resources, action opportunities and service learning projects, professional development educator workshops, and consulting services as described below:

Student Textbooks and Assessments

Facing the Future student textbooks include an intermediate textbook, ***Global Issues and Sustainable Solutions: Population, Poverty, Consumption, Conflict, and the Environment*** (GISS) and an advanced textbook, ***It's All Connected: A Comprehensive Guide to Global Issues and Sustainable Solutions*** (IAC). Our student textbooks are fully-referenced, engaging, and highlight positive youth-centered solutions to complex global issues. We also offer free downloadable ***Teacher's Companion Reading Review and Assessments*** which include chapter-by-chapter short answer and essay questions to accompany the textbooks. To preview and order our student textbooks and to download the free *Teacher's Companions* please visit **www.facingthefuture.org.**

Activity-Based Lessons

A core component of *Facing the Future* resources is engaging hands-on activities to help students understand complex global issues and inspire them to take action. ***Engaging Students through Global Issues: Activity-Based Lessons and Action Projects*** offers rigorous and relevant ways for you to bring global issues alive in your classroom. Each activity is designed to help students understand key concepts, internalize issues, develop critical thinking skills, and implement sustainable solutions.

Service Learning and Community Action Projects

Facing the Future offers research, tools, models, and ideas for incorporating service learning and action projects in your classroom. Each activity-based lesson includes an **Action Projects** section providing ideas that are directly related to the content addressed in the activity. You can also find action opportunities on our website for national and local projects that your students can participate in. For more information about *Facing the Future*'s service learning and action opportunities, see page 21.

Website

Facing the Future's website includes extensive resources for teachers and students, including downloadable lessons, service learning projects, youth-centered action opportunities, and additional information and resources on global issues and sustainable solutions. Please visit our site at **www.facingthefuture.org.**

Professional Development Educator Workshops

Facing the Future offers hands-on, interactive workshops and in-services for classroom teachers, pre-service teachers, and community educators. These workshops build global literacy; promote critical thinking and problem solving; explore strategies and tools to help educators integrate global sustainability into their curriculum; and provide educators with proven techniques to engage students through action and service learning. For more information about *Facing the Future* workshops, please visit our website.

Consulting Services

Facing the Future consults with schools, districts, and states interested in the integration of global issues and sustainability across the curriculum. Experienced *Facing the Future* staff is available to collaboratively assess your school and faculty needs and design an appropriate program. For more information about these and other professional development services, please visit our website.

Lesson Number and Title:

1. Crossword Puzzles
2. Global Issues Trivia
3. Sides Debate
4. Making Global Connections
5. From Issue to Opportunity
6. Is it Sustainable?
7. Systems Are Dynamic
8. Bears in the Air
9. How Big is a Billion?
10. Splash But Don't Crash
11. Seeking Asylum
12. Watch Where You Step
13. Now Hear This!
14. When the Chips Are Down
15. Farming for the Future
16. Every Drop Counts
17. Fueling the Future
18. Biodiversity Connections
19. Toil for Oil
20. Fishing for the Future

SUBJECT AREA	CLASS	1	2	3	4	5	6	7	8	9	10	11	12	13	14	15	16	17	18	19	20
SOCIAL STUDIES	World History		X	X	X						X	X		X		X		X			
	World Cultures		X	X																	
	Ancient Civilizations														X						
	Geography	X	X	X	X	X	X	X	X	X	X	X	X	X	X	X	X	X		X	X
	U.S. History											X								X	
	Civics/ Government		X	X			X	X	X									X			
	Economics		X	X	X	X	X	X	X	X		X	X	X	X	X				X	X
	Global Studies	X	X	X	X		X	X	X	X	X	X	X	X	X	X	X	X	X	X	X
	Contemporary World Problems		X	X		X			X					X		X	X	X		X	X
SCIENCE	Earth		X	X				X									X	X		X	
	Environmental	X	X	X	X	X	X	X	X	X	X	X	X	X	X	X	X	X	X	X	X
	Life		X	X	X	X		X	X	X	X		X	X	X	X			X		X
	Physical							X	X									X			
MATH			X							X	X			X	X	X	X	X		X	X
LANGUAGE ARTS		X		X														X			
JOURNALISM																					
BUSINESS / FINANCE			X						X												
HEALTH / NUTRITION																X					
GRADE LEVEL		5-12	5-12	5-12	5-10	9-12	7-12	5-12	5-12	5-8	5-9	6-11	5-11	5-12	7-11	5-12	5-12	7-12	5-9	5-9	6-12

© 2006 FACING THE FUTURE: PEOPLE AND THE PLANET   www.facingthefuture.org

Subject Area Chart — Lessons 21–40

Lesson Number and Title	21 What's Up With the GDP?	22 Livin' the Good Life?	23 What's In The News?	24 Are You Buying This?!	25 Life: The Long and Short of It	26 Partners for Health	27 Three Faces of Governance	28 Taxes: Choices and Trade-offs	29 Take a Step for Equity	30 Shop Till You Drop	31 Let Them Eat Cake	32 Everyone Does Better When Women Do Better	33 What's Debt Got to Do With It?	34 Microcredit for Sustainable Development	35 To Fight or Not to Fight?	36 Worldview Mingle	37 Who Are the Nacirema?	38 Metaphors for the Future	39 Deep Space 3000	40 Creating Our Future
SOCIAL STUDIES — World History			X											X	X		X			X
World Cultures			X											X	X	X	X			X
Ancient Civilizations																				
Geography	X	X	X		X		X		X	X	X	X		X	X	X	X	X	X	X
U.S. History			X				X	X									X			
Civics/Government		X	X			X	X						X	X	X			X		X
Economics	X	X	X		X	X	X	X	X	X	X	X	X	X	X					X
Global Studies	X	X	X	X	X	X	X		X	X	X	X	X	X	X	X	X	X	X	X
Contemporary World Problems		X	X	X	X	X	X		X	X	X	X	X	X	X	X	X		X	X
SCIENCE — Earth							X													X
Environmental	X	X	X	X			X	X	X	X	X				X	X	X	X	X	X
Life					X	X				X		X							X	X
Physical							X												X	X
MATH	X	X			X			X		X	X	X	X	X						
LANGUAGE ARTS			X	X													X	X		
JOURNALISM			X	X																
BUSINESS / FINANCE	X	X		X				X					X	X						
HEALTH / NUTRITION					X	X	X			X		X								
GRADE LEVEL	7-12	9-12	9-12	6-12	6-11	9-11	10-12	7-11	7-12	6-12	5-11	7-11	8-11	9-12	9-12	9-12	9-12	7-12	7-10	5-12

© 2006 FACING THE FUTURE: PEOPLE AND THE PLANET   www.facingthefuture.org

National and State Standards Consistency

Lessons in this book address national education standards including National Council for the Social Studies (NCSS) and National Science Education Standards (NSES). Specific consistency with NCSS and NSES standards is indicated in each lesson. *Facing the Future* curriculum is also aligned with several state educational standards. Visit **www.facingthefuture.org** for state-specific standards alignment.

NATIONAL SOCIAL STUDIES AND SCIENCE STANDARDS REFERENCED IN LESSONS

National Council for the Social Studies (NCSS) Standards

Strand 1– Culture

Strand 2– Time, Continuity, and Change

Strand 3– People, Places, and Environments

Strand 4– Individual Development and Identity

Strand 5– Individuals, Groups, and Institutions

Strand 6– Power, Authority, and Governance

Strand 7– Production, Distribution, and Consumption

Strand 8– Science, Technology, and Society

Strand 9– Global Connections

Strand 10– Civic Ideas and Practices

National Science Education Standards (NSES)

Content Standard A– Science as Inquiry

Content Standard B– Physical Science

Content Standard C– Life Science

Content Standard D– Earth and Space Science

Content Standard E– Science and Technology

Content Standard F– Science in Personal and Social Perspectives

Content Standard G– History and Nature of Science

© 2006 FACING THE FUTURE: PEOPLE AND THE PLANET   www.facingthefuture.org

SUBJECT	GRADE	CLASS	MODULE
Social Studies	Middle School	Geography	Where Do We Stand? Human Footprints on Earth

Activities / Reading / Homework / Additional Resources

Day 1	**Systems Thinking** – FTF Lesson: *Systems are Dynamic*. Homework: Read Chapter 2 from GISS and do questions from GISS Teachers' Reading Review and Assessment, or write response to question: "What future do you want to see?"
Day 2	**Ecological Footprints** – FTF Lesson: *Watch Where You Step*. Homework: Take the "Footprint Quiz" www.myfootprint.org; Write response to question: "Can everyone live the way I do? Why or why not?"
Day 3 & 4	**Modeling Growth: Envisioning a System** – FTF Lesson: *When the Chips are Down*. Homework: Respond to question: "What different choices would you have made in your country if you had known what was going to happen? How did the game make you feel? Why?" Read Chapter 4 from GISS.
Day 5	**Creative Action** –Discuss and commit to an action project. Examples: Make posters describing ways to lessen personal ecological footprints; Evaluate the cafeteria food and propose alternatives; Write an article for a school or local paper; Make a pledge and sign it: Do a "trash audit" for your school; Do "Destination Conservation" (find out how at www.facingthefuture.org).

Additional Resources
Books: *Stuff: the Secret Lives of Everyday Things* (Ryan and Durning, 1997)*; Material World* (Menzel, 1994)
Films: *Finding Balance; Jam Packed; Cost of Cool; World in Balance*

SUBJECT	GRADE	CLASS	MODULE
Social Studies	High School	Economics	For Love or Money?

Activities / Reading / Homework / Additional Resources

Day 1	**What is a Fair Share?** – FTF Lesson: *Let Them Eat Cake*. Homework: Read Unit 5, Chapter 2 from IAC and write a response to the question: "What is inequity? What are some consequences of the unequal distribution of wealth?"
Day 2	**Experiencing Economic Inequality** – FTF Lesson: *Take a Step for Equity*. Facilitate a discussion based on reflection questions. Homework: Read Unit 5, Chapter 3 from IAC. Write a response to the question: "What do you think are some solutions to the issue of inequity?"
Day 3 & 4	**How Can We Measure Progress?** – FTF Lesson: *What's Up with the GDP?* Homework: Read Unit 6 from IAC. Make a poster of possible solutions to the problems of economic inequality.
Day 5	**A Plan for Justice** –Present posters and commit to 1 or more action projects in small groups or as a class. Examples: Do a Hunger Banquet; students can write a letter to elected officials about a change in policy that unfairly hurts the poor; do Heifer Project International, a service learning project (find out more at www.facingthefuture.org)

Additional Resources
Books: *Stuff: the Secret Lives of Everyday Things* (Ryan and Durning, 1997); *Material World* (Menzel, 1994)
Films: *Finding Balance; Jam Packed; Cost of Cool; World in Balance*

SAMPLE LESSON MODULES

SUBJECT	GRADE	CLASS	MODULE
Science	Middle School	Integrated	Global Issues With Local Solutions

Activities / Reading / Homework / Additional Resources

Day 1	**Global Connections** – FTF Lesson: *Making Global Connections*. Homework: Read Chapter 1 from GISS and have students write a response to the question: "What global issues do you see in your own community and do you see any progress with sustainable solutions to these issues?"
Day 2	**Ecological Footprints** – FTF Lesson: *Watch Where You Step*. Homework: Read Chapter 4 from GISS and take the "Footprint Quiz" at www.myfootprint.org; Have students list ways in which they (or their family) could reduce their ecological footprint.
Day 3	**Subsistence Farming** – FTF Lesson: *Farming for the Future*. Homework: Read Chapter 5 from GISS and write a response to the following statement: "The way that I conduct my daily life at home influences the lives of people in other countries."
Day 4	**Making a Local Connection** – Discuss issues of food security, sustainable agriculture, and energy use in transportation methods with your students. Have them map out their ideal meal, trying to make the origin of their food as local as possible. Facilitate a class discussion about the advantages and drawbacks to creating local food systems.
Day 5	**Edible Garden and Community Farms** –Create an edible garden in your classroom or on your school grounds. Tour a local community gardening project and volunteer to get your hands dirty.

Additional Resources
Books: *Coming Home to Eat: The Pleasures and Politics of Local Foods* (Gary Paul Nabhan, 2002); *Fast Food Nation* (Eric Schlosser, 2002)
Films: *Santiago's Story; The Ecological Footprint: Accounting for a Small Planet*

SUBJECT	GRADE	CLASS	MODULE
Science	High School	Life	Global Health Issues

Activities / Reading / Homework / Additional Resources

Day 1	**Resource Distribution** – FTF Lesson: *Shop Till You Drop*. Homework: Read Chapters 3 & 4 from Unit 5 in IAC. Write a letter to your government or the government of a developing country proposing a solution to inequitable resource distribution.
Day 2	**Life Expectancy** – FTF Lesson: *Life: The Long and Short of It*. Homework: Read Chapters 6 & 7 from Unit 5 in IAC. Create a health policy for a fictitious country.
Day 3	**Global Health Issues** – FTF Lesson: *Partners for Health*. Homework: Read Chapter 5 from Unit 5 in IAC. Do the "Advocates for Health" writing assignment in the Partners for Health Lesson.
Day 4	**Government Policy and Action**– Facilitate a discussion about government action and policy and the role of nonprofits in social welfare.
Day 5	**Class Action** –Brainstorm ways in which students can participate in global health activism. Create awareness-raising posters to put up around school. Fundraise for a nonprofit working towards AIDS prevention or other global health issues.

Additional Resources
Books: *Mountains Beyond Mountains* (Kidder, 2003); *Invisible Enemies: Stories of Infectious Disease* (Farrell et. al., 2005)
Films: *Rx for Survival: A Global Health Challenge; Silent Killer: The Unfinished Campaign Against Hunger*

Service Learning and Community Action Projects

After building your students' awareness about global issues through *Facing the Future*'s engaging, hands-on lessons, they are likely to ask, "But what can we do to help?" Students today are inundated with stories about how global issues such as global warming, acid rain, HIV/AIDS, rainforest degradation, population growth, conflict, and global poverty are impacting people and the planet. The complexity and magnitude of these issues can leave young people feeling overwhelmed. **In fact, the global situation is one of the best arguments for incorporating service learning and personal action into your classroom.** Issues taking place in our local communities are often extensions of issues that are global in nature; so getting your students involved in their immediate environments is an empowering way to start addressing global issues.

Service Learning: What and Why?

Service learning is a teaching method that combines meaningful service with curriculum-based learning. Students improve their academic skills by applying what they learn in school to the real world and then reflecting on their experience, which reinforces the link between their service and in-school learning. The research suggesting the positive benefits of service learning for students includes improvement in academic achievement, personal and social development, civic engagement, and career exploration skills. For links to current research on service learning, visit the **Service Learning Research and Tools** area of our website.

Using Service Learning and Action in Your Classroom

Each activity-based lesson in this guide concludes with an **Action Projects** section providing ideas that are directly related to the content addressed in the activity. Use these ideas as short action opportunities for your students, or develop them into full service learning projects using the **Service Learning Framework** that can be downloaded for free from *Facing the Future*'s website.

For a complete student-driven project planning tool, use the ***Creating Our Future*** activity in this guide to encourage youth voice and ownership in your students' service learning projects. The activity provides a framework to walk students through visioning the future, developing a plan to realize the future they'd like to see, and implementing their plan.

Whether you and your students have 5 minutes, or an entire semester, the list of creative ways to engage your students on global issues is endless. In addition to the ideas listed at the end of each activity in this guide, check out the following resources in the **Take Action** area of our website:

- **Fast Facts, Quick Actions:** Click on specific global issues and find a list of current facts, actions students can take today, and organizations who are working on long-term, structural solutions to these issues.
- **Service Learning Projects:** Browse the service learning database to read about projects that your whole class can participate in. You'll find everything you need to get started.
- **Action Toolbox:** Get creative service learning project fundraising ideas, media tips, and download the *Facing the Future* **action pledge** (also on page 22).

Visit Facing the Future's Website www.facingthefuture.org

© 2006 FACING THE FUTURE: PEOPLE AND THE PLANET   www.facingthefuture.org

I'm taking the Facing the Future pledge!

I, _____

pledge to take action to help create a sustainable world by:

_____

_____

_____

_____

Signature: _____   Date: _____

WORDS ON THE WORLD
CROSSWORD PUZZLE

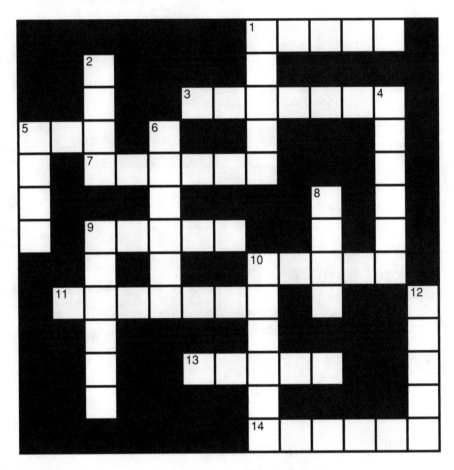

ACROSS

1. The whole wide...
3. Liberty and _____ for all
5. BIG fighting
7. Safe and sound
9. Opposite of #5 across
10. Pleased
11. Use resources
13. Energy from the sun
14. Not enough food

DOWN

1. Trash
2. Autos
4. The electrical kind turns lights on
5. A cool kind of energy
6. Atlantic and Pacific
8. Wish for
9. Human beings
10. Feeling good
12. Swim in it, drink it

IT'S OUR FUTURE
CROSSWORD PUZZLE

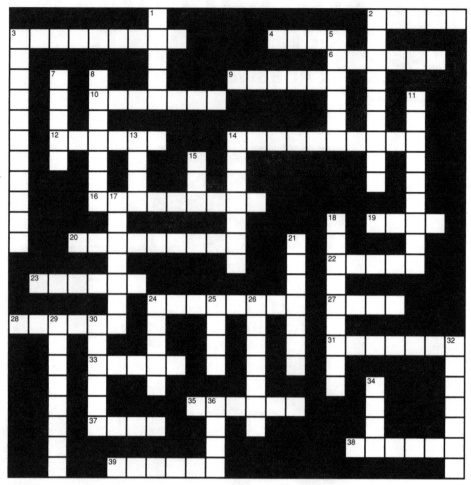

ACROSS

2. Something to drink when you're thirsty
3. Knowledge acquisition
4. Largest, most populous region of the world
6. Grower of food
9. Starvation
10. What geese and other birds do
12. Having an option
14. Over 6 billion worldwide
16. Raw materials
19. Cast a ballot
20. Your use of resources is your ecological _____
22. Wanderer
23. Country
24. Contentious disagreement
27. Air current
28. Wind and solar are 2 forms
31. Edges
33. Body of salt water
35. Make different
37. Lend a hand
38. Safe and sound
39. Folks

DOWN

1. Power from the sun
2. Cultural perspective
3. Our surroundings
5. Continent where Zambia is
7. Everyone living together happily
8. Give choices to
11. Linked
13. Gas guzzlers
14. Lack of wealth
15. Deadly combat
17. Study of balance in nature
18. A resource that regenerates is_____

21. Liberty and ____ ____ for all
24. Not dirty
25. Nourishment for the body
26. See in your mind's eye
29. Having the same rights
30. Getting bigger
32. Biological classification
34. 2-wheeled environmentally clean transport
36. Optimism

CROSSWORD PUZZLE ANSWER KEYS

WORDS ON THE WORLD

IT'S OUR FUTURE

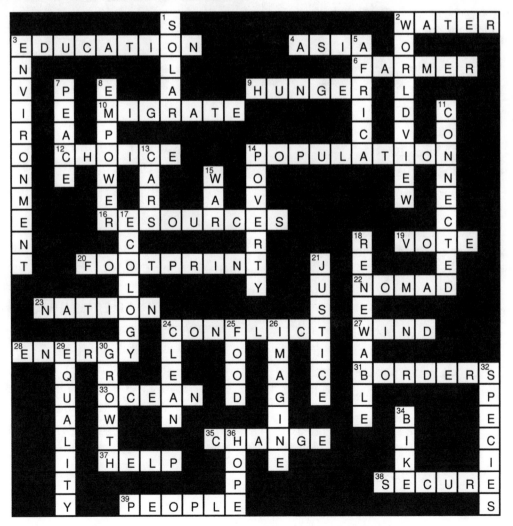

Global Issues Trivia

OVERVIEW

Use this trivia game as an introduction to the study of critical global issues. Students collaborate in teams to answer questions about world population, economics, and environmental issues.

INQUIRY/CRITICAL THINKING QUESTIONS

- How are the issues of population growth, resource consumption, poverty, conflict, and the environment connected?

OBJECTIVES

Students will:
- Collaborate and answer questions about critical global issues

TIME REQUIRED: 30 minutes

KEY ISSUES/CONCEPTS

- **Global Issues**
- **Interconnections**

SUBJECT AREAS

- **Social Studies** (World History, World Cultures, Geography, Civics/Government, Economics, Contemporary World Problems, Global Studies)
- **Science** (Life, Earth, Environmental)
- **Math**
- **Business/Finance**

NATIONAL STANDARDS CONSISTENCY

- **NCSS: 2, 3, 7, 9**
- **NSES: C, F**

GRADE LEVEL: 5–12

Materials/Preparation

Teacher Master: *Global Issues Trivia Questions*

Activity

1. Divide the class into 2 teams and have them arrange their seats so team members can discuss the trivia questions.

2. Give the following directions:
   - Each team will choose a spokesperson
   - Team 1 will be asked a question and then have 10 seconds to discuss the question among their team members and give their answer.
   - For each correct answer, they get 1 point
   - If the team that is asked the question gets it wrong, the other team gets to answer the question
   - Rotate questions between the 2 teams

3. Choose some or all of the trivia questions from the handout *Global Issues Trivia Questions* and begin the game (some questions are multiple-choice).

4. (Optional) You may want to have a prize for the winning team!

Assessment Reflection Questions

For Intermediate and Advanced Students

- What do you think are the most surprising and/or shocking facts?
- Discuss how the issues raised in the game are connected to each other.
- What issue(s) interest you the most and what would you like to learn more about?

Global Issues Trivia Questions

1. What is the current (2005) human population of the world?
    a. 3.5 billion; b. 6.5 billion;
    c. 10.5 billion; d. 18.5 billion

2. What was the world's human population in 1960?
    a. 0.5 billion; b. 1 billion;
    c. 3 billion; d. 5 billion

3. At current rates of growth, what will world population be in 2050?
    About 9 billion

4. What are the first, second, third, and fourth most-populous countries in the world?
    From first to fourth most populous: China, India, United States, Indonesia

5. By about how many people per year is world population growing?
    a. 25 million; b. 55 million;
    c. 80 million; d. 95 million

6. What percentage of the world's people today live in cities?
    a. 10%; b. 25%; c. 50%; d. 80%

7. What city in the world has the largest population?
    Tokyo with 33.2 million

8. Because of urban sprawl in the United States, an area the size of which state is paved over each year?
    a. Texas; b. Delaware;
    c. Rhode Island; d. Kansas

9. In 1950, average life expectancy worldwide was:
    a. 36; b. 49; c. 56; d. 66

10. In 2000, average life expectancy worldwide was:
    a. 46; b. 56; c. 65; d. 76

11. What is the measurement tool called that is used to describe the area of the Earth's surface necessary to support a given human lifestyle?
    Ecological Footprint

12. What country has the largest Ecological Footprint per person?
    a. United States; b. Italy;
    c. Japan; d. Afghanistan

13. What environmental concern is associated with habitat loss? Biodiversity—extinction of species

14. What are some humane methods proven to reduce population growth? Provide access to reproductive health care; educate and empower women; reduce poverty

15. Roughly what percentage of the world's people live on $2 a day or less?
    a. 15%; b. 30%; c. 40%; d. 65%

16. Roughly what percentage of the world's people live on $1 a day or less?
    a. 10%; b. 20%; c. 45%; d. 60%

17. What is the most widely spoken language on Earth? Mandarin Chinese

18. Roughly how many people in the world today are chronically hungry?
    800 million

19. Roughly what percentage of the world's people lack access to a safe water supply? a. 10%; b. 15%; c. 20%; d. 50%

20. Approximately what percentage of global energy do hydrocarbon fuels generate? a. 20%; b. 40%; c. 60%; d. 80%

21. What activity accounts for the highest water use worldwide - agriculture, industry, or domestic? Agriculture accounts for about 65-70% of water use; industry for about 20-25%; and domestic for about 13%

22. Worldwide, how many cars and trucks are in use each day?
    a. 10 million; b. 100 million;
    c. 200 million; d. 600 million

23. What is a renewable resource? A resource such as trees, wind, or fish that can be replaced as it is consumed

24. What element do many scientists believe can provide an unlimited source of clean energy? Hydrogen

Source: *It's All Connected: A Comprehensive Guide to Global Issues and Sustainable Solutions, 2005*

Sides Debate

OVERVIEW

Students debate a controversial global issue, standing on opposite sides of the room depending on whether they agree or disagree with a statement provided by the teacher. They debate the issue and can switch sides if they are convinced by students taking the opposite side. This exercise can be used as a "hook" to introduce several other *Facing the Future* activities.

INQUIRY/CRITICAL THINKING QUESTIONS

- How can we understand an issue from the perspective of another person?
- Can controversial issues always be resolved?

OBJECTIVES

Students will:
- Take a stand on an issue and state their reasons
- Listen to arguments for multiple sides of an issue
- Have the opportunity to change their mind on an issue

TIME REQUIRED: 5-10 minutes

KEY ISSUES/CONCEPTS

- **Controversial issues**
- **Debate**
- **Adopting perspectives**

SUBJECT AREAS

- **Social Studies** (World History, World Cultures, Geography, Civics/Government, Economics, Contemporary World Problems, Global Studies)
- **Science** (Life, Earth, Environmental)
- **Language Arts**

NATIONAL STANDARDS CONSISTENCY

- **NCSS: 2, 3, 7, 9**
- **NSES: C, F**

GRADE LEVEL: 5–12

Materials/Preparation

- Two 8.5 x 11 pieces of paper with "Agree" written on 1 and "Disagree" on the other, posted on opposite sides of the room
- Controversial statement (statements are listed in the activity introduction section of several *Facing the Future* lessons)

Activity

1. Show the class a controversial statement. There are Sides Debate statements included in the Introduction sections of several lessons throughout this guide. You can also develop your own statements based on controversial issues. However, when first introducing this activity, it is helpful to start with a non-controversial issue that the students can use to practice the debate exercise. For example, you can use a statement such as, "It would be better to be a dog than a cat" or "I'd rather live in the city than in the country". Follow the steps below using the non-controversial statement as an example, then move on to a controversial one. The first time you do a Sides Debate, take some time to establish the process and rules. Once students get the hang of it, they will be able to do Sides Debates quickly and effectively throughout the year.

Sides Debate

2. Tell students they will debate the statement standing by the "Agree" sign if they agree with the statement or by the "Disagree" sign if they do not agree with the statement. Give them the following rules (use an overhead or write these on the board):

- Everyone must take a side
- Everyone should be prepared to state their reason for agreeing or disagreeing with the statement
- Anyone can switch sides if they are convinced by the opposing side
- No one can speak a second time until everyone else has spoken once
- Be convincing but respectful of others when making your arguments

3. Have the students stand up and take a side (Note: If everyone takes the same side, ask a few students to try taking the other side and demonstrate how one might argue for that side).

4. Going back and forth from side-to-side, have students state their reasons for agreeing or disagreeing with the statement.

5. After everyone has spoken once (and/or the debate has been exhausted) and students have finished switching sides, bring the class back to their seats for either a reflection discussion or to begin a lesson related to that statement.

Assessment Reflection Questions

For Intermediate and Advanced Students

- What did you like/dislike about this debating process?
- Was everyone's opinion heard and respected? Why or why not?

For Advanced Students

- Would it have been difficult to take the other side? Why or why not?
- How does seeing it from someone else's perspective help to resolve an issue?
- Can controversial issues always be resolved?

Making Global Connections

OVERVIEW
Students demonstrate the interconnectedness of global issues and solutions through a kinesthetic exercise using global issue cards and a ball of yarn.

INQUIRY/CRITICAL THINKING QUESTIONS
- How are global issues interconnected?
- How does a change in one global issue affect other global issues?
- How are solutions to global problems interconnected?

OBJECTIVES
Students will:
- Kinesthetically experience the interconnectedness of global issues
- Understand how a change in one issue can positively and negatively affect a change in another issue

TIME REQUIRED: 1 hour

KEY ISSUES/CONCEPTS
- **Global issues**
- **Interconnections**
- **Systems thinking**

SUBJECT AREAS
- **Social Studies** (World History, World Cultures, Geography, Economics, Global Studies)
- **Science** (Life, Environmental)

NATIONAL STANDARDS CONSISTENCY
- **NCSS: 3, 7, 8, 9**
- **NSES: A, C, E, F**

GRADE LEVEL: 5–12

FTF Related Reading
- Intermediate: Chapter 1 from *Global Issues and Sustainable Solutions*
- Advanced: Unit 1, Chapter 1 from *It's All Connected*

Materials/Preparation
- Handout, *Global Issues Cards*, 1 card per student (or 1 per pair of students if you do the activity in pairs). For advanced students, mix in the *Advanced Global Issues Cards*
- Ball of yarn

Activity
Introduction
1. Write the following quote on the board or overhead and have students do a journal entry or "freewrite" (a short, ungraded, in-class writing that allows students to compose freely and fluently on a given word, quote, piece of art, etc.) on it:

> "When you try to pick out anything by itself, you find it hitched to everything else in the universe." - John Muir

After they write for a few minutes, lead a class discussion about the quote, having students share their writing.

2. Alternatively, you can introduce the activity by asking students to think about something they ate today. Then ask them to think about how the food/meal might be connected to the environment. Did the production, processing, or transportation have any

Making Global Connections

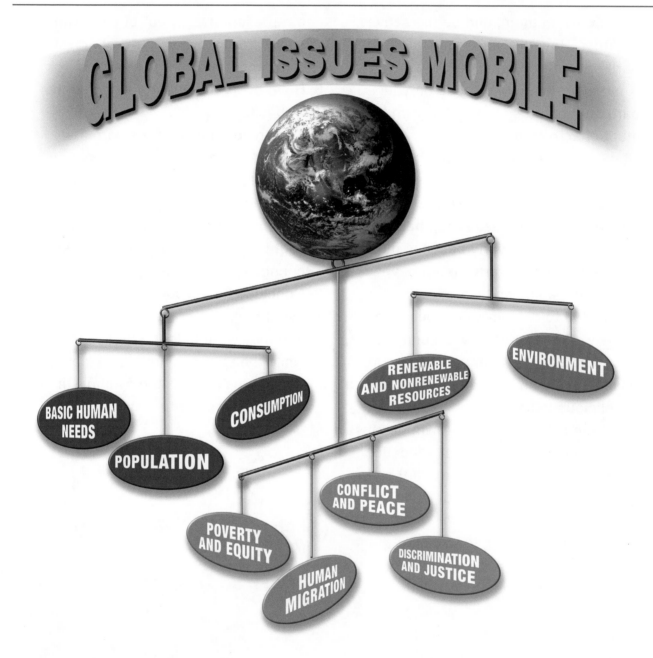

impact on the natural environment, including water, land, plants, or animals? Now ask them to choose 1 of these environmental connections and think about its human connection. Does the environmental impact have any effect on people? Do people use the environmental resource? After a few seconds, have 1 or 2 students share their series of connections.

3. Tell students they are going to do an exercise that will help them see and experience how global issues are interconnected.

Steps

1. Have students stand in a circle. Pass out the *Global Issues Cards* to each student and keep 1 card for yourself. In classes with more than 16 students, you can have students pair up, choose 1

Making Global Connections

card between them, and do the activity together. Have the pairs stand so that 1 partner is in front of the other.

2. Read aloud the global issue on your card and then toss the ball of yarn to a student across the circle.

3. Have that student (together with his/her partner) read the global issue on his/her card and state how this issue is connected to your issue (e.g. healthcare is connected to poverty because most people living in poverty do not have access to basic healthcare; conflict is connected to discrimination because some wars are started when one group of people does not like another group based strictly on their ethnic background or religious beliefs; education is connected to population growth because people with higher levels of education tend to have fewer children). If the student(s) cannot figure out how the 2 issues are connected, other students in the circle can help. If no one in the circle can think of a connection, the student(s) can pass and continue the activity.

4. Once the student(s) has stated how her/his issue is connected to the previous one, she/he holds onto a piece of the yarn and tosses the ball of yarn to someone else across the circle.

5. Continue the exercise until everyone has caught the ball of yarn, called out the interconnections, and is now holding a piece of the yarn. Have the last student throw the ball of yarn back to you. You should now have

a representative "web" of yarn with every student holding a Global Issues Card and a piece of the web.

6. Have everyone pull the string so the web is taut.

7. Tug on your piece of the yarn and ask if anyone felt the tug. Have some others tug on the yarn and see who else feels it. Try tugging harder and see who feels it then. Ask what that tug might represent or signify about the connections between global issues.

8. Conclude the lesson with a discussion using the reflection questions below. You may want to lead the discussion while the students are still standing and holding the yarn so the symbolism of the web is still present.

© 2006 FACING THE FUTURE: PEOPLE AND THE PLANET www.facingthefuture.org

Making Global Connections

Assessment
Reflection Questions

For Intermediate and Advanced Students

- Why might it be helpful to understand how and why global issues are interconnected?
- Can you think of other issues that might be interconnected like the ones raised in this activity?
- How can understanding the interconnectedness of global issues help us find solutions to the problems surrounding these issues?

For Advanced Students

- Understanding the interconnectedness of issues can often be the first step in solving problems. Interconnectedness is an important and key concept in "systems thinking"—a holistic way of thinking that takes into account the connections, interactions, and processes that link different elements together and form a complete "system". By understanding that issues are interconnected, we can begin to see when and where we can intervene in a system to make change (see *It's All Connected*, Units 1 and 7 for a detailed discussion of systems thinking). What are some examples of places we could intervene in a system and maximize positive connections between various issues? Have the students discuss the idea of intervening in a system and making positive changes.

- Identify not only where or when one could intervene in a system but how an individual's actions can "snowball" – i.e. trigger other reactions in the system that build upon and sustain the positive effects of the original action. What kind of small action might snowball into a large result? How can small changes replicate and multiply to produce widespread and lasting change?

Writing Connection

- Arrange students in groups of 5 or 6. Using a *Global Issues Card*, 1 student writes a short story (2-3 sentences) about his/her issue on the top of a piece of notebook paper and then passes the story to the next student. That student then writes a short story (1-2 sentence) that explains how the issue on his/her card is connected to the previous story. They then fold the paper so that only the last story is visible, and pass it on to someone else. Keep passing, writing, and folding the paper until everyone has written part of the connections story. Once everyone has written, have each group open the whole story and read it aloud to the class.

Art Connection

- Have students create a "global issues mobile" using photos or drawings (glued to cardboard) that represent different global issues. Find photos or create drawings, glue the pictures onto cardboard, and cut them into shapes. Write the global issues on the back of the cardboard. Use either wire or string to attach the pieces to cross bars made of either wooden dowels or sticks.

Making Global Connections

Action Projects

- Throw a "BeadWear Party" at your school through the BeadforLife project. BeadforLife is an organization that fights poverty by employing very poor women in Uganda to make beautiful jewelry out of recycled paper. This project gives students the opportunity to help women feed their children and send them to school by buying their products, while also educating students, their friends, parents, and community about Uganda and the plight of poor people around the world. For a detailed description of this and other service learning projects, visit **www.facingthefuture.org** and click on **Take Action** and then **Service Learning Projects**.

- Have students adopt a retirement home for the school year. Make 2-4 visits during the year to develop a relationship with the individuals living at the home. Students interview the residents to learn their perspectives on global issues, and make global issues mobiles with them that incorporate both the students' and the residents' perspectives. Through visits, interviews, and discussions, students find out what their needs are and develop a project that addresses those needs.

- Have students get involved in the issue they care about most with millions of other young people from around the world on Global Youth Service Day, which occurs every year in late April. Visit **www.gysd.net** for more information.

Additional Resources

Films

- *Finding Balance: Forests and Family Planning in Madagascar*, Population Action International, 2005, 9 minutes, **www.populationaction.org.** This short documentary explores the connections between women's health and environmental sustainability.

Books

- *The Web of Life: A New Scientific Understanding of Living Systems,* Fritjof Capra, Anchor, 1997. Capra sets forth a new scientific language to describe the interrelationships and interdependence of psychological, biological, physical, social, and cultural phenomena.

- *The Tipping Point: How Little Things Can Make a Big Difference,* Malcolm Gladwell, Back Bay Books, 2002. Gladwell's "Tipping Point" theory is based on three main principles: ideas are contagious, little causes can have big effects, and change does not happen gradually but at one pivotal moment. The challenge is to find the right leverage point and push or "tip" it, setting off a chain reaction of positive change.

Websites

- **www.facingthefuture.org** - Facing the Future's website focuses on the interconnectedness of global issues and sustainability.

- **www.pegasuscom.com** - Pegasus Communications' website provides systems thinking resources to help individuals, teams, and organizations understand and address the challenges and complexities of a changing world.

- **www.sustainabilityinstitute.org** – The Sustainability Institute focuses on understanding the root causes of unsustainable behavior in complex systems and, through projects and training, helps people shift their mindsets and restructure systems in ways that move us toward a sustainable society.

© 2006 FACING THE FUTURE: PEOPLE AND THE PLANET www.facingthefuture.org

© 2006 FACING THE FUTURE: PEOPLE AND THE PLANET   www.facingthefuture.org

Global Issues Cards (Page 1)
Use these with Intermediate and Advanced Class

Poverty

Consumption

Population Growth

Peace and Conflict

Human Migration

Environment

Technology

Healthcare

© 2006 FACING THE FUTURE: PEOPLE AND THE PLANET   www.facingthefuture.org

Global Issues Cards (Page 2)
Use these with Intermediate and Advanced Class

Education

Food

Water

Economics

Discrimination

Sustainability

Human Rights

Global Warming

© 2006 FACING THE FUTURE: PEOPLE AND THE PLANET   www.facingthefuture.org

Global Issues Cards (Page 3)
use these *additional* cards with Advanced Class

Governance

Culture

Social Justice

Biodiversity

Non-Renewable Resources

Renewable Resources

Media

Energy Use

From Issue to Opportunity

OVERVIEW

Help students understand and define global issues and their interconnections. Students develop criteria for determining what makes an issue global in scope, brainstorm and list global issues, group and prioritize the issues into categories to highlight interconnections, and explore solutions.

INQUIRY/CRITICAL THINKING QUESTIONS

- What defines a global issue?
- How are global issues connected to each other and to our own lives?
- What is the benefit of understanding the connections between global issues?

OBJECTIVES

Students will:
- Develop and discuss criteria for defining a global issue
- Identify, group, and prioritize global issues
- Explore and explain the interconnections between global issues as well as their solutions

TIME REQUIRED: 1 hour

KEY ISSUES/CONCEPTS

- **Global issues**
- **Interconnectedness**
- **Leverage**
- **Problems as opportunities**

SUBJECT AREAS

- **Social Studies** (Geography, Economics, Civics/Government, Contemporary World Problems)
- **Science** (Life, Environmental)

NATIONAL STANDARDS CONSISTENCY

- **NCSS: 3, 5, 7, 9**
- **NSES: C, F**

GRADE LEVEL: 9–12

FTF Related Reading

- Intermediate: Chapter 1 from *Global Issues and Sustainable Solutions*
- Advanced: Unit 1, Chapter 1 from *It's All Connected*

Materials/Preparation

- Overhead: *Defining a Global Issue*
- Butcher paper, 5–10 sheets
- Marking pens, 1 per student
- Sticker dots, 2 per student

Activity

Introduction

1. Ask students, "What makes an issue global versus local?" Brainstorm, list, and discuss the defining criteria of a

global issue. These may include the following: global issues have significant impacts, they are trans-boundary, they are persistent (occurring repeatedly over time), and they are interconnected. Use the overhead *Defining a Global Issue* to help lead this part of the discussion.

Steps

1. Have the class brainstorm and list on the board or overhead as many global issues they can think of, assessing each issue against the agreed-upon criteria for defining a global issue.

2. Look at the entire list and have the class develop categories into which similar issues can be grouped. For example, rain forest destruction, loss

From Issue to Opportunity

of natural habitat, global warming, and species extinction could all be categorized under "The Environment". Other possible categories include: Health, Human Rights, Energy, Food and Water Security, Peace and Conflict, Economics, Population, Governance, and Culture/Worldview. After deciding on 5 or more categories, write each category on the top of separate pieces of butcher paper and post them around the room.

3. Have the students go to each of the posted sheets and write the global issues from the brainstorm list under a relevant heading. There will likely be issues that fall under more than 1 category.

4. Give each student 2 sticker dots. Have him/her walk around the room, read all the posted sheets, and then place a

sticker on what he/she believes are the 2 most-important categories.

5. Conclude with the following reflection questions.

Assessment Reflection Questions

For Intermediate and Advanced Students

- Which category had the most votes (stickers)? Is there a clear majority? (If there is a clear majority, consider focusing a unit of study on the most popular global issue(s)).
- Which category ended up with the most issues?
- Which specific issue fell under the most categories?
- Why is it that some issues seem to have many connections? How might this information be useful and what might this tell us about the issue(s)?

For Advanced Students

- Explain the idea of "leverage". The global issues that seem to be most connected to other issues are probably ones that have the highest leverage. Working on 1 or 2 issues that have several connections, therefore, can help alleviate many other problems. Brainstorm possible solutions to the high-leverage global issues.
- Discuss the process of brainstorming, grouping, and prioritizing used in this activity. Discuss the potential this process has for solving other problems.

From Issue to Opportunity

Writing Connection

- Have students participate in a Model United Nations–style of assembly in which they act as country delegates, writing and presenting resolutions that address specific global issues.

- Have each student choose 1 issue from the class list (or a new one) and use either a diagram or a paragraph to demonstrate how it meets the criteria of a global issue (as defined in the activity). This assignment emphasizes students' ability to assess and apply criteria and illustrate interconnectedness. Students may want to have time to do some Internet research on their chosen issue in order to do a more thorough job. Give students the following instructions: Choose 1 of the global issues we have listed today. Then, draw a diagram or write 1-2 paragraphs that illustrate how this issue meets at least 3 of the criteria we established for a "global issue". You must include "interconnectedness" and "significant impacts" as 2 of the criteria. For each set of criteria, give 3 examples of how your issue qualifies as a global issue. One way to approach this might be to imagine that you are a legislator or a philanthropist setting out to work on this issue. Ask yourself which other interconnected issues you will need to take into account. Which groups might you want to collaborate with? In order to convince people to support your issue, you will need to be able to explain the impacts of the issue and why it is important.

Action Projects

- Interview members of the community to find out how global issues are affecting their local community. Findings can be shared with the local media.

- Create a service learning project guide for young people in your community. Research organizations that are addressing community needs and contact them to find out what service opportunities they provide for youth. Compile the information in a format that is accessible for young people and share it through a website, school districts in your area, or in hard copy.

- Visit **www.facingthefuture.org** and click on **Take Action**, and then **Fast Facts Quick Actions** for more information and action opportunities on a variety of global issues.

Additional Resources

Films

- *Spaceship Earth: Our Global Environment,* Kirk Bergstrom and Kit Thomas, 1999. Hosted by young people, this program travels around the world to explore 3 primary environmental issues: deforestation, global warming, and ozone depletion.

Websites

- **www.globalexchange.org** - Global Exchange is an international human rights organization dedicated to promoting social, economic, and environmental justice around the world.

- **www.conservationeconomy.net** - This website asks the question, "What does a sustainable society look like?" and provides frameworks for an ecologically restorative, socially just, and prosperous society and restructure systems in ways that move us toward a sustainable society.

DEFINING A GLOBAL ISSUE

What makes an issue "global"?

Global Issues Are:

- ## Significant

- ## Trans-national or trans-boundary

- ## Persistent or long-acting

- ## Interconnected

Is It Sustainable?

OVERVIEW

Students define and discuss sustainability and its 3 key components: the economy, the environment, and society. Students brainstorm, analyze, and write about the sustainability of a variety of actions taken by individuals, businesses, and governments, using a Venn diagram to help organize the process.

INQUIRY/CRITICAL THINKING QUESTIONS

- What does "sustainability" mean and how does it apply to human activity?
- How is the sustainability of an individual, business, or government activity determined?
- How can we balance the needs of people, protect the environment, and have a vibrant and equitable economy?
- How can an activity be made more sustainable?

OBJECTIVES

Students will:
- Define sustainability and its 3 key components: the economy, the environment, and society
- Identify and describe a range of activities undertaken by individuals, businesses, and governments (e.g. foods they eat, transportation they use, products they buy, services provided, laws passed, etc.)
- Determine the sustainability of these activities based on a set of criteria that includes impacts on the economy, the environment, and society
- Represent their findings using a Venn diagram
- Analyze if and how an unsustainable activity can be altered to adhere to the 3 components of sustainability

TIME REQUIRED: 1 hour

KEY ISSUES/CONCEPTS

- **Sustainability**
- **Three components of sustainability: economy, environment, and society**

SUBJECT AREAS

- **Social Studies** (World History, World Cultures, Geography, Economics, Global Studies)
- **Science** (Life, Environmental)

NATIONAL STANDARDS CONSISTENCY

- **NCSS: 1, 3, 4, 5, 6, 7, 8, 9**
- **NSES: B, C, E, F**

GRADE LEVEL: 7–12

Is It Sustainable?

FTF Related Reading

- Intermediate: Chapter 1 from *Global Issues and Sustainable Solutions*
- Advanced: Unit 1, Chapter 2 from *It's All Connected*

Materials/Preparation

- Overhead: *Components of Sustainability*
- 3 different colored sticky notes, 2"x2", enough for each student to have 1 sticky note of each color
- Draw a Venn diagram (like the one in the *Components of Sustainability* overhead) on a large sheet of butcher paper (or project the overhead onto a whiteboard)

Activity

Introduction

1. Ask the class what they think sustainability means. Have them first think quietly for a minute. Then have them pair up with a partner and discuss what they think sustainability means. Have them share their answers with the class. As they share, write down their ideas on the board or overhead. Ideally they will construct a definition that is close to this: Sustainability means meeting present needs without compromising the ability of future generations to meet their own needs. The meaning of this might be explored further, with "needs" or "needs of the present" defined more clearly by students. Have them brainstorm some needs and then discuss the potential conflicts that inevitably arise between needs (e.g. having affordable clothing versus livable wages for workers, or having clean air versus using a car as transportation).

2. Define the 3 components of sustainability using the overhead *Components of Sustainability*. Explain that in determining whether an action or product/good/service is sustainable, many people who study sustainability take into account 3 key elements: the environment, the economy, and society/equity. In order to determine whether or not something is sustainable, the activity being evaluated would be assessed in relation to each of these principles, or "standards of sustainability". This assessment reveals how the action or item impacts the economy, the environment, and society, in either negative, positive, or neutral ways. You may need to define economy, environment, and society. Do this using the same think, pair, share method used to define sustainability.

3. Using the Venn diagram (on the butcher paper or projected on the whiteboard) explain that its purpose is to demonstrate that issues overlap and share common traits.

Steps

1. Explain that they will list and analyze the sustainability of several different activities, products, and actions from the categories of: individual activities (e.g. eating breakfast, driving to school, attending school, and playing guitar), specific business products or services (e.g. clothes, housing, computers, restaurants) and specific government actions (e.g. passing laws and

Is It Sustainable?

regulations, provision of services such as utilities, trash, etc.).

2. Before breaking them into groups, choose 1 activity (such as driving to school) and walk through an analysis of the activity with the whole class, asking if it is sustainable using the 3 "components of sustainability" (Economics, Environment, and Society) as a guide. Questions to ask about the activity include:

Sustainability:
- Is the activity sustainable today?
- Can it be done without causing damage in the 3 areas (economics, environment, and society?)
- Can this activity be done so that people in the future will have the same opportunities to do this activity as people today?

Environment:
- How many resources does the activity use?
- Does the activity cause damage to plants or animals?
- Is biodiversity protected?
- Does it cause air pollution, water pollution, or soil erosion?
- Does it use resources at a rate that allows the resource to be renewed or regenerated?
- What happens to the waste created by the activity?
- Does the activity generate excessive waste?

Society:
- Does it contribute to people's quality of life?
- How does it affect culture(s)?
- Are individuals and communities involved in making decisions about the activity, and is the decision-making process fair and democratic?
- Is it an equitable activity; does it offer more options and opportunities to certain groups of people than others?

Economy:
- What is the economic impact of the activity?
- Does it create meaningful and satisfying work for individuals?
- Does it contribute to a community's economic development?
- Does the activity rely on products or services that have negative effects on the environment or society?
- Do some people benefit economically from this activity at the expense of others?
- Will this activity contribute to the conservation of natural resources?

3. Arrange students in groups of 3 and assign each group 1 category: individual activities, business products and services, or government actions.

4. Have them create a brainstorm list of activities that fall within their assigned category.

5. From their brainstorm list, have students choose 2 activities from their list and transfer these to individual color-coded sticky notes (use different color sticky notes for each category, such as blue for individual activities, yellow for business activities, and green for government activities).

6. Have students place their sticky notes on the Venn Diagram in the area they think the activity best fits, depending on whether the activity is economically, environmentally, and/or socially sustainable.

© 2006 FACING THE FUTURE: PEOPLE AND THE PLANET www.facingthefuture.org

Is It Sustainable?

7. Have each group explain to the class how they decided on the placement, giving concrete examples and evidence to support their decision. Encourage each member of the group to participate in the discussion and, if time permits, answer questions from the class.

8. Conclude with the following reflection questions.

Assessment Reflection Questions

For Intermediate and Advanced Students

* If someone asked you what sustainability meant, how would you respond?
* Explain whether it is easy or hard to decide whether an activity is sustainable.
* Can everything we do be measured against the standards of sustainability? What are some examples of activities that would be especially difficult to measure and especially easy to measure?
* Can something that is unsustainable be altered to become more sustainable?
* Choose an unsustainable activity from the Venn Diagram and explain how it could be made more sustainable.

For Advanced Students

* Why do you think people use the standards of sustainability to assess human activities? How and where could this process be useful?
* If you were a business owner or a government decision-maker, what would you think about sustainability?
* Ask whose needs should be met when there are trade-offs involved (e.g. between economic and environmental priorities) and how these contradictions can be resolved. This discussion will underscore the idea that working toward sustainability is a balancing act that requires long-term creative thinking and the ability to compromise and see through the eyes of others. Issues of choice and responsibility are also highlighted – students will learn that they have the ability to make choices that bring about positive change, and understand that their choices (e.g. whether or not to eat fast food or buy a brand of clothing that is manufactured in sweatshops) have concrete economic, environmental, and social impacts, even if these impacts are out of sight and felt far away.
* Discuss the difference between "economic development" and "economic growth" and the relationship between economic growth and consumption. What is the role of economic growth in fostering sustainable development?

Is It Sustainable?

Does economic development help nations focus more on conserving their resources or does it contribute to over-consumption? In some cases, economic development includes commitments to eradicating poverty and changing unsustainable patterns of consumption.

Technology Connection

- Compare the levels of sustainability of different nations by downloading the International Institute for Sustainable Development's "Dashboard of Sustainability." The Dashboard is a unique on-line tool that uses a vehicle's instrument panel to represent country-specific assessments of economic, environmental, social, and institutional performance toward (or away from) sustainability. Download at http://www.iisd.org/cgsdi/intro_dashboard.htm.

Action Projects

- Visit **www.facingthefuture.org,** click on **Take Action**, and then **Fast Facts Quick Actions** for sustainability information and action opportunities.

- Have your students take the **Facing the Future Pledge** to help create a sustainable world. Pledge form is on page 22 or can be downloaded at www.facingthefuture.org. Post the pledges in the classroom and have students track and then report later in the year how they are doing on their pledge.

Additional Resources

Films
- *Ecological Design: Inventing the Future,* Brian Danitz and Chris Zelov, 1994, 60 minutes. What do flying bicycles, Rocky Mountain jungles, "living machines", and recyclable homes with their own "metabolism" all have in common? They are unique, inexpensive solutions to the design dilemma of sustainable living and are all featured in this film.

- *Visions of Utopia: Experiments in Sustainable Culture,* Geoph Kozeny, 2002, 94 minutes. This documentary looks at different ways people are bringing more community into their lives and their work.

- *Ancient Futures: Learning from Ladakh,* The International Society for Ecology & Culture, 1993, 59 minutes. **www.isec.org.uk** A documentary video on the changes that Western development brought to the high mountain city of Ladakh in northern India. Ladakh, a culture of Tibetan Buddhism and sustainable agricultural practices, struggled with the coming of television, drugs, consumerism, and industry.

Websites
- **www.iisd.org** - The International Institute for Sustainable Development (IISD) engages decision-makers in government, business, NGOs and other sectors to advance policies that are beneficial to the global economy, environment, and social well-being.

- **www.naturalstep.org** - A non-profit international organization working to build an ecologically and economically sustainable society through education, scientific research, and services for business and government.

Lesson 6 Overhead:
Components of Sustainability

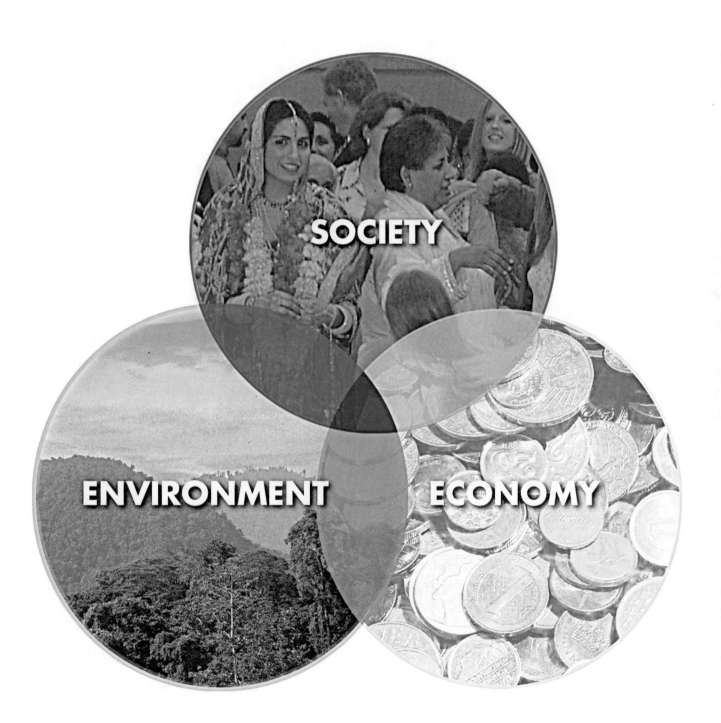

Systems Are Dynamic

(Variations of this activity have been used for many years, in a variety of educational settings, to provide a direct experience of the dynamic nature of systems.)

OVERVIEW

Students experience the dynamic, interconnected, and self-organizing nature of systems through an exercise in which they move around an open space trying to keep an equal distance between themselves and 2 other people.

INQUIRY/CRITICAL THINKING QUESTIONS

- What is the inherent nature of a system?
- How can understanding the nature of systems help us find solutions to large, complex problems?

OBJECTIVES

Students will:
- Experience and discuss the dynamic, interconnected, and self-organizing nature of systems
- Consider how understanding the nature of systems can help us find sustainable solutions

TIME REQUIRED: 30 minutes

KEY ISSUES/CONCEPTS

- **Systems dynamics**
- **Interconnectedness**
- **Self-organizing systems**

SUBJECT AREAS

- **Social Studies (Geography, Economics, Global Studies)**
- **Science (Life, Environmental, Physical)**

NATIONAL STANDARDS CONSISTENCY

- **NCSS: 3, 7, 8, 9**
- **NSES: A, C, E, F**

GRADE LEVEL: 5–12

FTF Related Reading

- Intermediate: Chapter 1 from *Global Issues and Sustainable Solutions*
- Advanced: Unit 1 from *It's All Connected*

Materials/Preparation

- No materials needed, but you will need a large open space to conduct the activity
- This activity works best if students have a very basic understanding of systems. *Facing the Future* related readings (above) provide more than enough background to conduct this activity.

Activity

Introduction

1. Ask students to define a "system". What are some of the defining features of a system? (e.g. a system has many parts that work together; if you change 1 part it affects other parts; if you remove or add something it can change the whole system; a system is made of interconnected parts; a system can be something in nature, or it can be mechanical or human). Ask for examples of systems that they encounter, use, or are a part of.

2. Explain to the students that they are

© 2006 FACING THE FUTURE: PEOPLE AND THE PLANET www.facingthefuture.org

Systems Are Dynamic

going to do an exercise to help them understand the dynamic nature of systems.

Steps

1. Have the students stand randomly in a large open space either indoors or outside.

2. Give the following 2 instructions:
   - Mentally select 2 other people in the group, without indicating whom you have chosen.
   - Move so as to keep an equal distance between you and each of these 2 people at all times. This does not mean simply remaining at the midpoint between them.

3. To pursue this objective, students will begin to circulate, each movement triggering many others in an active, interdependent fashion. Movement may speed up for a while, then may abate, accelerate, and again slow down toward equilibrium, but it rarely reaches stasis.

4. Let the movement continue for 3 or 4 minutes, then, as activity lessens, have students pause where they are and begin the reflection questions.

Lesson Variation: Have 2 students stay outside the room during instructions, then call them in at a certain point during the activity and ask them to try

to detect what is happening. When the process halts and they learn (or have discovered) the principle guiding people's movements, ask the observers if they could organize this complex process from the outside. This highlights the principle that relations within systems are so complex that they can only self-regulate. You can also invite the observers to walk quietly through the game while it is in progress. The observers and the players will notice that this pass-through does not affect or disrupt the game, since the players are moving solely in relation to each other. This models how humans can pass through a system (such as a forest or a swamp) and not disrupt its defining relations.

Assessment
Reflection Questions

For Intermediate and Advanced Students

- Have the students describe what happened. Begin by asking, "What did you experience?" Their reflection may bring out some key features of self-regulating systems, such as the interdependence of all parts and the continuous process of seeking and maintaining balance. Students may realize that they thought the point of the game was to achieve stasis, whereas in fact the game demonstrated that self-regulating systems

Systems Are Dynamic

require constant internal activity.

- Where was your attention focused when you were doing this activity? Were you focused on the big picture or the small details? Were you focused on your own actions or the actions of others? Why is this perception important?
- What other systems can you think of that are interconnected, dynamic, and self regulating? (e.g. the human body, an automobile, a natural habitat, etc.)
- Why and how is it helpful to understand these aspects of a system? How can this understanding of systems help us to figure out solutions to large and complicated global issues?
- How far-reaching are the effects of one small, intentional change within a system? What might the implications of this be for making positive changes to a system?

For Advanced Students

- What kinds of feedback helped us to fulfill the function of the activity (staying equidistant from 2 others)? Could we have done it with our eyes closed? The ensuing discussion can address how not only visual perceptions, but feedback of all kinds, guide us in our daily lives in the systems we co-create at home, work, and school.
- Would anyone volunteer to organize this process? It is obvious that no party or person on the outside could direct the movements necessary to keep this system in balance.

Writing Connection

Have students create a "cluster" graphic organizer following these guidelines: Choose a global issue and write that in the center of the paper. Write as many connecting issues as you can think of around the issue. Write as many other issues you can think of that affect or are affected by these issues and connect them with lines. Write a short summary explaining the cluster.

Action Projects

- Have students identify a local system (e.g. your school or classroom, watershed, park, or forest) and the changes that could be introduced to that system to make a positive difference.
- Visit **www.facingthefuture.org**, click on **Take Action**, then **Fast Facts and Quick Actions** for information and action opportunities on a variety of local and global issues.

Additional Resources

Films

- *MindWalk,* Bernt Capra (based on the *book The Turning Point* by Fritjof Capra), 1990, 112 minutes. A U.S. politician, a poet, and a scientist discuss their philosophies of life while walking through an island off the coast of France.
  http://www.fritjofcapra.net/mindwalk.html

Books

- *The Web of Life: A New Scientific Understanding of Living Systems,* Fritjof Capra, Anchor, 1997. Capra sets forth a new scientific language to describe the interrelationships and interdependence of psychological, biological, physical, social, and cultural phenomena.

Websites

- **www.pegasuscom.com** - Pegasus Communications' website provides systems thinking resources to help individuals, teams, and organizations understand and address the challenges and complexities of a changing world.
- **www.sustainabilityinstitute.org** – The Sustainability Institute focuses on understanding the root causes of unsustainable behavior in complex systems and, through projects and training, helps people shift their mindsets and restructure systems in ways that move us toward a sustainable society.

Bears in the Air

OVERVIEW

Through a game in which an object is tossed as fast as possible around a circle, students experience the limits of success, redesign their "tossing system" to meet their goal, and begin to identify assumptions that drive behavior.

INQUIRY/CRITICAL THINKING QUESTIONS

- How do mental models and assumptions keep us from reaching our goals?
- How can we redesign a system that is not functioning well to achieve our desired outcome?

OBJECTIVES

Students will:
- Experience how mental models can limit our success and keep us from reaching our goals
- Redesign a system to accomplish a shared goal
- Discuss how this activity models real-world systems and explore possible redesigns of those systems

TIME REQUIRED: 30 min - 1 hr

KEY ISSUES/CONCEPTS

- **System dynamics and redesign**
- **Mental models**
- **Limits to success**

SUBJECT AREAS

- **Social Studies** (Geography, Civics/Government, Economics, Global Studies, Contemporary World Problems)
- **Science** (Life, Environmental, Physical)
- **Business/Finance**

NATIONAL STANDARDS CONSISTENCY

- **NCSS: 5, 10**
- **NSES: F, G**

GRADE LEVEL: 5–12

FTF Related Reading

- Intermediate: Chapter 9 from *Global Issues and Sustainable Solutions*
- Advanced: Unit 1 Chapter 3 and Unit 7 from *It's All Connected*

Materials/Preparation

- A stuffed bear or other easy and safe-to-throw-and-catch object
- Watch with a second hand to time activity
- Clear an area in the classroom large enough for students to stand in a circle

Activity

Introduction

1. Arrange students so they are standing shoulder- to-shoulder in a circle. Stand in the circle with them and show them the stuffed bear or other object.

2. Tell students they are going to play a game in which they toss the bear around the circle. Tell them there are

Bears in the Air

only 2 rules to the game: (1) Everyone must touch the bear and (2) They must touch it in the same sequence each time.

3. Have everyone hold their hands out in front so they are ready to catch the bear.

4. Gently toss the bear to someone across the circle.

5. Have that person toss the bear to someone else and drop his or her hands after tossing. The last person tosses the bear back to you.

6. Practice once so they are comfortable with the sequence.

7. Now tell them you are going to time the activity to see how fast they can do it. You will need to either time it yourself or designate a student for that job ahead of time.

8. Run the activity and time it. After the first timed run-through, tell students that you are sure they can do it much faster. Run and time the activity a few more times, telling them after each run-through that they can do it even faster. Most likely they will be able to do it faster in the beginning just by tossing faster; however, once they reach a certain level of success, they will not get any faster without a system redesign. In fact, they may even get slower if they get sloppy and toss the bear outside the circle or drop it in their attempt to go faster. This part of the activity models the concept of "limits to success".

9. If students ask if they can do the activity differently, just repeat the 2 rules above.

10. Continue until students figure out how to redesign the system to achieve the desired goal. There are several redesigns that will accomplish the task much faster, such as standing next to each other and passing the bear along the line, or lining their hands up vertically in the correct order and cascading the bear down the vertical line.

11. Conclude with the following reflection questions.

Assessment
Reflection Questions

For Intermediate and Advanced Students

- What happened the first few times through? Did you succeed in doing it faster? Why?
- Was there anyone who thought about other ways of doing it but did not speak up? What kept that person from offering a solution?
- Did anyone offer a solution that was ignored? Why was their solution ignored?

For Advanced Students

- What were the assumptions in the activity and how did these assumptions limit your ability to achieve your goal (there might have been some assumptions that there were unstated rules about how the activity could be done)?
- What are some examples of real-world situations in which people experience the limits to success by doing something harder and faster? What are the assumptions associated with how that system functions, and how could that system be redesigned to achieve a common goal?

© 2006 FACING THE FUTURE: PEOPLE AND THE PLANET   www.facingthefuture.org

Bears in the Air

Action Projects

- Have students choose a "system" that they think is not working well. This could be something going on at home, in their school, in their community, or in the larger world. Have them analyze and write about the system using the *Bears in the Air* activity as a model. They should identify and explore the system's goals, assumptions, mental models, limits to success, and possible redesigns.

Additional Resources

Books

- *The Lorax*, Dr. Seuss, Random House, 1971. This children's story about the wise Lorax who warns the Once-ler not to cut down all the Truffula trees models several systems thinking concepts, including interconnectedness, limits to success, and unintended consequences.

Websites

- **www.thesystemsthinker.com** - Newsletter of Pegasus Communications, an organization that provides resources to help individuals, teams, and organizations understand and address the challenges they face in managing the complexities of a changing world.

How Big is a Billion?

OVERVIEW
A short demonstration of how much 1 billion is, using increasing amounts of rice to represent the world's population. Students then create their own representations of 1 billion.

INQUIRY/CRITICAL THINKING QUESTIONS
- How much is 1 billion?
- How can we represent the number "1 billion"?
- How many people can the planet support?

OBJECTIVES
Students will:
- Observe a demonstration of how much 1 billion is
- Gain an understanding of the significance of global population
- Create their own representation of 1 billion

TIME REQUIRED: 30 minutes

KEY ISSUES/CONCEPTS
- Population
- Exponential growth

SUBJECT AREAS
- **Social Studies** (Geography, Economics, Global Studies)
- **Science** (Life, Environmental)
- **Math**

NATIONAL STANDARDS CONSISTENCY
- NCSS: 3, 9
- NSES: C, F

GRADE LEVEL: 5–8

FTF Related Reading
- Intermediate: Chapter 2 from *Global Issues and Sustainable Solutions*
- Advanced: Unit 2 from *It's All Connected*

Materials/Preparation
- 1 small bag of uncooked rice
- Teaspoon, 1 cup measuring cup, gallon jar

Activity
Introduction
1. The purpose of this exercise is to put into perspective how many people there are in the world. To get started, ask students what the population of the world is (about 6.5 billion).
2. Ask them if they can imagine how big the number 1 billion is. Tell them you are going to help them see how big 1 billion is.

Steps
1. Scoop out a level teaspoon of rice from a bag of uncooked grains and show to the class. Tell them that there are about 200 grains of rice in 1 teaspoon.
2. Show them a cup of rice and explain that there are approximately 9,600 grains of rice (48 teaspoons) in 1 cup. Ask how many cups are in 1 gallon (16 cups). Then ask how many grains of rice there are in 16 cups (9,600 x 16 = 153,600 grains of rice).
3. Ask how many gallons it would take to equal 1 million grains of rice. Answer: 1,000,000 divided by 153,600 = 6.5 gallons = 1 million grains of rice.
4. Ask students: If 6.5 gallons equals 1 million grains of rice, how many gallons would it take to equal 1 billion grains of rice? Answer: 6.5 gallons (1 million) times 1,000

How Big is a Billion?

would be 6,500 gallons, which equals approximately 1 billion.

5. Ask how many gallons of rice it would take to equal 6 billion (the approximate number of people on the planet). Answer: It would take approximately 39,000 gallons of rice to equal 6 billion!.

6. Arrange students in groups of 3-4 and have each group come up with another way to demonstrate how much 1 billion is. Encourage them to think about creative and different ways to demonstrate this number. For example, the number of kids jumping up and down for a length of time, or the number of sugar cubes laid end to end, etc.

7. Have each group make a poster showing their "1 Billion" representation and present it to the class.

8. Conclude with the following reflection questions.

Assessment
Reflection Questions

For Intermediate and Advanced Students

• Which of the examples created by students was the most effective in demonstrating 1 billion?

• What is the significance of having 6.5 billion people in the world?

• Of the 6.5 billion people on the planet, how many live in the United States? (280 million) China? (1.2 billion) India? (1 billion)

• How many people do you think the planet could support?

Action Projects

• Visit **www.facingthefuture.org**, click on **Take Action**, then **Fast Facts and Quick Actions** for more information and action opportunities related to population growth.

Additional Resources

Films

• *Jam Packed: The Challenge of Human Overpopulation,* The Video Project, 1997, 28 minutes. Jam Packed explores human population growth from the perspective of a young adult.

• *World Population,* ZPG, 2000, 7 minutes. This short video presents a visual representation of population growth throughout history.

Books

• *Anno's Magic Seeds,* Mitsumasa Anno, Puffin Books, 1995. A children's story about a man who plants seeds that double every year, incorporating concepts in math, economics, and the environment.

Websites

• **www.prb.org** - The Population Reference Bureau informs people around the world about population, health, and the environment, and empowers them to use that information to advance the well-being of current and future generations.

• **www.populationaction.org** – Population Action International (PAI) is an independent policy advocacy group working to strengthen political and financial support worldwide for population programs grounded in individual rights.

• **http://www.unfpa.org** – The United Nations Population Fund (UNFPA) is an international development agency that supports countries in using population data for policies and programmes to reduce poverty, to prevent HIV/AIDS, to promote reproductive health, and to promote dignity and respect for women and girls.

Splash But Don't Crash

OVERVIEW

Help students see the effect of population growth rates on the Earth's carrying capacity through a simulation in which they move water from a container representing births and deaths into another container representing the Earth.

INQUIRY/CRITICAL THINKING QUESTIONS

- What is the Earth's carrying capacity?
- What are the potential impacts of different rates of natural population increase on the Earth's carrying capacity?
- What can we do to reduce these impacts?

OBJECTIVES

Students will:
- Model population growth rates of selected nations and regions
- Consider and discuss the social, environmental, and economic impacts of such growth and possible solutions

TIME REQUIRED: 1 hour

KEY ISSUES/CONCEPTS

- **Carrying Capacity**
- **Population growth rate**
- **Natural increase**

SUBJECT AREAS

- **Social Studies**(Geography, World History, Global Studies)
- **Science** (Life, Environmental)
- **Math**

NATIONAL STANDARDS CONSISTENCY

- **NCSS: 2, 3 7, 9**
- **NSES: A, C, F**

GRADE LEVEL: 5–9

FTF Related Reading

- Intermediate: Chapter 4 from *Global Issues and Sustainable Solutions*
- Advanced: Unit 2, Chapters 3 and 4 from *It's All Connected*

Materials/Preparation

- 2 clear containers, at least 1-gallon size, with an open top large enough to reach into to remove water
- Blue food coloring to tint water
- Fill 1 container half full with water and add enough food coloring to make the water appear blue, and fill the second container about 3/4 full with water (do not add food coloring to second container)
- Several measuring cups, ranging from 1/4 cup to 1 cup in size
- Towel or tray to catch spills
- Population Reference Bureau's "World Population Data Sheet" found at **www.prb.org** under Quick Links.

Activity

Introduction

1. (Optional) Do a Sides Debate using the statement below (see Sides Debate lesson on page 28):
- "Human population does not yet seriously affect our natural environment because there is still so much open, uninhabited land in our world."
2. Explain and discuss the definition

Splash But Don't Crash

and concept of carrying capacity (the maximum number of people the Earth can support indefinitely).

3. Ask students how many people they think the Earth can support. Discuss how the carrying capacity of the Earth is a much-studied and hotly contested issue. Some people think that the Earth can support many more people than we have now, while others believe that we have already exceeded Earth's capacity.

4. Tell the class that they will do an activity to model natural increase (population growth and death rates) of a specific region and its effect on the Earth.

Steps

1. Have the class choose a country or region from Population Reference Bureau's "World Population Data Sheet" as a model for the simulation.

2. Explain that the container with the tinted water represents the Earth, the tinted water itself represents current population, and the air in the container above the tinted water represents the habitat for all other species on the planet. Explain that the clear water container represents population supply (i.e. births).

3. Divide the class into 2 groups: 1 representing birth rates and the other death rates.

4. Give each group 1 measuring cup. Base the size of each group's cup on relative birth and death rates of the chosen country or region. For example, if the class chooses Africa as the demonstration region, have them look up the birth and death rates for Africa in the PRB "World Population Data Sheet" (41 per 1,000 birth rate and 15 per 1,000 death rate) and select measuring cups representing the relative percentages. For

Splash But Don't Crash

convenience, the group representing births might be given a 1-cup measure, and those representing deaths given a 1/3-cup measure. If North America is chosen (14 per 1,000 birth rate and 9 per 1,000 death rate), use a 1-cup and 1/2-cup measure to approximate those values.

5. Have each group line up on opposite sides of the room. Call on individual students to come forward and do the following:

a. A student from the birth-rate group fills his or her cup from the supply container and adds it to the "Earth" container.

b. A student from the death-rate group then fills his or her cup from the "Earth" container and dumps it back into the supply bucket.

6. Keep the process going until the "Earth" container is dangerously full, and any more increase will cause an overflow.

7. Conclude with the following reflection questions.

Assessment
Reflection Questions

For Intermediate and Advanced Students

- What did you observe happening during the exercise? (The "Earth" container's water level rose, and as "population" increased, habitat for the other species decreased.)
- What would have happened if we had continued the exercise? (If population increase continued, the water would have reached the top, and all other species would be displaced. If population had increased further, the container would

have overflowed. If that overflow were real people, the results would likely be death from famine, war, and disease.)
- What signs could we look for as we approach the point of "overflow"?
- What happened to the color of the water in the "Earth" container and how might that compare to depletion of the Earth's resources as carrying capacity is approached?
- Discuss how this scenario might impact students' own lives.

For Advanced Students

- Elaborate on how this scenario would impact your own life in terms of your environment, economy, and social institutions, both locally and globally.
- Discuss what policies you might implement to prevent the loss of habitat, the extinction of species, and the depletion of resources.

Writing Connection

- Students write an essay or illustrated short story about a crowded situation such as in an elevator, on a boat or airplane, or in a classroom full of students. Have them explain the effects that crowding has on them and the people around them. Is it uncomfortable or stressful? If so, how do they respond, and what would happen if everyone reacted that way? How do the ways they and others respond to crowding play out in a larger global context? Have them explain what it would be like if that situation was permanent. How does this relate to areas of the world that we think of as crowded?

Splash But Don't Crash

Math Connection

- Have the class calculate the doubling time of different regions and countries listed in the Population Reference Bureau's "World Population Data Sheet". Divide 70 by the rate of natural increase listed in the data sheet. For example, in 2001, Somalia had a natural increase rate of 3 percent. 70 divided by 3 percent equals a doubling time of 23 years. Select at least 1 country from an industrialized region such as Europe or North America and at least 1 from a developing region such as Africa, Asia, or Latin America and compare the results. Have the students graph the comparative doubling times of several regions. Discuss how these doubling times might affect future availability of resources, such as food, water, and energy in these regions. What effects might these doubling times have on the environment?

Action Projects

- Do "Heifer Project International", a Service Learning Project in which students raise money to buy farm animals for poor families to help them become more self-sufficient. For a detailed description of this project, visit **www. facingthefuture.org** and click on **Take Action**, then **Service Learning Projects**.
- Plant an organic school garden using

locally appropriate fruits and vegetables. Start a school composting program and use the compost to improve the soil in your new garden.

- Find alternative uses for materials currently being landfilled (like tires, cell phones, computers, etc.) in your community. Students can develop a project to support the reuse of landfilled items. Search the Internet to find organizations that support this work by offering recycle bins, outreach materials, etc.
- Visit **www.facingthefuture.org** and click on **Take Action**, then **Fast Facts Quick Actions** for more information and action opportunities on population growth and related issues.

Additional Resources

Films

- *World in the Balance,* NOVA & The WGBH Educational Foundation, 2004,120 minutes. In Japan, Europe, and Russia, birth rates are shrinking and the population is aging. In parts of India and Africa, more than half of the still growing population is under 25. The world population is now careening in 2 dramatically different directions. This video explores these directions. **www.wgbh.org**

Websites

- **www.prb.org** - The Population Reference Bureau publishes an annual "World Population Data Sheet" which can be downloaded for free from their website.

- **www.populationaction.org**- Population Action International is an independent policy advocacy group working to strengthen political and financial support worldwide for population programs grounded in individual rights.

Seeking Asylum

OVERVIEW

Through a simulation, students experience the difficult choices and struggles facing refugees and internally displaced persons (IDPs) when they are forced to leave their homes. Students learn about the root causes of refugee and IDP crises, and the options and obstacles each group faces.

INQUIRY/CRITICAL THINKING QUESTIONS

- Why and how does someone become a refugee or IDP?
- How do nations determine who qualifies as a refugee?
- How are refugee issues tied to other global issues?
- What are the impacts (negative and positive) of refugee and IDP populations on the environment, economies, and social fabrics of their host and home countries?
- What are some sustainable solutions to addressing the root causes of refugee and IDP crises?

OBJECTIVES

Students will:
- Gain a sense of empathy for the hard choices facing refugee and IDP families
- Understand the root causes of refugee and IDP crises, and the root solutions for preventing these crises
- Learn about the asylum process, and the differences in protection offered to refugees and IDPs
- Be introduced to the debate within developed nations over setting immigration policies

KEY ISSUES/CONCEPTS

- **Refugees and Internally Displaced Persons**
- **Asylum**
- **Resettlement**

SUBJECT AREAS

- **Social Studies** (World History, Geography, U.S. History, Economics, Global Studies)
- **Science** (Environmental)

NATIONAL STANDARDS CONSISTENCY

- **NCSS: 1, 3, 5, 6, 9, 10**
- **NSES: F**

GRADE LEVEL: 6–11

TIME REQUIRED: 1 hour

© 2006 FACING THE FUTURE: PEOPLE AND THE PLANET   www.facingthefuture.org

Seeking Asylum

FTF Related Reading

- Intermediate: Chapter 7 from *Global Issues and Sustainable Solutions*
- Advanced: Unit 2, Chapter 3 from *It's All Connected*

Materials/Preparation

- Handout/Overhead: *Defining Refugees, IDPs, and Migrants*, overhead or 1 copy per student
- Handout: *Seeking Asylum - Items*, 1 copy per 4 students
- Handout: *Citizenship Certificate*, 1 copy
- 2 large pieces of blank paper with "Asylum in Petrus" written in large letters on 1 piece and "Internally Displaced Persons" on the other. Tape the 2 signs on opposite sides of the classroom
- 2 sheets of butcher paper and pens, place 1 sheet and pens by each area
- A jug of water and crackers (enough for 1 or 2 crackers per student for about half your class) placed in an area by the "Asylum in Petrus" sign

Activity

Introduction

1. (Optional) Do a Sides Debate using the following prompt (see Sides Debate description on page 28):

    "The U.S. should allow more refugees into this country."

2. Show and review the Overhead or Handout, *Defining Refugees, IDPs, and Migrants*.

Steps

1. Divide the class into "families" of 3-4 students.
2. Explain to the class that, due to an outbreak of civil war, all the families have to leave their homes immediately.
3. Tell them that each family can only take 5 items with them, selected from the Handout *Seeking Asylum – Items* that you will pass out to them. They will only have 2 minutes to agree on what to bring and then flee before the fighting reaches their home. They can only choose items that are on the list.
4. Pass out the list quickly and start timing for 2 minutes. Keep the pressure on them to complete their selections within the allotted time.
5. After the 2 minute period, have them put their pens down. Have a representative from each family read off their 5 items. Make a note to yourself of which families chose to bring Identification Cards.
6. After all families read off their lists, take those families that chose Identification Cards to the "Asylum in Petrus" section of the room. Take those families that did not list Identification Cards to the "Internally Displaced Persons" section of the room.
- Note: If no families have chosen to bring Identification Cards, have everyone go to the IDP side. Randomly choose 2 families and tell them that if they can prove they are from their home country and are in need of asylum, they can go to the refugee camp. Or, have a family that brought money "buy" their way into the camp. The goal is to have at least a couple of families in the refugee camp. Alternatively, if all the families bring identification cards, randomly select some families and move them to the IDP side of the room, telling them that their identification papers are not in order.

Seeking Asylum

7. Explain that families often need to be able to prove where they come from in order to be granted asylum (protection) by a neighboring country. Inform the families in the Asylum section that they are now in the fictional country of Petrus, housed in a refugee camp operated by The United Nations High Commissioner for Refugees. This is why they have been given some basic food and drink (the water and crackers). The Asylum families may eat the crackers and drink water.

8. Explain that people in refugee camps are often assigned jobs, so those in the refugee camp are going to brainstorm and write on the butcher paper, what their camp will need to function (e.g. kitchens, schools, doctors, etc.), and then identify the different types of jobs they might be doing.

9. Explain to those in the IDP area that families without identification papers were not granted asylum, and are stuck in the middle of the civil war in their home country. No United Nations agency has the authority to look after these families so, at the moment, they do not have any food or drink. Tell the IDP families to brainstorm and write on the butcher paper, what they will do to survive – they could try to set up their own camp using the items they chose to take with them, or they could try to enter Petrus illegally by bribing border guards with their items, etc.

10. After the students have brainstormed for a few minutes, take all but 1 of the families from the Asylum section and explain that the government of Petrus has determined that the civil war in the refugees' home country has calmed down enough for them to return home. Explain that while Petrus is sorry the families have nothing, and their homes are probably gone, the refugees are using up the limited resources of their country and every family cannot be granted asylum forever. Take the families to the IDP section.

11. Finally, tell the 1 family remaining in the Asylum section that Petrus has agreed to resettle them, offering permanent residency. A local agency will help them find a home and a job. Give them the *Citizenship Certificate*.

12. Bring the class back together for reflection questions.

Assessment
Reflection Questions
For Intermediate and Advanced Students

- How did you decide what to bring with you?
- How did you feel having such a short time to decide?
- Did you feel the asylum process was fair?
- Why do you think it is important to have identification cards?
- If you were to change the rules for countries granting refugees asylum, what would you do? Would you accept anyone who claimed they were a refugee?
- Are there refugees in your community? Where are they from? How are they treated? What agencies exist to help refugees in your community?

Seeking Asylum

For Advanced Students

- Would you feel different about accepting someone who was not physically threatened with violence, but couldn't find any work in their own country?

- How do you think refugee and IDP crises affect other global issues like environmental destruction, poverty, and education?

- If the situation that caused a family to seek asylum is resolved, but the family has nothing to go back to in their home country, should they still be sent home? Why? Under what conditions should refugees be sent home?

- Why do you think the United Nations helps refugees, but is not authorized to help internally displaced persons?

- If the United Nations cannot help IDPs, can you think of any organization that could help IDPs?

- What could be a sustainable solution to preventing large scale refugee and IDP crises? Economic development? Participatory and effective governance? Who should be in charge of implementing this solution?

Writing Connections

- Have students write a poem based on their experience in the activity, keeping in mind the things their family chose to bring, and where they ended up. Have them use imagery, senses, metaphors, and descriptive words in their poems.

- Have students write a short "memoir" as if they were a refugee or IDP. Have the class share their stories with younger students, perhaps at a local elementary school.

Art Connection

• Create a family tree collage using photos of a student's family and images from magazines, the Internet, newspapers, and other sources that depict places in the world where the student's family originally came from.

Technology Connection

- Visit www.itvs.org/beyondthefire/master.html for an interactive experience in which students listen to the stories of refugee teens from around the world.

Action Projects

- Partner with a refugee or internally displaced person (IDP) school either through pen-pal relationships with their students or by raising money to send school supplies and equipment. When you partner with "RESPECT International" you'll get everything you need to get started and to find a partner school. For a detailed description of this and other service learning projects, visit www.facingthefuture.org and click on **Take Action,** and then click **Service Learning Projects.**

Seeking Asylum

- Research and contact resettlement organizations in your community to learn more about local refugee and IDP issues and to seek volunteer opportunities. The International Rescue Committee (IRC) at www.theirc.org is a good place to start your search.
- Visit www.facingthefuture.org, click on **Take Action**, then click **Fast Facts Quick Actions** for refugee-related information and action opportunities listed in the "peace and conflict" section.

Additional Resources

Films

- *Refugee*, Spencer Nakasako, 2002, 60 minutes. Focuses on a boy from a tough neighborhood in San Francisco returning to Cambodia to meet his dad, who did not escape during Pol Pot's regime. www.refugeethemovie.com

Books

- *Of Beetles and Angels: A Boy's Remarkable Journey from a Refugee Camp to Harvard,* Mawi Asgedom, Little, Brown and Company, 2002.

- *Under the Persimmon Tree,* Suzanne Fisher Staples, Farrar Straus Giroux, 2005. This young adult novel offers a new level of insight into Afghanistan in the months following the September 11, 2001 attacks. The author alternately expresses the views of two survivors: young Najmah, a villager living in the Kunduz Hills, and Nusrat, the American wife of an Afghan doctor.

Websites

- www.unhcr.org - The Office of the United Nations High Commissioner for Refugees official website.
- www.theirc.org - Official website of the International Rescue Committee. The IRC provides emergency relief, rehabilitation, protection of human rights, post-conflict development, resettlement services, and advocacy for those uprooted or affected by conflict and oppression.

© 2006 FACING THE FUTURE: PEOPLE AND THE PLANET   www.facingthefuture.org

Lesson 11 Overhead/Handout:

DEFINING REFUGEES, INTERNALLY DISPLACED PERSONS, AND MIGRANTS

Refugee - A person who flees his/her country because he/she has a well-founded fear of being persecuted for reasons of race, religion, nationality, membership of a particular social group, or political opinion. A refugee, under this technical definition, is someone who crosses an international border to seek refuge in another country.

Asylum - Refugees who cross a border are seeking asylum, or protection within the country they entered. Under international law, a person who can prove he/she qualifies as a refugee must be granted asylum until he/she either chooses to return home, or conditions improve enough that it is determined he/she is no longer in immediate danger, and can be told to leave by the country that granted the protection.

Resettlement - Countries can choose to resettle refugees, officially granting them permanent residency within their borders.

Internally Displaced Person (IDP) - someone who is forced to leave his/her home for the same reasons as a refugee, but is unable to cross an international border to obtain asylum. IDPs currently do not have the same rights and protections offered to refugees by international law. Their plight is often not monitored by international agencies, since they have not left their home country. While intra-state conflicts are the most common source of mass IDP movements, in recent years large-scale economic and public works projects in developing countries have resulted in forced mass evacuations of citizens to make room for dams, logging, and other land use purposes.

Migrant - Someone who chooses to leave his/her home and obtain citizenship in a different country through an official citizenship process, or chooses to leave his/her home and enter a new country by circumventing the citizenship process (illegally). The most common reason for emigration is a lack of economic opportunity and/ or quality of life in the person's home country. In recent years there has been a movement to change how destination countries treat migrants from the poorest parts of the world, dubbing them economic or environmental refugees.

© 2006 FACING THE FUTURE: PEOPLE AND THE PLANET   www.facingthefuture.org

Seeking Asylum – Items

Directions:

There has been an outbreak of civil war in your country and you are being forced to leave immediately. Your "family" must choose only 5 of the items below to take with you. Review the list together and circle the 5 items you agree to take.

You have 2 minutes to reach a decision!

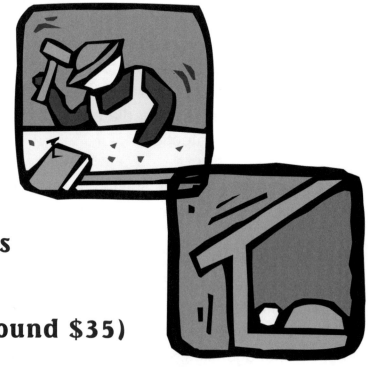

- **Cooking pot**
- **Hammer and nails**
- **Water jug**
- **Radio**
- **Sack of grain**
- **Waterproof tarp**
- **Identification cards**
- **Cooking stove**
- **Family savings (around $35)**
- **Soap**
- **Machete (large curved knife)**
- **Photo album**
- **Pet dog**
- **Rifle**
- **Blankets**
- **Lantern**

Certificate of Citizenship

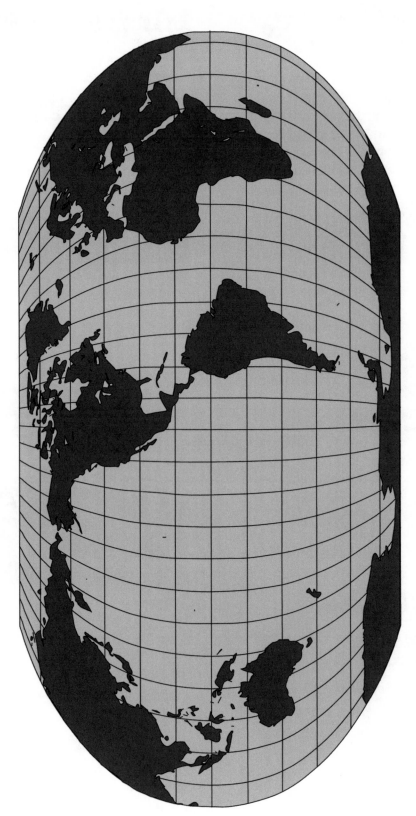

For the Country of Petrus

ENGAGING STUDENTS THROUGH GLOBAL ISSUES

© 2006 FACING THE FUTURE: PEOPLE AND THE PLANET   www.facingthefuture.org

Watch Where You Step

OVERVIEW

Students identify the components of an Ecological Footprint by creating a web diagram of all the resources they use in their everyday lives and the mark or "footprint" this consumption leaves on the environment. The activity emphasizes the interconnectedness of lifestyle, population, and environmental impacts, and focuses on solutions to reduce Ecological Footprints.

INQUIRY/CRITICAL THINKING QUESTIONS

- What are the environmental, economic, and social impacts of a typical U.S. diet and lifestyle?
- What would be the consequences if the rest of the world adopted a U.S. lifestyle?
- What can we do to reduce impacts associated with resource consumption?

OBJECTIVES

Students will:
- Identify the resources, processes, and impacts embodied in everyday activities
- Describe the interconnectedness of population, lifestyle, economics, and environmental issues
- Discuss, create, and implement ways to reduce Ecological Footprints

TIME REQUIRED: 1 hour

KEY ISSUES/CONCEPTS

- **Ecological Footprint**
- **Carrying Capacity**

SUBJECT AREAS

- **Social Studies**
  (Geography, Economics, Global Studies)
- **Science** (Life, Environmental)
- **Math**

NATIONAL STANDARDS CONSISTENCY

- **NCSS: 2, 3, 7, 9**
- **NSES: C, F**

GRADE LEVEL: 5–11

FTF Related Reading

- Intermediate: Chapter 4 from *Global Issues and Sustainable Solutions*
- Advanced: Unit 2, Chapters 3 and 4 from *It's All Connected*

Materials/Preparation

- Butcher paper, 1 sheet per group of 3-4 students
- Marking pens, colored, 2–3 pens per group of 3-4 students

- Overhead: *Definition and Components of an Ecological Footprint*
- (Optional) Handout: *Hamburger, Fries, and a Cola*

Activity

Introduction

1. (Optional) Do a Sides Debate using the statements below (see Sides Debate lesson on page 28):
   - "There are enough resources to meet the

Watch Where You Step

needs of everyone on the planet."
- "The U.S. gives more to the world, and therefore can take more from the world."

2. Introduce the concept of Ecological Footprint using the overhead, *Definition and Components of an Ecological Footprint.* Tell students that in order to understand this concept, they will create a diagram illustrating everything that is associated with 1 component of their Ecological Footprint.

Steps

1. Give the following directions before grouping students and assigning their Footprint component: In groups, brainstorm and map all of the resources, processes, and impacts associated with 1 component of your Ecological Footprint, such as a meal, mode of transport, favorite object, or item of clothing. For example, for 'My Favorite Meal,' you would first agree on a meal you like, write and/or draw it in the center of the paper, and then write and/or draw the resources and processes it took to produce it.

2. Do a short verbal example together with the class. Ask them what it takes to create a hamburger (cow, bun, lettuce, etc.). There are a few steps between the cow and the burger itself. What are they? (e.g. grass, butcher, meat grinder). Between the cow and the burger, we have the slaughterhouse, the transportation of the beef to the restaurant, the energy to heat the stove to cook the burger, and so on. Now, think about all the steps required to make your item, including the resources needed to produce, process, deliver, serve, and dispose of it (e.g. farmland, water, farm

machinery, fertilizer, pesticides, petroleum fuels, electrical energy, transportation, refrigeration, markets, and restaurants). What impacts result from each of those processes and technologies (e.g. soil erosion, pesticide runoff, air pollution, freeway crowding, and urban sprawl)? Use the optional handout Hamburger, Fries, and a Cola as an example of what goes into producing this common U.S. meal.

3. Arrange students in groups of 3-4.

4. Assign each group 1 of the following scenarios that illustrate 1 component of an Ecological Footprint, and have them begin their web diagrams (if you have a large class, you can assign items to more than one group):
   - My Favorite Food
   - How I Traveled Here Today (a mode of transportation)
   - My Favorite Object (a toy, sports equipment, etc.)
   - My Favorite Piece of Clothing

5. Allow about 20 minutes for this portion of the activity. Encourage students to be creative and think of everything that is related to the object. Remind them to include items such as transportation of a product, the marketing of popular brand items, health issues, and waste disposal.

6. After completing their diagrams, have students brainstorm and list, on the back of their butcher paper, 10 things that they can do personally to reduce their Ecological Footprint (in relation to the item they mapped).

7. Have each group present their diagrams and report their findings and solutions to the class. As students present their footprint

Watch Where You Step

reduction solutions, be sure to emphasize that they do not need to give up everything they like, but rather should focus on ways to reduce their impacts. For example, they do not need to say that people should never drive cars; rather, they could say that people could ride a bike to school when possible, or once a week.

8. Bring the class back together for reflection questions.

Assessment
Reflection Questions

For Intermediate and Advanced Students

- Discuss the average size of an Ecological Footprint of a person living in the United States (about 24 acres) as compared to someone living in India (about 2 acres).
- What impacts might result if twice as many people lived in our community and enjoyed the

same meals, transportation, clothing, etc.?
- What impacts might result if everyone in the world were to enjoy the same lifestyle? How would that impact you economically, environmentally, socially, and politically? How might that impact your access to education, employment, and recreation?
- What would be the consequences of 12 billion people having the same lifestyle? Would that be sustainable? How might your life change in response?

For Advanced Students

- If only a small percentage of the world's people were able to enjoy such a meal, mode of transportation, or clothing while the rest of the world did without, what might the environmental, social, and security consequences be?
- Why would stabilizing the U.S. population have a major impact on trends in global

© 2006 FACING THE FUTURE: PEOPLE AND THE PLANET   www.facingthefuture.org

Watch Where You Step

resource consumption and environmental damage (despite the fact that the United States constitutes less than 5 percent of global population)?

- Does lessening our impacts necessarily mean reducing our quality of life? Are there ways of enhancing your quality of life while reducing your impacts (e.g. driving a higher mileage car, generating less waste, saving money by using more efficient appliances)?
- How else could you maintain a comfortable and fulfilling lifestyle, but lower the associated environmental impacts?

Lesson Extensions

- For younger students, you may want to have the class focus on 1 component of an Ecological Footprint rather than those listed above. For example, you could have the whole class choose a meal and then assign 1 part of the meal to each group.
- Bring in an everyday item in its original packaging (such as a juice box, CD, cookies, drink cup, small appliance, toy, etc.) and have the class analyze the Ecological Footprint created by producing, distributing, and disposing of the item. Discuss alternatives to using the item and/or how the item could be produced in a more sustainable manner. Then assign students to do the same (individually or in small groups) with an item of their choice. Have them propose their sustainable solution to other users and/or the manufacturer of the item.
- Have students do a "trash carry" activity. Give each student a large, empty trash bag and have them carry it with them, putting into it all of the trash they generate in 1, 2, or 3 days. Have them weigh their bag of trash at the end of the day(s). Brainstorm ways they could reduce the amount of trash they generate. Repeat the exercise on another day, implementing their trash-reduction ideas. Have them then weigh their second bag of trash. Did they succeed in

reducing the amount of their trash? Discuss other ways trash can be reduced.

Writing/Art Connection

- Use the book *Material World* by Peter Menzel to analyze the Ecological Footprints of people around the world. Have the students create their own "material world" picture of their bedroom at home, either as a photo or a drawing, and write a short paper describing the project.
- Have students write a letter to someone about the Ecological Footprint concept. By writing a letter, students demonstrate that they understand what an Ecological Footprint is, why the concept is an important one, and how one's footprint might be reduced. Alternatively, if a student feels it is not important to reduce one's footprint, they may explain why they feel that way. Give students the following instructions: Write a letter to a friend, cousin, parent, or someone else that you know. In your letter, you must:
  - Briefly explain what an Ecological Footprint is. What have you learned about it?
  - Suggest ways that you and the recipient of your letter might reduce your Ecological Footprints. Be realistic. What are some things you might really try?
  - Try to convince the other person that it is worth trying these suggestions. Explain why you think it is important to reduce the size of your Ecological Footprint. Alternatively, if you believe that it is not important to do so, then explain why not. Try calculating your own Ecological Footprint, as described below, before writing your letter.

Math/Technology Connection

- Students can calculate the size of their own Ecological Footprint and compare it with people around the world by visiting **www.myfootprint.org**.

Watch Where You Step

Action Projects

- Do an Ecological Footprint Awareness Campaign. Have the students post their Footprint diagrams around the school with titles such as, "This Is What It Takes to Bring You Your Lunch" or "Have You Ever Wondered What Resources It Takes to Get You to School Every Day?"

- Have the students evaluate the food prepared in the school cafeteria and present a proposal to the school administration and their peers with alternatives to high resource consumption and wasteful practices.

- Have your students take the Facing the Future Pledge to help create a just and sustainable world. Reprint the pledge form on page 22 or download it from **www.facingthefuture.org**. Post the pledges in the classroom and revisit them throughout the year. Have students write in their journals about the activity and how their pledge is going.

- Do a "trash audit" and develop (or improve) a recycling program for the school. Include how much and what kind of trash is produced, where and how it is disposed of, and the associated impacts. Determine the school's financial cost of the wasted materials and the handling and disposal of the trash. Set up or improve the existing structure for recycling (who can take it, provide bins, etc.), educate the school on how and what to recycle, and track results.

- Visit **www.facingthefuture.org**, click on **Take Action**, then **Fast Facts and Quick Actions** for more information and action opportunities on reducing consumption and Ecological Footprints.

Additional Resources

Films

- *The Ecological Footprint: Accounting for a Small Planet,* Global Footprint Network, Bullfrog Films, **www.bullfrogfilms.com**, 2005, 30 minutes. In this documentary film,

Mathis Wackernagel introduces the Ecological Footprint and paints a picture of our current global situation. Wackernagel explores the implications of ecological deficits and provides examples of how governments, communities, and businesses are using the Ecological Footprint to help improve their ecological performance.

Books

- *Stuff: The Secret Lives of Everyday Things,* John C. Ryan and Alan Thein Durning, Northwest Environmental Watch, 1997. Stuff follows a typical day in the life of a fictional, middle-class North American, and tracks her consumption. **www.northwestwatch.org**.

- *Material World: A Global Family Portrait,* Peter Menzel, Sierra Club Books, 1994. Award-winning photojournalist Peter Menzel brought together 16 of the world's leading photographers to create a visual portrait of life in 30 nations.

Websites

- **www.rprogress.org** - Redefining Progress works with a broad array of partners to shift the economy and public policy towards sustainability.

- **www.footprintnetwork.org** – Global Footprint Network supports a sustainable economy by advancing the Ecological Footprint, a measurement and management tool that makes the reality of planetary limits relevant to decision-makers around the world.

© 2006 FACING THE FUTURE: PEOPLE AND THE PLANET   www.facingthefuture.org

Lesson 12 Overhead:

Definition and Components of an Ecological Footprint

Ecological Footprint:

The area of the Earth's productive surface (land and sea) that it takes to produce the goods and services necessary to support a person's lifestyle

Components of an Ecological Footprint:

- **Oxygen** (e.g. trees for absorbing carbon dioxide)

- **Food** (e.g. meat, dairy, fish, fruits and veggies)

- **Water** (e.g. drinking, cooking, washing)

- **Fiber** (e.g. clothes, wood, upholstery)

- **Energy** (e.g. fuel for cars, heat for cooking)

- **Infrastructure** (e.g. highways, hospitals, water facilities)

- **Waste Disposal** (e.g. garbage dumps, landfills)

- **Recreation** (e.g. soccer fields, golf courses)

© 2006 FACING THE FUTURE: PEOPLE AND THE PLANET   www.facingthefuture.org

Hamburger, Fries, and a Cola
What Did it Take To Produce This American Meal?

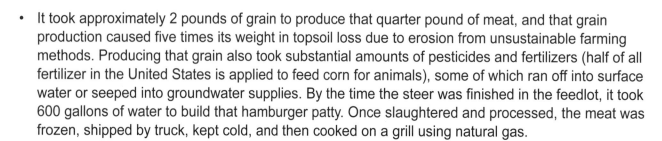

- The meat came from cattle grazed initially on public or private land, and later fed grain. About 10 percent of all public lands in the western United States have been turned to desert by overgrazing, and about two-thirds of those public lands are significantly degraded. Streamside lands, where cattle graze, have been especially damaged.

- It took approximately 2 pounds of grain to produce that quarter pound of meat, and that grain production caused five times its weight in topsoil loss due to erosion from unsustainable farming methods. Producing that grain also took substantial amounts of pesticides and fertilizers (half of all fertilizer in the United States is applied to feed corn for animals), some of which ran off into surface water or seeped into groundwater supplies. By the time the steer was finished in the feedlot, it took 600 gallons of water to build that hamburger patty. Once slaughtered and processed, the meat was frozen, shipped by truck, kept cold, and then cooked on a grill using natural gas.

- The 5-ounce order of fries came from one 10-ounce potato grown in Idaho on half a square foot of soil. It took 7.5 gallons of water to raise that potato, plus quantities of fertilizer and pesticides, some of which ran off into the Columbia or Snake Rivers. Because of that, and dams that generate power and divert water for irrigation, the Snake River sockeye salmon is virtually extinct. A number of other species are also in decline because of these production practices.

- The potato was dug with a diesel-powered harvester and then trucked to a processing plant where it was dehydrated, sliced, and frozen. The freezing was done by a cooling unit containing hydrofluorocarbons, some of which escaped into the atmosphere and likely contributed to global climate change. The frozen fries were then trucked to a distribution center, then on to a fast-food restaurant where they were stored in a freezer and then fried in corn oil heated by electricity generated by hydropower.

- The meal was served in a fast-food restaurant built on what once was originally forest, then farmland, then converted to commercial/industrial uses as the city expanded. The ketchup in aluminum-foil packets came from Pittsburgh and was made from Florida tomatoes. The salt came from Louisiana.

- The cola came from a Seattle processing plant. It is made of 90 percent water from the Cedar River. The high-fructose corn syrup came from Iowa, as did the carbon dioxide used to produce the fizz, which is produced by fermenting corn. The caffeine came from a processing plant that makes decaffeinated coffee. The cola can was made from one-third recycled aluminum and two-thirds bauxite ore strip-mined in Australia. It came to Washington State on a Korean freighter, and was processed into aluminum using an amount of energy equivalent to a quart of gasoline. The energy came from some of the same dams mentioned earlier that have contributed to a 97 percent decrease in the salmon runs of the Columbia Basin.

- The typical mouthful of food consumed in the United States traveled 1,200 miles for us to eat it. Along the way, it required packaging, energy, roads, bridges, and warehouses, and contributed to atmospheric pollution, adverse health effects, and traffic congestion.

Now Hear This!

OVERVIEW

Students literally see and hear a comparison of an average U.S. citizen's and sub-Saharan African citizen's Ecological Footprint through a demonstration in which popcorn kernels – representing Ecological Footprints – are poured into a metal pan. This demonstration lesson can be conducted on its own or as a companion to our other Ecological Footprint activities, "Watch Where You Step!" and "When the Chips Are Down".

INQUIRY/CRITICAL THINKING QUESTIONS

• How does the Ecological Footprint of an average U.S. citizen compare to that of an average sub-Saharan African citizen?
• How can people reduce the size and impact of their Ecological Footprint?

OBJECTIVES

Students will:
• Hear a comparison between the environmental impact of an American lifestyle and that of a citizen of a country with a smaller Ecological Footprint
• Brainstorm ideas for reducing personal Ecological Footprints

TIME REQUIRED: 5–10 min / 1 hr

5–10 minutes for demonstration; 1 hour if poster making is included

KEY ISSUES/CONCEPTS

• **Ecological Footprint**
• **Carrying Capacity**

SUBJECT AREAS

• **Social Studies** (Geography, Economics, World History, Global Studies, Contemporary World Problems)
• **Science** (Life, Environmental)
• **Math**

NATIONAL STANDARDS CONSISTENCY

• **NCSS: 3, 7, 9**
• **NSES: C, F**

GRADE LEVEL: 5–12

FTF Related Reading

• Intermediate: Chapter 4 from *Global Issues and Sustainable Solutions*
• Advanced: Unit 2, Chapter 3 from *It's All Connected*

Materials/Preparation

• Overhead: *Definition and Components of an Ecological Footprint* (page 73)
• 2,500 popcorn kernels (about 2 cups) placed in a container from which you can easily pour

© 2006 FACING THE FUTURE: PEOPLE AND THE PLANET www.facingthefuture.org

Now Hear This!

Activity

Introduction

1. Explain and discuss the concept of Ecological Footprints using the overhead, *Definition and Components of an Ecological Footprint*.

2. Explain that people around the world have different environmental impacts or Ecological Footprints. Ask students which citizens they think have the largest Ecological Footprint (Answer: U.S. citizens). Tell them that the average U.S. citizen has an Ecological Footprint of 24 acres. An acre is about the size of a football field, so imagine standing in the middle of 24 football fields. There might be some cows grazing on part of the area for your beef consumption, and grain planted on another part for your bread and cereal. There would be an area for producing metal for your bicycle, car, refrigerator, and oven. There would be an area for fresh water and a landfill for all of the trash you create. By contrast, the Ecological Footprint of an average person living in India is just 2 acres. Their space is much smaller. They would likely have no cows, and the only metal they might have is for a bicycle and/or a watch.

Steps

1. Tell the class that you are going to demonstrate the relative impact of 2 countries' Ecological Footprints (be sure the class is quiet before you begin).

2. Hold 10 popcorn kernels in your hand and tell the students: "This is the impact of 1 person living in sub-Saharan Africa over the course of his or her lifetime." Slowly drop the 10 kernels into the pan.

3. Now tell them: "By contrast, this is the impact of 1 person living in the United States over the course of his or her lifetime." Very slowly, pour the rest of the kernels into the metal pan. The slower you pour, the more dramatic the demonstration.

4. Conclude with the following reflection questions.

Now Hear This!

Assessment
Reflection Questions

For Intermediate and Advanced Students

- Ask the students why the average U.S. citizen's Ecological Footprint sounded so much louder.

- Discuss that although the average person living in sub-Saharan Africa may have a smaller impact, he or she does not have enough resources to survive. On the other hand, if everyone on the planet were to use the same amount of resources as the average U.S. citizen, we would need 4 more planet Earths to support all of us.

- Have the class brainstorm ways to bring the 2 Footprints in the activity to a closer balance and ways to reduce their personal Ecological Footprints.

For Advanced Students

- Discuss issues or problems in our world today that may be the result of, or fueled by, disproportionate consumption patterns throughout the world.

Technology Connection

- Have students calculate their individual Ecological Footprints by visiting **www.myfootprint.org.**

Action Projects

- Have each student, or small groups of students, make a poster describing ways to reduce personal Ecological Footprints. Display the posters around campus as part of a peer education campaign.

- Do "Destination Conservation", a Service Learning Project in which students measure and track energy use and conservation practices in their school and home. Visit **www.facingthefuture.org,** click on **Take Action**, and then **Service Learning Projects** for everything you need to do this project with your class.

- Visit **www.facingthefuture.org** and click on **Take Action**, and then **Fast Facts Quick** Actions for more information and action opportunities on consumption.

Additional Resources

Films

- *The Ecological Footprint: Accounting for a Small Planet,* Global Footprint Network, 2005, 30 minutes. In this documentary film, Mathis Wackernagel introduces the Ecological Footprint and paints a picture of our current global situation. Wackernagel explores the implications of ecological deficits and provides examples of how governments, communities, and businesses are using the Footprint to help improve their ecological performance.

Books

- *Radical Simplicity: Small Footprints on a Finite Earth,* Jim Merkel, New Society Publishers, 2003.

Websites

- **www.rprogress.org** - Redefining Progress' website has extensive information about Ecological Footprints around the world.

- **www.footprintnetwork.org** – Global Footprint Network's goal is to increase the effectiveness of the Ecological Footprint as a tool for promoting ecological, social, and economic sustainability.

When the Chips Are Down

OVERVIEW

Students model 3 patterns of Ecological Footprint growth over 4 generations, using poker chips to represent Ecological Footprints and maps that they create to represent countries. The activity emphasizes the impact of changes in population growth rates and consumption patterns over relatively few generations, and possible solutions to these impacts.

INQUIRY/CRITICAL THINKING QUESTIONS

- How does an increase in Ecological Footprints impact countries?
- What are the impacts of different Ecological Footprint growth rates when carried out over several generations?
- What personal and structural solutions could be implemented to address impacts identified in this activity?

OBJECTIVES

Students will:
- Design and draw maps of their ideal country
- Model different Ecological Footprint growth rates over 4 generations
- Consider and discuss impacts of the different Ecological Footprint growth rates
- Consider, discuss, and debate a number of "structural" solutions to impacts associated with Ecological Footprint growth

TIME REQUIRED: 1.5 hours

KEY ISSUES/CONCEPTS

- **Ecological Footprint**
- **Carrying Capacity**
- **Resource scarcity and impacts** (migration, discrimination, and conflict)

SUBJECT AREAS

- **Social Studies** (Ancient Civilizations, Geography, Economics, Global Studies)
- **Science** (Life, Environmental)
- **Math**

NATIONAL STANDARDS CONSISTENCY

- **NCSS: 2, 3, 7, 9**
- **NSES: C, F**

GRADE LEVEL: 7–11

FTF Related Reading

- Intermediate: Chapters 2 and 8 from *Global Issues and Sustainable Solutions*
- Advanced: Unit 2 from *It's All Connected*

Materials/Preparation

- Overhead, *Definition and Components of an Ecological Footprint* (page 73)
- Butcher paper, 1 sheet per group (each sheet should be no larger than 25" x 30")
- Marking pens, colored, 3–4 pens per group

When the Chips Are Down

- Poker chips, 500 for a class of 20 or fewer, 1,000 for a class of more than 20
- Count out the poker chips for each group and each generation according to the table below, and put the larger stacks in labeled plastic bags

Generation	Group 1 (doubling)	Group 2 (tripling)	Group 3 (quadrupling)
1st	2	3	4
2nd	4	9	16
3rd	8	27	64
4th	16	81	256
Total Chips	30	120	340

Activity

Introduction

1. Use the overhead, *Definition and Components of an Ecological Footprint* on page 73, to discuss the concept of Ecological Footprint (or do the Facing the Future demonstration activity "Now Hear This!" to introduce the concept of Ecological Footprint).

Steps

1. Explain the following directions: In groups, design and draw a map of your "ideal" country, including the following components: farmland, housing, water, forests, recreation, energy sources, infrastructure, waste disposal, defense, and open space/wilderness. Decide on a name for your country and the type of government you want, and write those on the map.

2. Divide the class into 3 groups for a class of 20 or less, 6 groups for a class over 20 (with 6 groups, you will need to double the number of chips indicated in the above table. You will have 2 groups model

doubling, 2 groups model tripling, and 2 groups model quadrupling).

3. Give each group a piece of butcher paper and a set of marking pens. Have them brainstorm, discuss the components to be included, and then draw their country maps. Instruct them to draw their maps as if they were looking down on it from an airplane flying above (e.g. small squares for houses, areas for food cultivation, roads, etc.). Encourage students to be creative and to think about everything they might want to include in their ideal country. Give them plenty of time to create their maps so they are proud of their country and have an emotional connection to it.

4. When the groups are finished creating their countries, place the maps side by side (with edges touching) on a large table or on the floor, and have each group (or 2 representatives from each group) stand next to their country maps. Be sure that all the students can see the maps.

5. With the students gathered around, have each group briefly present their country map to the class.

6. Read (or paraphrase) the following directions to the students:

    You will model 3 different patterns of Ecological Footprint growth (based on population and consumption increase) over 4 generations, using poker chips to represent Ecological Footprints and the maps to represent countries. Each poker chip represents an Ecological Footprint. Ecological Footprints of individuals and nations vary depending on both population size and consumption patterns. Larger populations have a larger footprint

When the Chips Are Down

because more people require more resources to support them. Higher consumption lifestyles have a larger footprint because they require more resources per person to support those lifestyles. For example, eating an animal protein–intensive diet requires much more farmland than a vegetarian diet. Automobile use requires roads, repair shops, and parking lots, thus eliminating habitat for other species. You will place the Ecological Footprints (chips) on areas of the map where you want your impacts to be. For example, you might want to place the chips in areas designated for housing, roads, or farmland, since those are areas you have designed to be impacted. On the other hand, you probably do not want to place Ecological Footprints in your wilderness areas, if you want to keep them undeveloped.

7. Point to 1 map and tell them that this country represents a traditional agrarian society. They are doubling in population each generation, but their average consumption per person remains the same so their Ecological Footprint is doubling each generation. Place 2 chips, representing the first generation, on this country.

8. Point to the next country and tell them that this country represents a more developed society that has reduced its population growth rate, but is still experiencing a 50 percent increase in population and is doubling its consumption, so its total Ecological Footprint is tripling each generation. This is representative of some rapidly industrializing "Asian Tiger" nations, such as Thailand. Place 3 chips, representing the first generation, on this country.

9. Point to the third country and tell them that this country represents a society that is doubling both its population and its per capita consumption each generation. Therefore, its Ecological Footprint will quadruple each generation. This is representative of highly affluent societies such as the United States. Place 4 chips, representing the first generation, on this country.

10. Emphasize that chips cannot be placed outside the borders of countries and that chips cannot be placed on top of each other since an Ecological Footprint is a measurement of surface area and cannot be stacked (Note: Be careful not to say that they must keep their chips on their own country; placing chips, which represent Ecological Footprints, on other countries is allowed and even encouraged).

11. Hand out the second generation of chips and have the groups place the chips on their maps, modeling 1 "generation" of Ecological Footprint growth at a time. After each cycle is complete, hand out bags of pre-counted chips (as indicated in the above table) for the next

© 2006 FACING THE FUTURE: PEOPLE AND THE PLANET www.facingthefuture.org

When the Chips Are Down

generation. As you hand out the bags of chips, tell each group to decide where they want to place the Footprints. As they progress through the generations, they will have to decide which resources they want to impact or "cover up" with the Footprints.

12. Have the students briefly stop and observe the progression of the 3 models after each generation cycle. The group modeling a doubling of Footprint size will finish their task quite soon, and with minimal difficulty. The group modeling a tripling of Footprint size will probably take somewhat longer, and will confront decisions about how to handle growth and how to allocate impacts. The group modeling a quadrupling of Footprint size will take much longer and need much more room. Allow enough time for students to consider alternatives, but force the play rapidly enough so there is a sense of urgency and stress.

13. Students modeling the faster growth patterns (tripling and quadrupling) will be forced to decide which resources to deplete to accommodate their needs, since not all of the chips will fit on their maps without overrunning the resource base (you may need to remind students that the only rules are that they cannot stack the chips or place them off the paper; however, there is no rule about putting chips on another country). Situations that may arise include deforestation, loss of habitat, migration, border incursions, "brain-drain" (migration of educated people in search of better jobs), and invasion of neighboring countries to support population and consumption needs. Students may decide they need to impose draconian policies to halt population and consumption growth and "suspend" democratic principles. Some students may

decide to build border walls and store weapons to deter invasion of neighbors. The game will likely end in frantic activity, such as students pushing piles of chips across borders, other students throwing chips off the table, students trying to block other countries from placing chips on theirs, etc.

14. Bring the class back together for reflection questions.

Assessment
Reflection Questions

For Intermediate and Advanced Students

- What 2 things can make a country's total Ecological Footprint bigger?
- How did you feel when you saw how the other countries were dealing with their growth?
- What would happen if the chips game continued for 2 more cycles? What other decisions might each country have to make?
- What different choices would you have made in your country if you had known what was going to happen?
- How would careful planning have changed the outcome of the activity?

For Advanced Students

- Which decisions made in the activity actually occur in real life? What are the real-life impacts of those decisions, and what effect might they have on quality of life and social institutions? What type of government might emerge in response to the increased stress?
- Discuss the difference between personal and structural solutions to the impacts produced in the activity (e.g. a personal solution may be to reduce your own Footprint size by using alternative transportation rather than driving a car solo to school or work everyday. Structural solutions may include helping people in developing nations become economically self-sufficient, providing access to reproductive and community health care, and developing sustainable technologies).

When the Chips Are Down

Writing Connection

- Use the Population Reference Bureau's World Population Data Sheet at www.prb.org to determine the projected increase in global population in 1 year. Then identify 1 or more countries with approximately that population size. Look at a world map and determine where a new country with this population size could be placed every year for 10 years. Using the following questions, have students write a response paper on the feasibility of creating these new countries:
  - What resources and infrastructure would be required to support this new country?
  - What sort of geography and environment does the new country's projected location have?
  - How would the geography and environment change if a country of that size were placed there?
  - Does the existing geography and environment offer the resources that you determined were necessary to support the new country?
  - If not, how might those resources be provided?

Technology Connection

- Have students visit Annenberg Media's website at www.learner.org/exhibits/collapse/ and do the excellent web-based lesson titled "Collapse: Why Do Civilizations Fall?"

Language Arts/Math Connection

- This activity models exponential growth. To help students gain an understanding of exponential growth rates, have students read the children's story, Anno's Magic Seeds, by Mitsumasa Anno, in which a man plants seeds which double every year.

Action Projects

- Do a "Trickle-Up" Service Learning Project in which students raise money to provide small business grants for people living in poverty in developing countries. For a detailed description of this project, visit www.facingthefuture.org, click on Take Action, and then click on Service Learning Projects.
- Remove invasive plant species in a public area near your school and replant the area with native plants. Check to see if your city or county has a department that will work with you on this (e.g. Department of Parks, Department of Soil & Conservation, or Department of Natural Resources).
- Visit www.facingthefuture.org and click on Take Action, and then Fast Facts Quick Actions for more information and action opportunities.

Additional Resources

Books

- Anno's Magic Seeds, Mitsumasa Anno, Puffin Books, 1995. A children's story about a man who plants seeds that double every year, incorporating concepts in math, economics, and the environment.

- Collapse: How Societies Choose to Fail or Succeed, Jared Diamond, Viking Adult, 2004. Diamond examines how ancient and modern societies have collapsed due in large part to over-consumption of resources and population growth.

Websites

- www.rprogress.org - Redefining Progress is one of the creators of the Ecological Footprint calculator.

- www.prb.org – Population Reference Bureau's website includes extensive country-specific demographic data.

Farming for the Future

(Adapted with permission from the lesson Starvation or Survival developed by Barby and Vic Ulmer of Our Developing World. For related activities please visit Our Developing World's website at www.magiclink.net/~odw)

OVERVIEW

Through a simulation activity, students experience the challenges, decisions, choices, and impacts that subsistence farmers in the developing world face. In "village" groups, students decide which crops they will plant over 2 seasons, during which time there are randomly assigned dry and wet years.

INQUIRY/CRITICAL THINKING QUESTIONS

- What are some of the challenges that subsistence farmers face in growing enough food to feed their families?
- What are the root causes of hunger and poverty, and how can they be addressed sustainably?

OBJECTIVES

Students will:
- Experience the challenges, decisions, choices, and impacts that subsistence farmers in the developing world face
- Understand some of the root causes of hunger
- Consider sustainable solutions to help alleviate poverty and hunger

TIME REQUIRED: 1 hour

KEY ISSUES/CONCEPTS

- **Food security**
- **Subsistence farming**
- **Hunger and malnutrition**
- **Sustainable agriculture**

SUBJECT AREAS

- **Social Studies** (World History, Economics, Geography, Global Studies, Contemporary World Problems)
- **Science** (Life, Environmental)
- **Health and Nutrition**
- **Math**

NATIONAL STANDARDS CONSISTENCY

- **NCSS: 2, 3, 7, 9**
- **NSES: C, F**

GRADE LEVEL: 5–12

FTF Related Reading

- Intermediate: Chapter 5 from *Global Issues and Sustainable Solutions*
- Advanced: Unit 3, Chapters 1, 2, and 3 from *It's All Connected*

Vocabulary

- **Food Security** – Access by all people at all times to enough food for an active, healthy life (about 2,000 calories per day). Food security includes, at a minimum, availability of nutritionally adequate and safe foods, and an assured ability to acquire food in socially acceptable ways.
- **Subsistence Farming** – Small scale farming for the purpose of growing food to meet the needs of the family and/or community, as opposed to commercial for-profit farming.
- **Malnutrition** – A state of poor nutrition resulting from an insufficient, excessive, or unbalanced diet, or from an inability to absorb food.

Farming for the Future

Materials/Preparation

- Handout/Overhead: *Farming for the Future Directions and Worksheet,* 1 copy per group of 3-4 students and 1 overhead
- Handout: *Effects of Malnutrition,* 1 copy per group of 3-4 students
- Handout: *Impact and Solution Cards*, make 1 copy and cut out cards, keep the Year 1 and Year 2 cards separate
- 1 six-sided dice

Activity

Introduction

1. Start out with an introduction question, such as "Do you remember a time when you were not sure where your next meal would come from and what did you do?" Or "have you ever grown your own food or worked on a farm?"
2. Go over the vocabulary words. Begin by asking the students to define: food security, subsistence farming, and malnutrition.
3. Tell the class they are going to do an activity to simulate subsistence farming in small villages in Africa.

Steps

1. Go over the directions using an overhead of the handout *Farming for the Future Directions and Worksheet.*
2. Arrange the class into "village" groups of 3-4 students and have each group choose a name for their village.
3. Give each group 1 *Farming for the Future Directions and Worksheet* and 1 *Effects of Malnutrition Chart.*
4. Villages have about 5 minutes to select the number and type of food crops they will

plant and fill in the "# of Fields" column on the worksheet.
5. Throw the dice (or have 1 student throw it) to determine Year 1 weather: 1, 2, 3, or 4 = a dry year; 5 or 6 = a wet year (typically there are more dry years than wet years in Africa).
6. Villages compute their food yields based on the weather and, in pencil, fill out the first part of the worksheet (up to the Total Yield line).
7. Have villages read off their village name, the crops they planted, and their total yield.
8. Have each village, one at a time, select a *Year 1 Impact Card* and read it aloud to the class. Tell them that some cards affect all the villages and some only apply to the village that draws the card.
9. Students fill out the Impact Loss line of their worksheet after each *Impact Card* is read. If students draw *Impact Cards* that impact *all* villages, then the Impact Loss line will need to be revised accordingly. Be sure they use a pencil so they can erase and rewrite the loss.
10. After all villages have selected and read an *Impact Card*, have students calculate the "Total Yield After Impact" and fill in that line of their worksheet.
11. Have students calculate malnutrition based on the *Effects of Malnutrition Chart* and fill in that line of the worksheet. Ask students why malnutrition effects will be felt the following year.
12. Call on each village to read aloud their calculated "Total Yield After Impact" and record it on the board or overhead so you can compare the different villages' yields.

© 2006 FACING THE FUTURE: PEOPLE AND THE PLANET   www.facingthefuture.org

Farming for the Future

13. Repeat the activity for Year 2 using the *Year 2 Solution Cards* in place of the *Year 1 Impact Cards*. There are 2 basic differences between Year 1 and 2. For Year 2, the effects of malnutrition from the previous year are included in the yield calculations, and the *Solution Cards* suggest sustainable practices to increase crop yield and improve quality of life (you do not need to tell the students that the Year 2 cards are all solutions).

14. Conclude with the following reflection questions via a class discussion and/or journal writing.

Assessment Reflection Questions

For Intermediate and Advanced Students

• How did the village yields compare to one another? Who fared the best and who fared the worst? What were the primary reasons for the differing yields?

• How did the *Impact Cards* change your situation as a subsistence farmer?

• What are the practical effects of living a life in which the line between starvation and survival is so fine?

• What do you think it would be like if this simulation represented your own life, year in and year out?

• The activity provides all villagers with *Solution Cards* in Year 2. How realistic are the solution cards?

• What are some other solutions to the challenges faced by the farmers (other than the ones offered on the *Solution Cards*)?

For Advanced Students

• What do you think would have happened if this cycle of low food production and malnutrition were to continue for several years?

• What are structural solutions to the issues of hunger and food security?

• What are some factors affecting whether or not solutions can be implemented (e.g. governance, NGOs, community-based development)?

• Do people in the developed world impact food production in the developing world? If so, how? (e.g. type and amount of food we consume, water we use, or where we choose to buy our food).

• What other global issues are connected to the issue of food security?

Farming for the Future

Writing Connection

- Research and write a paper or create a brochure about a developing world country, focusing on its food security and agricultural practices. Include a brief background on the country's demographics, hunger and poverty statistics, current agricultural practices, and recommendations for sustainable practices to improve quality of life.

- Research and write an essay or article for the school paper about where your food comes from and how it reaches your community. Visit your local supermarkets, check the shelves, and talk to store managers. If you live in a farming/rural area, talk to farmers in your community and interview your parents and grandparents about the ways farming has changed in recent times. Find out if any food crops are grown in your area. Find out how much is grown locally and how much is transported from other states and countries. If much of your food is transported from locations far away, determine the impacts a shortage of fuel would have on food availability and price.

- Research and write a report on trade agreements (like NAFTA), focusing on how these affect both subsistence farmers in developing countries and people in the developed world.

Action Projects

- Define your "foodshed" by finding out what foods are grown in your region. What other food crops could be supported in your environment? Research

community supported agriculture (CSA) **www.nal.usda.gov/afsic/csa/**, farmers' markets, and other local food production and distribution efforts in your community. Identify local individuals and organizations supporting these efforts and work with them to develop or improve your community's farmers' market to provide safe, local food for everyone in your community.

- Team up with a local food bank to develop a cookbook that includes tasty and nutritious recipes using the ingredients commonly found at the food bank. Students can also do live "cooking shows" at the food bank to demonstrate how to make the recipes.

- Visit **www.facingthefuture.org**, click on **Take Action**, then **Fast Facts and Quick Actions** for information and action opportunities related to poverty and hunger.

Farming for the Future

Additional Resources

Films
- *Silent Killer: The Unfinished Campaign Against Hunger,* John DeGraaf, Bullfrog Films, 2005, 57 minutes. Highlights promising attempts in Africa, and in South and Central America, to end world hunger.

- *Santiago's Story,* TransFair USA, 2000, 15 minutes. This short film demonstrates how fair trade can make a difference in local communities.

Books
- *Hope's Edge: The Next Diet for a Small Planet*, Frances Moore Lappé and Anna Lappé, Jeremy P. Tarcher/Putnam, 2002. Hope's Edge includes the stories of subsistence farmers from 5 continents as well as an analysis of hunger, calls for action, learning resources, and recipes too.

- *Coming Home to Eat: The Pleasures and Politics of Local Foods,* Gary Paul Nabhan, W.W. Norton & Company, 2002. Chronicles a year spent by the author eating only from his local foodshed (growing, fishing, and gathering).

Websites
- **www.oxfamamerica.org** - Oxfam America is an international development and relief agency committed to developing lasting solutions to poverty, hunger, and social justice.

- **www.fao.org** – The Food and Agriculture Organization of the United Nations leads internationalefforts to defeat hunger, serving both developed and developing countries.

- **www.transfairusa.org** - Website of TransFair USA, a nonprofit organization that promotes and certifies fair trade products.

- **www.foodfirst.org/12myths** – Food First includes an online publication, 12 Myths About Hunger, Institute for Food and Development Policy, 1998.

- **www.localharvest.org** – A nationwide directory of farmers markets, CSAs, and other local food sources.

- **www.foodsecurity.org** - The Community Food Security Coalition (CFSC) is a North American organization dedicated to building strong, sustainable, local and regional food systems that ensure access to affordable, nutritious, and culturally appropriate food to all people at all times.

- **http://www.fian.org/fian/index.php** – FIAN International, the FoodFirst Information and Action Network, is a human rights organization that campaigns for the right to adequate food in over 60 countries in Africa, the Americas, Asia, and Europe.

© 2006 FACING THE FUTURE: PEOPLE AND THE PLANET   www.facingthefuture.org

Farming for the Future Directions and Worksheets

Student Names: _____

_____

Village Name: _____

Directions:

- Your village has **10 small fields to plant**
- You must plant at l**east 3 different crops** to ensure a variety of food types and **at least 2 fields must be protein crops**
- Determine your yields based on the **weather dice roll**: 1, 2, 3, 4 = dry year; 5, 6 = wet year
- Use a pencil to fill out the worksheet
- Chose an *Impact Card*, read it aloud, and calculate impact losses (some impacts will affect all villages and some will affect only your village)
- Determine the effect of malnutrition based on your final total yield and the *Effects of Malnutrition* chart
- Repeat activity for Year 2

Worksheet Year 1

Type/Crops	# of Fields	Wet Yield Units	Dry Yield Units	Total Yields
ROOTS				
Yams		70	20	
Cassava		40	60	
CEREAL				
Maize		60	30	
Millet		30	60	
PROTEIN				
Groundnuts		50	30	
Peas		50	30	
Total Yield				
Impact loss (from card)				
Total Yield After Impact				
Next year's loss from malnutrition				

Worksheet Year 2

Type/Crops	# of Fields	Wet Yield Units	Dry Yield Units	Total Yields
ROOTS				
Yams		70	20	
Cassava		40	60	
CEREAL				
Maize		60	30	
Millet		30	60	
PROTEIN				
Groundnuts		50	30	
Peas		50	30	
Total Yield				
Impact loss (from card)				
Loss from last year's malnutrition				
Total Yield After Impact and Malnutrition Loss				

© 2006 FACING THE FUTURE: PEOPLE AND THE PLANET   www.facingthefuture.org

Effects of Malnutrition

If food production falls below 450 units, your village will suffer from malnutrition and illness, affecting the residents' ability to work in the fields the following year. Use this chart to calculate malnutrition in your village based on the total food unit yield for each year.

Food Units	Loss from Malnutrition Next Year
450 and above	Lose 0 units
400-449	Lose 25 units
350-399	Lose 40 units
300-349	Lose 55 units
250-299	Lose 65 units
0-249	Lose 70 units

Impact Cards – Year 1

Flood

River bursts its banks, and since your village is located close to the river, your fields are flooded.

Your village loses 50 units

Normal Harvest

However "rust", a plant disease, affects your village, reducing maize yield to 50 units for a wet year and 30 units for a dry year.

Your village calculates the loss of maize yield

Normal Harvest

However your village's food storage has become damp, causing rot in 25% of your yams.

Your village calculates the loss of yam yield

Normal Harvest

However failure to rotate crops has lowered your yield. Cassava is very filling, easy to grow, and does not require much water but it depletes soil.

Your village reduces units by 60 if you grew 2 or more fields of cassava

Normal Harvest

However there has been political corruption in your village and a local government official has demanded that you pay him with food units.

Your village loses 40 units

Global Warming

Temperatures have been rising steadily. Many seeds are temperature sensitive and will not germinate at higher temperatures.

Each villages loses 50 units

AIDS

Several working-age villagers have contracted HIV/AIDS, reducing the number of workers available to grow crops.

Your village loses 70 units

Population Growth

More children were born in your village this year, requiring extra food to survive.

Your village subtracts an additional 40 units from the "loss from next year's malnutrition" line

War

A civil war erupts in the region and soldiers from both sides overrun fields in all of the villages.

Each village loses 100 units

Debt Repayment

International lenders, who have given you loans, need to be repaid immediately. Your village must grow "cash crops" of flowers for export, reducing food crops for your people.

Your village loses 70 units

© 2006 FACING THE FUTURE: PEOPLE AND THE PLANET   www.facingthefuture.org

Solution Cards – Year 2

Farming Collective

All the villages form a
collective to learn and share
sustainable farming practices.

Each village's yield increases
by 50 units

A Community Well

After several years of drought,
a non-governmental organization (NGO)
offers to work with your village to
construct a well.

Your yield increases by 60 units

Experimental Field

You plant a field of maize using
compost and drip irrigation.
The irrigation water is from a
rooftop water catchment system,
since rain is your only water source.

Your village gains 20 units
for each maize field planted

Digging Ditches

You spend several weeks
digging contour ditches, which
help conserve water and
prevent soil erosion.

Your village's yield increases
by 30 units

Rotate Crops

Your village decides to rotate
maize and groundnut crops.
Groundnuts enrich the soil with
nitrogen, doubling the yield of
your maize crops.

Your village doubles its maize
crop units

Literacy Class

Several people in your village join a
literacy class and, now able to read the
directions on a natural pesticide sack,
they find that you need less than you
have been using.

Your village gains 10 units because of
the money saved on pesticide

Composting

Your village decides to start
using compost and can thus reduce
the buying of expensive fertilizers.

Your village saves money and is able to
increase crop yield by 20 units

Health Center

A regional health center opens, providing
primary and reproductive healthcare to all villages.
The health center teaches reproductive health
classes. After time, birth rates begin to stabilize
and all villages require less food to survive.

All villages revise the malnutrition chart
so only 400 food units are needed
to prevent malnutrition

Every Drop Counts!

OVERVIEW

A series of water-related lessons beginning with a water trivia game and a short demonstration of how much of the Earth's water is available for human and other species' needs. The series includes a "water walk" and a personal water-use audit.

INQUIRY/CRITICAL THINKING QUESTIONS

- How much available fresh water exists worldwide?
- What are the causes and consequences of unequal water use around the world?
- How is water availability and use connected to other global issues?
- What can be done to conserve water resources and increase water availability?

OBJECTIVES

Students will:
- Understand that the world's fresh water supply is finite
- Understand what it might be like if they had to haul their own water daily
- Consider the global implications of fresh water use and discuss solutions to water scarcity

TIME REQUIRED: 1-2 hours

(depending on if you do all or part of the lessons)

KEY ISSUES/CONCEPTS

- **Water scarcity**
- **Water distribution and use**
- **Water conservation and productivity**

SUBJECT AREAS

- **Social Studies**
  (Geography, Global Studies, Contemporary World Problems)
- **Science** (Environmental, Earth)
- **Math**

NATIONAL STANDARDS CONSISTENCY

- **NCSS: 3, 7, 9**
- **NSES: A, C, D, F**

GRADE LEVEL: 5–12

FTF Related Reading

- Intermediate: Chapter 5 from *Global Issues and Sustainable Solutions*
- Advanced: Unit 3, Chapters 1, 2, and 3 from *It's All Connected*

Materials/Preparation

- Teacher Master, *Water Trivia*
- 1 gallon of water
- Clear, wide mouth container about the size of 1 pint (Optional: Add a drop of blue food coloring to the cup so that when you add the water it will be more visible from the back of the class)
- 1-cup measuring cup, tablespoon, and teaspoon
- Overhead: *Water Facts*
- Bucket of water or several gallon containers of water
- Handout: *Personal Water Use Audit*

© 2006 FACING THE FUTURE: PEOPLE AND THE PLANET   www.facingthefuture.org

Every Drop Counts!

Activity

Introduction

1. Do a trivia game using the *Water Trivia* teacher master sheet. Ask students all or part of the trivia questions. If you want to set it up as a competition, see the directions for the *Global Issues Trivia* in the beginning of this book (page 26).
2. Have students brainstorm all the things they do or use that require water. Create a list on the board or overhead under the headings: Domestic, Agricultural, and Industrial.
3. Ask students if they know how much fresh water there is on the planet.
4. Tell them you are going to demonstrate how much fresh and available water there is on the planet.

Steps - Part 1

1. Show the class a gallon of water.
2. Take out 2.5 percent (6 tablespoons plus 1 teaspoon) and place it in a clear container to represent the amount of fresh water on Earth.
3. Of this amount, remove 70 percent (4.5 tablespoons) to represent the amount of water trapped in glaciers or too deep in the ground to realistically be recovered. The remainder – less than 1 percent of the Earth's total water supply – is left to support human needs for agriculture, drinking, and washing as well as for lakes, rivers, and fresh water ecosystems.
4. Conclude with the following reflection questions.

Assessment Reflection Questions - Part 1

For Intermediate and
Advanced Students

• Given that there is a fixed amount of fresh water on the planet, what will happen to the distribution of water resources as global population grows?
• What happens when people do not have enough water to meet their basic needs?
• What happens when a fresh water resource is polluted? Why is it important to protect fresh water resources from pollution?
• What are some other purposes/uses of fresh water aside from human consumption?
• How can we reduce our personal water use?

For Advanced Students

• Does the greater use of water resources in developed countries (U.S., Canada, and Europe) affect the availability of water resources in water-scarce countries?
• How can water productivity (more crop per drop) be increased so that more water is available in areas that need it?

Activity

Steps - Part 2

1. Show and discuss the *Water Facts* overhead.
2. Create a scenario of a water-scarce country by having students walk around the classroom several times carrying a bucket (or gallon) of water (or have them go outside and carry the bucket around the track or playfield). You can do this activity with either 1 bucket and have 1 student at a time carry it, or use several gallon containers and have a number of students do the activity simultaneously.
3. Pass out and go over the *Personal Water Use Audit* worksheet with students so they can measure how much water they and their family uses.
4. Conclude with the following reflection questions.

Every Drop Counts!

Assessment Reflection Questions - Part 2

For Intermediate and Advanced Students

- How hard was it to carry the bucket of water?
- How would your life be different if you had to walk 3 hours every day for your water?
- What would life be like if you didn't have a safe, adequate water supply?

For Advanced Students

- Have you ever known anyone who had a water-related illness? Why aren't water-related illnesses very common in the developed world?
- Can water rich countries help provide water resources to water poor countries? How?
- Why do people in the developing world spend such a large percentage of their income on water?
- How is water availability and use connected to other global issues? (food production, health, environment, global warming, poverty, etc.)

Lesson Extensions

- Have the class determine and diagram the source of their community's fresh water. Graph the available limits of the community's water resources over the period of an average year. Predict events or circumstances that could negatively affect the availability of the community's drinking water. What would the impact be if the community water source ran dry? Brainstorm ways in which the community could reduce its fresh water consumption.
- Have students brainstorm a sustainable management plan for a watershed containing farmland, forest resources, salmon spawning streams, and other wildlife habitat. They should attempt to preserve each of the elements listed, while providing for economic and recreational opportunities for the area's human population.

Writing Connection

- Have students write a story as if they were a drop of water moving through the hydrologic cycle. They should describe what they see, hear, smell, taste, etc.

Every Drop Counts!

Technology Connection

- Have students research water use issues in a specific country including use, quality, conservation, and productivity measures and then prepare a PowerPoint presentation for the class based on the research and findings.

Action Projects

- Do a service learning project that helps WaterPartners International bring safe, accessible drinking water to those who do not have it. To learn more go to **www.facingthefuture.org**, click on **Take Action,** then click on **Service Learning Projects.**
- Collect and share data on your local rivers, lakes, and estuaries by contacting a local water quality monitoring agency or becoming part of a global initiative called "World Water Monitoring Day": **www.worldwatermonitoringday.org**.
- Let your neighbors know how natural waterways and marine species can be harmed by storm water runoff. You can help by labeling storm drains in the neighborhood around your school or home. By painting a warning next to a street's storm drain, you will educate others about where street waste flows – into local natural waterways. Stencils and information on labeling are usually available through local utility companies or other local entities.
- Organize a river or beach clean-up in your neighborhood.
- Visit **www.facingthefuture.org** and click on **Take Action**, then **Fast Facts Quick Actions** for more information and action opportunities related to water issues.

Additional Resources

Films

- *Environmental Ethics: Examining Your Connection to the Environment and Your Community,* The Video Project, 2005, 62 minutes, **www.videoproject.com**. This documentary profiles a diverse group of courageous Goldman Environmental Prize winners who have made it their duty to protect their local environments. Download an accompanying study guide at **www.envethics.org**.

Books

- *Water: The Fate of Our Most Precious Resource*, Marq de Villiers, Mariner Books, 2001. An eye-opening account of how global population growth, unchecked development, and cross-border struggles are stressing and depleting the world's fresh water supply.

Websites

- **www.water.org** – Water Partners International is committed to providing clean drinking water to communities in developing countries. Working in partnership with donors and those in need of safe water, they have helped thousands of people develop accessible, sustainable, community-level water supplies.
- **www.unep.org** – The Food and Agriculture Organization of the United Nations leads international efforts to defeat hunger, serving both developed and developing countries.

Water Trivia

1. What percent of the Earth's water is available for people to use?

   a. less than 1%; b. 5%; c. 10%; d. 20%

2. What percentage of people in the world lack access to safe drinking water? [1]

   a.15%; b. 25%; c. 35%; d. 45% (or 1.5 billion people)

3. What is the total amount of water (in gallons) consumed per day by the average person in the U.S.? [2]

   a. 55; b.150; c.750; d.1,300

4. About how many gallons/day are needed to sustain life (including the minimum water needed to produce the food we consume)? [3]

   a. 5; b. 13; c. 21; d. 33

5. What percentage of the adult human body is comprised of water? [4]

   a. 10%; b. 20%; c. 50-65%; d. 75-80%

6. What activity accounts for the highest water use worldwide - agriculture, industry, or domestic?[1]

   agriculture accounts for about 65-70% of water use; industry for about 20-25%; and domestic for about 13%

7. What is a proven technology or practice that can decrease agricultural water use?

   drip irrigation, planting low water use crops

8. What are other uses and benefits of fresh water aside from human consumption?

   stream flow, provides animal and plant nutrients and habitat, wetland filtration, recreation

9. What percent of his/her income does the average U.S. citizen spend on drinking water? [2]

   a. 0.5%; b. 2%; c. 10%; d. 25%

10. What percent of his/her income does the average Honduran living in the slums of that country's capital city spend on drinking water?[2]

    a. 0.5%; b. 2%; c. 10%; d. 25%

11. Approximately how many people in developing countries die each year from water-related disease?[2]

    a. 100; b. 1,000; c. 10,000; d. 10,000,000 (over 25,000 people every day!)

12. How many gallons of water does it take to produce 1 pound of corn?

    a. 68; b. 168; c. 568; d. 1268

13. How much water does it take to produce 1 pound a beef?[4]

    a. 40; b. 400; c. 4,000; d. 40,000

14. What are 2 things you can do personally to reduce your water use?

    turn off the water when brushing teeth, plant drought tolerant landscaping, reduce meat consumption

15. What is one benefit of a dam?

    produce hydroelectricity, prevent flooding, control water storage; make navigation easier

16. What is one negative impact of a dam?[6]

    impede the flow of soil nutrients, impede fish migration, flood rivers upstream

17. Name 3 sources of fresh water.[6]

    melting snow, aquifers, groundwater, rainwater, icebergs, desalinization of salt water

1 United Nations Environment Program www.unep.org

2 Water Partners International www.water.org

3 World Meteorological Organization

4 Mad Sci Network www.madsci.org

5 Environmental Protection Agency http://www.epa.gov/OGWDW/kids/games.html

6 American Forum for Global Education www.globaled.org

© 2006 FACING THE FUTURE: PEOPLE AND THE PLANET   www.facingthefuture.org

Lesson 16 Overhead:

Water Facts

- Every day more than 1 billion people make a 3-hour journey on foot just to collect water.

- More than 1.2 billion people (25% of the world's total population) do not have access to a safe and adequate water supply.

- 14,000 people die every day from water-related illnesses. This includes diseases transmitted via water such as giardia and dysentery, from lack of water (dehydration), and from parasites that breed in water (e.g. malaria).

- An average U.S. citizen will spend 0.5% of his/her annual income on water; while a citizen of Honduras will spend 25% of his/her annual income on water.

© 2006 FACING THE FUTURE: PEOPLE AND THE PLANET   www.facingthefuture.org

Personal Water Use Audit

Keep track of how many times you do each activity in 1 day. Keep a running tally throughout the day and then calculate your total times and gallons used at the end of the day.

Activity	Tally times doing activity	Total number	Estimated Water Use (multiply total number by the amount listed to get total gallons)
Washed hands			0.1 gallons =_____gallons
Showered (regular showerhead)			30 gallons =_____gallons
Showered (low-flow showerhead)			15 gallons =_____gallons
Tub bath			20 gallons =_____gallons
Brushed teeth			0.2 gallons =_____gallons
Drank a glass of water			0.008 gallons =_____gallons
Boiled pot of water for cooking			0.25 gallons =_____gallons
Flushed toilet (conventional toilet)			5 gallons =_____gallons
Flushed toilet (ultra-low flush toilet)			1.6 gallons =_____gallons
Washed a load of dishes in dishwasher			15 gallons =_____gallons
Washed a load of dishes in sink (not running the tap)			10 gallons =_____gallons
Washed load of laundry in conventional machine			40 gallons =_____gallons
Washed load of laundry in high efficiency washer			25 gallons =_____gallons
Washed a car			15 gallons =_____gallons
Other activity:			
Other activity:			
Other activity:			
Total daily gallons			

Adapted from WaterPartners International "Tap Tally Sheet" (http://water.org/assets/PDF/ODsplishsplash.pdf)

Fueling the Future

OVERVIEW

Students compare energy use and CO2 emissions by sector in the United States and China (and optionally in another country). They research and discuss energy impacts and sustainable energy solutions, write a resolution addressing energy use, and present their resolutions at a "World Energy Summit".

INQUIRY/CRITICAL THINKING QUESTIONS

- How does energy use by different sectors compare between the U.S. and China?
- How is energy use connected to other global issues?
- What can be done to conserve energy resources and reduce CO2 emissions?

OBJECTIVES

Students will:
- Calculate and compare the percentage of energy use and emissions by country and sector to world average energy use and emissions
- Brainstorm and research impacts of energy use by sector
- Brainstorm and research sustainable energy solutions
- Write a resolution
- Present their resolution at a mock "World Energy Summit"

TIME REQUIRED: 2 hours

KEY ISSUES/CONCEPTS

- **Energy use**
- **Renewable and non-renewable energy resources**
- **Climate change**
- **Energy conservation**

SUBJECT AREAS

- **Social Studies**
  (World History, Geography, Civics/ Government, Global Studies, Contemporary World Problems)
- **Science**
  (Earth, Environmental, Physical)
- **Math**
- **Language Arts**

NATIONAL STANDARDS CONSISTENCY

- **NCSS: 3, 6, 7, 8, 9, 10**
- **NSES: D, E, F**

GRADE LEVEL: 7–12

FTF Related Reading

- Intermediate: Chapter 6 from
  Global Issues and Sustainable Solutions
- Advanced: Unit 3, Chapter 4 from
  It's All Connected

Materials/Preparation

- A few items to show during the introduction segment of the activity (e.g. food, clothing, a book, computer, etc.)
- Handout: *Energy Use by Country and Sectors Table*, 1 per 2-4 students
- Handout: *Fueling the Future Role Cards*, copy and cut
- Handout/Overhead: *Writing a Resolution Worksheet*, 1 per student
- Calculators, 1 per group of 2-4 students

Fueling the Future

Activity – Day 1

Introduction

1. Show students some items (e.g. food, clothing, a book, computer, etc.) 1 at a time and ask them how energy is connected to the manufacturing and use of the item.
2. Tell the class they are going to do an activity that examines and compares the type and amount of energy use and emissions in the U.S. and China.

Steps

1. Write on the board or overhead these 3 energy sectors: Transportation, Residential, and Industrial/ Commercial.
2. Have students brainstorm different uses of energy (e.g. cars, home heating and cooling, lights, food production, etc.) and list them below the appropriate sector.
3. Divide the class into 6 groups of 2-4 students representing the 3 energy use sectors (transportation, residential, and industrial/commercial) for both the U.S. and China (Note: For classes with more than 24 students, divide into 9 groups representing the U.S., China, and another country's energy sectors. For country profiles of energy use by sector visit the World Resource Institute's website at **www.earthtrends.wri.org**).
4. Give each group a copy of *Energy Use by Country and Sectors Table* and 1 Role Card (there will be 2 groups of each energy sector – 1 for the U.S. and 1 for China).
5. Give groups about 15 minutes to complete the table for their country and sector, following the prompts on the Role Cards (calculate percent, list uses and impacts, and brainstorm sustainable energy solutions). Each group will need a calculator to figure

out their percentages. Sustainable energy solution ideas can be found in Unit 3, Chapter 5 of *It's All Connected*.
6. Have a representative from each group report to the class on the percentages in the first section of the table and have students fill in their tables based on the reported data from the other groups.
7. Bring the class back together for the following discussion prompts and questions (after the discussion, have the students either hold onto their completed *Energy Use by Country and Sectors Table* or collect the worksheets and pass them out again on Day 2 of the activity).

Assessment – Day 1 Reflection Questions

For Intermediate and Advanced Students

- Discuss the difference in percentages between U.S. and China energy use and emissions.
- Which sectors use the most energy? Which country uses the most energy?
- Why should we care about energy use and emissions? What effects does it have on people and the planet?
- Have students share and discuss their brainstorm lists of energy uses by different sectors.
- Have students share and discuss their sustainable energy solutions.

Activity – Day 2

Introduction

1. Tell the class that they are going to participate in a "World Energy Summit" in which they will work together in U.S./China sector groups to develop a policy addressing energy consumption, conservation, and

Fueling the Future

emission reductions. Tell them that they will be writing a resolution about their energy policy.

Steps

1. Put up the overhead, *Writing a Resolution Worksheet*, and go over what a resolution is with the class.

2. Arrange the class so that each sector joins together with the same sector from the other country. There will be 3 larger groups comprised of a U.S./China transportation sector, a U.S./China residential sector, and a U.S./China industrial/commercial sector.

Give 1 *Writing a Resolution Worksheet* to each group. Have the groups assign roles: facilitator, timekeeper, note taker, and reporter.

3. Give the groups about 10-15 minutes to discuss and decide on 1 or 2 polices to address energy consumption, conservation, and emission reductions. They will need to refer to the "Sustainable Energy Solutions" section of the *Energy Use by Country and Sectors Table* that they completed on Day 1 of the activity.

4. Give the groups about 15-20 minutes to write a resolution and to prepare to present

Fueling the Future

their resolution to the class.

5. Hold a "World Energy Summit" in which each group has 3-5 minutes to present their resolution to the class.

6. Each student should take notes on the resolutions that are presented so they can discuss and vote on the resolutions later.

7. After all groups present, facilitate a discussion on the pros and cons of each resolution.

8. Have students vote on each resolution.

9. Conclude with the following reflection questions.

their growing energy needs in a sustainable manner? Discuss the concept of "leapfrog technology" in which modern, sustainable technologies are transferred to developing countries, avoiding the unsustainable stage of industrial development that developed countries experienced.

Technology Extension

• Have students visit the Climate Analysis Indicators Tool (CAIT) developed by the World Resources Institute at **http://cait.wri.org,** where they can research and create a multitude of charts and graphs on global climate change and energy use by sector and country.

Assessment Reflection Questions

For Intermediate and Advanced Students

• Did the resolution process work? Were we able to develop some good energy policies?

• What are the limitations of this process?

• What are some other ways that governments, groups, and individuals can effect change in energy use and emissions?

• What other global issues are connected to energy?

For Advanced Students

• What are some of the hidden costs of using non-renewable energy?

• How can developing countries meet

Action Projects

• Have students write an essay explaining what they would do if they were unable to use any oil- or gasoline-powered vehicles once a week. Then have them plan and implement "fossil-fuel free" activity days for their family and neighborhood.

• Create a more energy-efficient learning environment. Many local energy companies or city utility agencies are teaming together with students to save schools and districts energy and money and to beautify learning environments.

© 2006 FACING THE FUTURE: PEOPLE AND THE PLANET www.facingthefuture.org

Fueling the Future

By providing energy audits, technical assistance with retrofit plans, information about financing methods, staff training, and educational programs, these companies and agencies can help schools identify many ways to save energy and money. Have students investigate local energy and utility companies to identify the resources and opportunities that are available to address energy consumption in their school or district. Your students can play a critical role in educating their peers and community on the many benefits of creating a more energy-efficient learning environment.

• Visit **www.facingthefuture.org** and click on **Take Action**, and then **Fast Facts Quick Actions** for more information and action opportunities related to energy use.

Additional Resources

Films

• *Rising Waters: Global Warming and the Fate of the Pacific Islands*, directed by Andrea Torrice, 2000, 57 minutes. Through personal stories of Pacific Islanders in Kiribati, the Samoas, the atolls of Micronesia, and Hawaii, as well as researchers in the continental United States, this documentary film puts a human face on the international climate change debate.

• *Silent Sentinels*, directed by Richard Smith, produced by the Australian Broadcasting Corporation, 1999, 57 minutes. This documentary film takes a broad look at coral reefs and how the coral organism has coped with climate change over time.

Books

• *Stormy Weather: 101 Solutions to Global Climate Change,* Guy Dauncey with Patrick Mazza, New Society Publishers, 2001. This book provides a comprehensive view of energy issues and practical solutions.

Websites

• **www.earthtrends.wri.org** – World Resources Institute's "Earth Trends" is a comprehensive on-line database that focuses on environmental, economic, and social trends. "Country Profiles" present environmental information about key variables for several topic areas. View charts and graphs to find statistics for over 220 countries.

• **http://cait.wri.org** – The Climate Analysis Indicators Tool (CAIT) is an information and analysis tool on global climate change developed by the World Resources Institute.

Sample from CAIT Resources & Links:
Annual sources (+) and sinks (-) of carbon from 10 world regions.

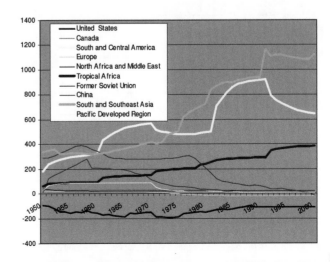

Fueling the Future
Energy Use by Countries and Sectors Table

Energy Consumption/Year * (million metric tons of oil equivalent) †	United States (1999)	U.S. %‡ of World Energy Use	China (1999)	China %‡ of World Energy Use	Total World Energy Use (1999)	Other Country (use, emissions, and % of world energy use)
Transportation	601,275		69,176		1,755,505	
Residential	254,209		289,489		1,845,475	
Industrial/Commercial§	554,076		363,523		2,818,316	
CO2 Emissions/Year (million metric tons)						
Transportation	1,693		221		5,505	
Residential	352		211		1,802	
Industrial/Commercial**	3,225		2,399		14,235	

Energy Uses and Impacts *Brainstorm different ways that energy is used in each sector and their impacts*

Transportation Uses	Transportation Impacts
Residential Uses	Residential Impacts
Industrial/Commercial Uses	Industrial/Commercial Impacts Uses

Sustainable Energy Solutions *Brainstorm alternatives to reduce and conserve energy use for each sector*

Transportation

Residential

Industrial/Commercial

* SOURCE: World Resource Institute EarthTrends www.earthtrends.wri.org

† A 'million metric ton of oil equivalent' is a measurement of energy. It is equal to the amount of energy in 1 metric ton of crude oil, 107 kilocalories or 41.868 gigajoules.

‡ To find % of World Energy Use divide U.S. total and China total by Total World Energy Use.

§ This category includes industry, agriculture, commercial, and public services.

** This category includes public electricity, heat production, auto producers, other energy industries, manufacturing industries, and construction.

© 2006 FACING THE FUTURE: PEOPLE AND THE PLANET   www.facingthefuture.org

Fueling the Future Role Cards
(country and energy sectors)

Country: **China**	Country: **United States**	Country:
Energy Sector: **Transportation**	Energy Sector: **Transportation**	Energy Sector: **Transportation**
1. Calculate your sector's percentage of the world's energy use and emissions 2. List uses and impacts of your sector 3. Brainstorm sustainable energy solutions for your sector	1. Calculate your sector's percentage of the world's energy use and emissions 2. List uses and impacts of your sector 3. Brainstorm sustainable energy solutions for your sector	1. Calculate your sector's percentage of the world's energy use and emissions 2. List uses and impacts of your sector 3. Brainstorm sustainable energy solutions for your sector
Country: **China**	Country: **United States**	Country:
Energy Sector: **Residential**	Energy Sector: **Residential**	Energy Sector: **Residential**
1. Calculate your sector's percentage of the world's energy use and emissions 2. List uses and impacts of your sector 3. Brainstorm sustainable energy solutions for your sector	1. Calculate your sector's percentage of the world's energy use and emissions 2. List uses and impacts of your sector 3. Brainstorm sustainable energy solutions for your sector	1. Calculate your sector's percentage of the world's energy use and emissions 2. List uses and impacts of your sector 3. Brainstorm sustainable energy solutions for your sector
Country: **China**	Country: **United States**	Country:
Energy Sector: **Industrial/Commercial**	Energy Sector: **Industrial/Commercial**	Energy Sector: **Industrial/Commercial**
1. Calculate your sector's percentage of the world's energy use and emissions 2. List uses and impacts of your sector 3. Brainstorm sustainable energy solutions for your sector	1. Calculate your sector's percentage of the world's energy use and emissions 2. List uses and impacts of your sector 3. Brainstorm sustainable energy solutions for your sector	1. Calculate your sector's percentage of the world's energy use and emissions 2. List uses and impacts of your sector 3. Brainstorm sustainable energy solutions for your sector

Lesson 17 Handout:

Fueling the Future–Writing a Resolution

What is a Resolution?

A resolution is a formal way of stating intended action by a group. Resolutions are used by decision-making bodies ranging from local school boards to the United Nations. A resolution usually consists of 2 main parts:

1. **PREAMBLE**: The *Whereas* clause(s) contains background information and reasons for the resolution.
2. **REQUEST FOR ACTION**: The Resolved clause(s) contains the request for action.

Steps in Preparing a Resolution

1. Identify the issue of concern.
2. Research and gather supporting background materials which are sufficient to allow a person with no prior knowledge of the subject to make an informed, intelligent decision.
3. Write a draft and then a final resolution in the proposed format, taking care to ensure that:
    - Each "**Whereas"** clause is accompanied by sufficient background material.
    - At least 1 of the "**be it Resolved**" clauses directs government (or other entity) to take action.
4. Select a representative(s) from your group to present and provide rationale in support of your resolution at the World Energy Summit.

How to Write a Resolution

Write the sections of your resolution in the following format:

1. The *Heading* serves as identification for the resolution and states WHERE the resolution will be submitted, WHAT the subject of the resolution is, and WHO is proposing the action.
2. The *Preamble* is used to explain WHY the action in the *Resolved* section should be taken. It states past action, reasons for the action, and reasons for concern. Each *Preamble* clause should be written as a separate paragraph, beginning with *Whereas* and ending with a semi-colon. The last paragraph of the *Preamble* should end with a connecting phrase such as "Therefore be it..."
3. The *Resolved* section indicates what action is proposed. The word *RESOLVED* is underlined and printed in capital letters, followed by a comma and the word "that". Each resolved clause is a separate paragraph and ends with a semi-colon, and in the case of the next to the last clause should be followed by "*and*".

Sample Resolution:

SUBMITTED TO: Our Class

SUBJECT: Writing a Resolution

PROPOSED BY: Our Teacher

Whereas we are studying energy use and emissions;

Whereas we have become experts on energy use and emissions for specific countries and energy use sectors;

Whereas we are holding a World Energy Summit;

Whereas we are learning to write a resolution for the World Energy Summit;

therefore, be it *RESOLVED*, that:

We agree to follow these guidelines in writing a resolution for the World Energy Summit;

We promise to work together to write a great resolution;

We will develop policies to conserve energy use and reduce emissions; and

We will present our findings at the World Energy Summit.

For more information on writing a resolution, visit the United Nations Online website at
http://www.unol.org/res/rw3.shtml

Biodiversity Connections

OVERVIEW

Students simulate biodiversity within an ecosystem by assuming the identities of resident plant and animal species in a forest stream ecosystem. Students investigate the functions of plant and animal species in the ecosystem, discover their interdependent relationships, and consider the importance of preserving biodiversity in nature.

INQUIRY/CRITICAL THINKING QUESTIONS

- What is biodiversity and why is it important in an ecosystem?
- What factors threaten biodiversity?
- What can people do to help protect and conserve the Earth's ecosystems?

OBJECTIVES

Students will:
- Identify the functions of plant and animal species in a forest stream ecosystem
- Explore species interdependency
- Consider what can be done to help protect biodiversity

TIME REQUIRED: 1 hour

KEY ISSUES/CONCEPTS

- **Ecosystems**
- **Biodiversity**
- **Sustainability**

SUBJECT AREAS

- **Social Studies** (Global Studies)
- **Science** (Life, Environmental)

NATIONAL STANDARDS CONSISTENCY

- **NSES: C, F**
- **NCSS: 9**

GRADE LEVEL: 5–9

FTF Related Reading

- Intermediate: Chapter 6 from
  Global Issues and Sustainable Solutions
- Advanced: Unit 4, Chapters 1, 2, 3, and 5 from
  It's All Connected

Vocabulary

- **Ecosystem** – A community of organisms (plant, animal, and other living organisms) together with their environment, functioning as a unit.
- **Habitat** – The environment in which an organism or biological population lives or grows.
- **Biodiversity** – The variety of life in all its forms, levels, and combinations, including ecosystem diversity, species diversity, and genetic diversity.

Biodiversity Connections

Materials/Preparation

- Handout: *Plant/Animal Identity Cards*, copy and cut into 15 cards (1 per every 2 students)
- (Optional) See the "Technology Connection" below for a good website with information about the species in this activity

Activity

Introduction

1. Tell the class that they are going to do an activity in which they take on the identity of a plant or animal species in a forest stream ecosystem and explore species interdependency.
2. If necessary, go over the vocabulary words.

Steps

1. Brainstorm with the students what a forest stream ecosystem might look like and what plant and animal species might live there. (You want students to give general answers here such as trees, insects, birds, fish, shrubs, etc.)
2. Arrange students in pairs. Have each pair randomly draw a *Plant/Animal Identity Card* and tell them that it is their job to figure out how the different plants and animals in the ecosystem function and interact.
3. Have each pair discuss and then answer the first question on their card – "What is your function in this ecosystem?"

4. Give students about 10 minutes to move about the room with their partner and interview other student pairs to investigate what other plant and animal species exist in the ecosystem and how they interact. Have them provide at least 2 answers to the second and third questions on their role cards – "What/Who do you depend on in this ecosystem?" and "What/Who depends on you in this ecosystem?"

- Optional: When the students are walking around "meeting" the other ecosystem parts, have them act out their plant/animal rather than tell each other what they are. This can be very straightforward – if someone figures out that they are a tree, for example, they could simply say "Yes, I'm a big leaf maple."

5. Call the class to attention. As a group, discuss the ecosystem and how it functions. How are the different plant and animal species interacting to ensure each others' survival? As students share their species and connections, draw or write the ecosystem components on the board and draw lines between the different species as the connections are stated.

© 2006 FACING THE FUTURE: PEOPLE AND THE PLANET   www.facingthefuture.org

Biodiversity Connections

6. Select a few students to explain their function within the ecosystem. Have students share which plant and animal species they depend on and which plant and animal species depend on them within the ecosystem.
7. Conclude with the following reflection questions.

Assessment Reflection Questions

For Intermediate and Advanced Students

• Why is biodiversity in an ecosystem important?
• What impact does removing even 1 species from an ecosystem have on the ecosystem as a whole?
• How might the ecosystem be affected if a new plant or animal species were introduced?
• How do human beings affect an ecosystem? What are some negative and positive effects?
• What is 1 example of an ecosystem in your community or region?
• What can you do as an individual, and what can be done on a systemic level, to protect and conserve the Earth's ecosystems?

For Advanced Students

• What factors threaten biodiversity in an ecosystem (e.g. climate change, a mining operation, etc.)?
• How might a contaminated or destroyed ecosystem impact a local community?
• What does 2004 Nobel Peace Prize Laureate Wangari Maathai mean when she says, "In making sure that other species survive, we will be ensuring the survival of our own"?

Technology Connection

• Have students research their species using the National Wildlife Federation field guide website at **www.eNature.com**, where they will find detailed information, including description, habitat, range, food source, and even some sounds!

Art Connection

• Have students draw or make a collage of the forest stream ecosystem including the plant and animal species inhabitants.

Action Projects

• Remove invasive plant species in a public area near your school and replant the area with native plants. Many city and county agencies will work with you and your students on this (Department of Parks, Department of Soil & Conservation, Department of Natural Resources, etc.).
• Join the Rainforest Action Network – a non-profit group working to protect tropical rainforests and the human rights of those living in and around those forests. For more information, visit Rainforest Action Network at **www.ran.org**.

Biodiversity Connections

* Visit **www.facingthefuture.org** and click on **Take Action** and then **Fast Facts Quick Actions** for more action opportunities on biodiversity issues.

Additional Resources

Films

* *Biodiversity: the Variety of Life*, Dal Neitzel, The Greater Ecosystem Alliance, 1992, 42 minutes, **www.bullfrogfilms.com**. Through the use of maps, diagrams and examples, this video offers important insight into preserving the balance of dynamic ecosystems.

* *Natural Connections*, Sharon Howard & Michael Rosen, 2000, 46 minutes (Also available as a 5-part series for schools), **www.bullfrogfilms.com**. Natural Connections makes effective use of interviews with well-spoken scientists, beautiful photography, top quality graphics, and original music to underline the importance of maintaining biodiversity if we as a species want to survive and thrive on our home planet.

Books

* *Biodiversity*, Dorothy Hinshaw Patent & William Allen Munoz (Illustrator), Clarion Books, 2003. A photo essay that illustrates not only what biodiversity is, but why it is important to maintain.

* *The Future of Life*, E.O. Wilson, Knopf, 2002. Eminent biologist and expert on biodiversity, E.O. Wilson argues that the integrity and diversity of the planet are under grave threat in the 21st century and then outlines a strategy for protecting most of the world's remaining ecosystems and species.

Websites

* **www.conservation.org** – Conservation International's mission is to conserve the Earth's living heritage, our global biodiversity, and to demonstrate that human societies are able to live harmoniously with nature.

* **www.wri.org** – The World Resources Institute is an environmental think tank whose mission is to move human society to live in ways that protect Earth's environment for current and future generations.

* **www.biodiv.org**– The Convention on Biological Diversity (CBD) is an agreement adopted by the majority of the world's governments at the 1992 Earth Summit. The Convention establishes 3 main goals: the conservation of biological diversity, the sustainable use of its components, and the fair and equitable sharing of the benefits from the use of genetic resources.

© 2006 FACING THE FUTURE: PEOPLE AND THE PLANET   www.facingthefuture.org

© 2006 FACING THE FUTURE: PEOPLE AND THE PLANET   www.facingthefuture.org

Plant/Animal Identity Cards

GREEN BACKED HERON (bird)
What is your function in this ecosystem?

What/Who do you depend on in this ecosystem?

What/Who depends on you in this ecosystem?

BIGLEAF MAPLE TREE
What is your function in this ecosystem?

What/Who do you depend on in this ecosystem?

What/Who depends on you in this ecosystem?

MAYFLY (aquatic insect)
What is your function in this ecosystem?

What/Who do you depend on in this ecosystem?

What/Who depends on you in this ecosystem?

DOUGLAS FIR TREE
What is your function in this ecosystem?

What/Who do you depend on in this ecosystem?

What/Who depends on you in this ecosystem?

GARTER SNAKE
What is your function in this ecosystem?

What/Who do you depend on in this ecosystem?

What/Who depends on you in this ecosystem?

© 2006 FACING THE FUTURE: PEOPLE AND THE PLANET   www.facingthefuture.org

Plant/Animal Identity Cards

CRAYFISH

What is your function in this ecosystem?

What/Who do you depend on in this ecosystem?

What/Who depends on you in this ecosystem?

RUFOUS HUMMINGBIRD

What is your function in this ecosystem?

What/Who do you depend on in this ecosystem?

What/Who depends on you in this ecosystem?

HONEYSUCKLE BUSH (shrub typically found along the banks of a forest stream)

What is your function in this ecosystem?

What/Who do you depend on in this ecosystem?

What/Who depends on you in this ecosystem?

RIVER OTTER

What is your function in this ecosystem?

What/Who do you depend on in this ecosystem?

What/Who depends on you in this ecosystem?

MOSQUITO

What is your function in this ecosystem?

What/Who do you depend on in this ecosystem?

What/Who depends on you in this ecosystem?

© 2006 FACING THE FUTURE: PEOPLE AND THE PLANET   www.facingthefuture.org

Plant/Animal Identity Cards

COHO SALMON (fish)
What is your function in this ecosystem?

What/Who do you depend on in this ecosystem?

What/Who depends on you in this ecosystem?

SPIKE RUSH (green, grass-like plant growing along shorelines or in shallow water)
What is your function in this ecosystem?

What/Who do you depend on in this ecosystem?

What/Who depends on you in this ecosystem?

COOPER'S HAWK (raptor type bird)
What is your function in this ecosystem?

What/Who do you depend on in this ecosystem?

What/Who depends on you in this ecosystem?

SPOTTED FROG
What is your function in this ecosystem?

What/Who do you depend on in this ecosystem?

What/Who depends on you in this ecosystem?

BLACK BEAR
What is your function in this ecosystem?

What/Who do you depend on in this ecosystem?

What/Who depends on you in this ecosystem?

© 2006 FACING THE FUTURE: PEOPLE AND THE PLANET   www.facingthefuture.org

Plant/Animal Identity Cards

RAINBOW TROUT

What is your function in this ecosystem?

What/Who do you depend on in this ecosystem?

What/Who depends on you in this ecosystem?

HUMAN

What is your function in this ecosystem?

What/Who do you depend on in this ecosystem?

What/Who depends on you in this ecosystem?

Toil for Oil

OVERVIEW

In this oil extraction simulation, students experience the increasing difficulty of extracting a limited, nonrenewable resource over several years. Students consider and discuss renewable energy sources.

INQUIRY/CRITICAL THINKING QUESTIONS

- What happens when a nonrenewable resource is extracted over several generations?
- What are the impacts of exploiting a natural resource?
- What renewable energy sources can be used to meet our energy needs, and what are the benefits of those sources?

OBJECTIVES

Students will:
- Experience the increasing difficulty of extracting nonrenewable oil resources over time
- Consider the social, environmental, and economic impacts of using a nonrenewable energy resource
- Identify clean, renewable, and sustainable energy sources

TIME REQUIRED: 1 hour

KEY ISSUES/CONCEPTS

- **Renewable and nonrenewable resources**
- **Population growth**
- **Scarcity**
- **Sustainability**

SUBJECT AREAS

- **Social Studies** (Geography, Global Studies, U.S. History, Economics, Contemporary World Problems)
- **Science** (Earth, Environmental)
- **Math**

NATIONAL STANDARDS CONSISTENCY

- **NCSS: 3, 5, 7, 8, 9**
- **NSES: B, C, D, E, F**

GRADE LEVEL: 5–9

FTF Related Reading

- Intermediate: Chapter 6 from *Global Issues and Sustainable Solutions*
- Advanced: Unit 3, Chapter 4 from *It's All Connected*

Vocabulary

- **Nonrenewable Resource** – A resource, such as coal or oil, that cannot be replenished as it is consumed.
- **Renewable Resource** – A resource, such as wind, solar, or geothermal energy, that can be replenished as it is consumed.

Materials/Preparation

- 2 pounds of dried red beans, for a class of 25 or fewer students
- 2/3 cup of dried black beans, for a class of 25 or fewer students
- 2 medium size bowls per 25 students, (put 1 pound of red beans and 1/3 cup black beans in each bowl)
- Timer, or watch with a second hand, to time activity
- Handout: *Oil Extraction Data Sheet*, 1 copy per student

Toil for Oil

Activity

Introduction

1. (Optional) Do a Sides Debate using the following statement (see Sides Debate description on page 28):

   "As humans, it is our right to extract as much oil as we want to meet our everyday energy needs and strengthen our economies."

2. Review the vocabulary, introducing the concept of renewable and nonrenewable resources.

3. Tell the class that today they are going to "drill" for oil, a nonrenewable resource, and they will model the extraction of oil reserves over 3 years.

Steps

1. Give each student 1 copy of the handout, *Oil Extraction Data Sheet* and go over it with them. Show them the bowls, explaining that the red beans represent dirt and the black beans represent oil.

2. For a class of 25 or fewer, divide the class into 2 groups. Each group will represent an oil company.

3. Have each oil company choose a name.

4. Place the bowls with the red and black beans in different areas of the room.

5. For each oil company, have 4 students representing the first year gather around the bowl filled with the mixed beans. The remaining students will wait while the year 1 students extract the oil.

6. Give students 30 seconds to extract the oil by picking out the black beans from the bowl and leaving the red beans in the bowl.

7. At the end of the 30-second period, have the

Toil for Oil

students stop extracting, count their barrels of oil, and record their oil extraction on their data sheets (each black bean is equal to 1 barrel of oil).

8. Have the same 4 students, plus 3 more students representing year 2 oil drillers, gather around the same bowls and repeat the activity for 30 more seconds, extracting and recording.

9. Have those same students, plus the remaining students in each oil company representing the 3rd year, gather around the same bowls and repeat the activity for 30 more seconds.

10. Have each oil company report their total number of barrels.

11. Have students individually or in their groups complete the questions on the *Oil Extraction Data Sheet*.

12. Conclude with the following reflection questions.

Assessment Reflection Questions

For Intermediate and Advanced Students

• What happened to the oil production as the number of oil drillers increased with each year? What might this simulate? (e.g. population increases, increased use per person.)

• With each year, was it easier or harder to extract the oil? (More drillers are able to extract more oil but then oil also runs out faster. It becomes increasingly more difficult to extract the oil, thus simulating the difficulty of extracting oil as the nonrenewable resource depletes and wells have to be dug deeper and deeper.)

• Are there any resources that are less available now than there were for your grandparents? What are some of these resources? How does this affect you? Do you ever think about future generations (your potential children and grandchildren) when you use resources today?

• Discuss and list ways to reduce the use of nonrenewable resources.

• Discuss and list clean, renewable energy sources (and their benefits) that could be used in place of nonrenewable sources.

For Advanced Students

• How is this activity similar to the extraction of real nonrenewable oil reserves?

• How is the use of a nonrenewable resource different from the use of a renewable resource?

• What happens to a resource when you have infinite population growth and a finite resource?

Writing Connection

• Have students research, prepare a poster or paper, and do a presentation on their community's current energy use, including nonrenewable and renewable sources. What are the processes and resources necessary to deliver that energy? What are the associated costs and impacts of that energy production? Is energy use subsidized? If so, how and why? How can energy consumption be reduced? Have them identify and describe several sources of renewable energy and the availability of those renewable energy technologies in the community. How can the community support the use of renewable energy technologies?

Toil for Oil

Action Projects

- Have students develop a display for their school or for the larger community promoting the sustainable use of energy resources.
- Do "Destination Conservation", a Service Learning project in which students track energy use and encourage conservation in their school and home. For a detailed description of this project, visit **www.facingthefuture.org** and click on **Take Action**, then **Service Learning Projects**.
- Organize a walk or bike-to-school day as part of an awareness campaign about the health benefits of walking and biking as well as air quality and the environment. Link up with a national initiative online at: **www.walktoschool-usa.org**.
- Visit **www.facingthefuture.org** and click on **Take Action**, then **Fast Facts Quick Actions** for more information and action opportunities on energy.

Additional Resources

Films

- *French Fries to Go*, Howard Donner, 2003, 15 minutes, **www.greenplanetfilms.org**. French Fries is the story about a guy, his truck, and a bunch of used vegetable oil. This funny and inspiring piece follows Charris Ford as he makes the rounds in his veggie fuel powered rig.

- *Oil on Ice*, Dale Djerassi/Bo Boudart Productions, 2004, 90 minutes, **www.greenplanetfilms.org**. A vivid, compelling, and comprehensive documentary connecting the fate of the Arctic National Wildlife Refuge to decisions the U.S. makes about energy policy, transportation choices, and other seemingly unrelated matters. Caught in the balance are the culture and livelihood of the Gwich'in people and the migratory wildlife in this fragile ecosystem.

Websites

- **www.wri.org** – World Resources Institute is an environmental think tank that goes beyond research to find practical ways to protect the earth and improve people's lives. Their website includes extensive data on renewable and nonrenewable energy use worldwide.

© 2006 FACING THE FUTURE: PEOPLE AND THE PLANET   www.facingthefuture.org

Oil Extraction Data Sheet

Student Name: _____

Oil Company: _____

Keep track of your oil company's total barrel extraction. Each black bean is equal to 1 barrel of oil.

	Year 1 (total from all oil drillers in your company)	Year 2 (total from all oil drillers in your company)	Year 3 (total from all oil drillers in your company)
Barrels of oil extracted			

1. How many drillers did your company have in year 1?_____ in year 2?_____ in year 3?_____

2. In which year was the largest number of barrels extracted?_____

_____

3. In which year was the second largest number of barrels extracted? _____

_____

4. Which year had the least number of barrels extracted?_____

_____

5. How does this activity mirror real oil extraction? _____

_____

6. Explain the difference between a nonrenewable energy source and a renewable energy source.

_____

_____

7. List 5 things you can do personally to conserve energy_____

_____

_____

_____

_____

8. List 3 policies, laws, manufacturing practices, or other types of legislation that could be implemented to reduce dependency on nonrenewable energy sources.

_____

_____

_____

Fishing for the Future

(Adapted with permission from "Fishing with Jim" by Jim Hartmann and Ben Smith)

OVERVIEW

Through a fishing simulation, students model several consecutive seasons of a fishery and explore how technology, population growth, and sustainable practices impact fish catch and fisheries management. As the students progress through the fishing seasons, they will likely overfish their oceans and will have to migrate to other oceans to meet their basic needs.

INQUIRY/CRITICAL THINKING QUESTIONS

- What happens when a commonly owned resource is overused?
- What are the impacts of overfishing or exploiting a natural resource?
- How can we establish and maintain the sustainable use of a resource?

OBJECTIVES

Students will:
- Experience the "tragedy of the commons" as it relates to fishing resources
- Consider social, environmental, and economic impacts of overfishing
- Identify sustainable fishing practices
- Determine and explain purchasing/consumption choices

TIME REQUIRED: 1 hour

KEY ISSUES/CONCEPTS

- **Tragedy of the Commons**
- **Sustainability**

SUBJECT AREAS

- **Social Studies** (Geography, Economics, Global Studies, Contemporary World Problems)
- **Science** (Life, Environmental)
- **Math**

NATIONAL STANDARDS CONSISTENCY

- **NCSS: 3, 5, 7, 9**
- **NSES: C, F**

GRADE LEVEL: 6–12

FTF Related Reading

- Intermediate: Chapter 5 from *Global Issues and Sustainable Solutions*
- Advanced: Unit 4, Chapter 4 from *It's All Connected*

Vocabulary

- **Tragedy of the Commons:** Occurs when resources—such as the air we breathe, the water we drink, and the fish we eat—shared by everyone (or held in common) are used at a rate that exceeds the resources' sustainable limit. Ultimately, as population grows and consumption increases, the "commons" collapse.

Materials/Preparation

- Plain, small candy-covered chocolate candies, one 16-ounce bag for up to 20 students
- Small plastic bowls, 1 per 4-5 students
- Put about 20 candies in 1 bowl per 4-5 students
- Spoons, 1 per 4-5 students
- Straws, 1 per student
- Watch, for timing activity
- Handout: *Fishing Log*, 1 per student

© 2006 FACING THE FUTURE: PEOPLE AND THE PLANET   www.facingthefuture.org

Fishing for the Future

Activity

Introduction

1. Introduce and discuss the concept of sustainability using the following definition: "Sustainability is meeting the needs of the present without limiting the ability of people, other species, and future generations to meet their needs." Ask why sustainability might be an important goal for a society and what might be some of the challenges in realizing this goal.

2. Tell students that today they are going to go fishing and explore some of these sustainability issues.

Steps

1. Explain the game rules:
   a. Each student will be a "fisher" whose livelihood depends on catching fish.
   b. The candies represent ocean fish such as cod, salmon, tuna, etc.
   c. Each fisher must catch at least 2 fish in each round to survive (i.e. get enough fish to either eat or sell).
   d. When the fishing begins, students must hold their hands behind their backs and use the "fishing rod" (straw) to suck "fish" (candies) from the "ocean" (bowl) and deposit them into their "boat" (i.e. on the table in front of them).
   e. The fish remaining in the ocean after each fishing season represent the breeding population, thus, 1 new fish will be added for every fish left in the ocean (bowl).

2. Divide the class into groups of 4 or 5 students and have each group choose an ocean name, such as North Atlantic, North Pacific, Arctic, Mediterranean, etc.

3. Give each group 1 serving bowl and give each student 1 straw and 1 copy of the handout *Fishing Log*.

4. Put one bowl with the candies by each group.

5. Say "Start fishing" and give the students about 20 seconds for the first "season" of fishing.

6. Have each fisher count his or her catch and record the data in their *Fishing Log*.

7. Fishers who did not catch the 2-fish minimum must sit out the following round.

8. Add 1 new fish (candy from the bag) for every fish left in the ocean (bowl).

9. Allow fishers to use their hands on the straws during the second session to represent "new technology".

10. After the second fishing season, give 1 fisher from each group a spoon representing more new fishing technology such as trawl nets, sonar equipment, etc. Continue the game for round 3.

11. Ask the students what happened when ocean group [name] ran out of fish. How are the fishers going to survive now (one option is to move to another ocean)? Allow students to "invade" other ocean groups when their ocean is depleted, but do not tell them that they can do this beforehand. Fishers may either go as a group to another ocean or they may disperse to other oceans.

12. Repeat fishing, recording, and replenishing fish stocks until either sustainable fishing levels are achieved or until all (or most) groups fish out their ocean.

13. (Optional) Repeat the activity after the class has experienced the "tragedy of the commons" and discuss sustainable practices to see if they can harvest in a sustainable manner.

14. Conclude with the following reflection questions.

Fishing for the Future

Assessment
Reflection Questions

For Intermediate and Advanced Students

- How did you feel when you realized that you had depleted your fish stock?
- How did you feel when other fishers joined your ocean group?
- How does this activity relate to real ocean and fishery issues?
- Have students brainstorm ways to have a sustainable fishery. What rules could be developed (e.g., limit the types of equipment allowed, limit the amount and type of fish, institute shorter seasons)?

For Advanced Students

- What is missing in this game (impacts on animals that rely on fish for their survival, population growth, etc.)?
- What happens to a resource when you have infinite population growth, rapidly developing technology, and a finite resource?
- Are there any commonly owned resources in our region or community? If so, what are some similar issues that arise, and how can they best be managed? (For example, air is a commonly used resource—how do we deal with air pollution? Forestry or animal grazing rights sometimes prompt similar discussion points. You might also talk about city parks, national parks, and other public lands, and their competing uses and needs.)

© 2006 FACING THE FUTURE: PEOPLE AND THE PLANET www.facingthefuture.org

Fishing for the Future

Writing Connections

- Have students do a freewrite and follow-up discussion on the following quote by John C. Sawhill, relating it to the fishing activity: "In the end, our society will be defined not only by what we create, but by what we refuse to destroy."
- Have students research a local fishery and include interviews with local fishers, biologists, and other people involved with the fishery.
- Have students choose 1 of the major world fisheries, such as salmon, cod, or tuna, and develop a sustainable fishing plan, paying attention to international laws and treaties.
- Have students investigate fish farming and its environmental and economic impacts.

Action Projects

- Students can research which fish are harvested in a sustainable manner and which are being depleted. Have them do an advertising campaign in their school promoting the consumption of sustainable fish and avoiding the consumption of threatened fish. This might include researching the kind of fish served in your school cafeteria and then recommending a sustainable seafood purchasing program to cafeteria staff and school principal. For recommendations about which seafood to buy or avoid, check out the Monterey Bay Aquarium's website "Seafood Watch" at http://www.montereybayaquarium.org/cr/
- Do a watershed planning/protection project to help protect local fisheries from environmental damage.
- Participate in a beach or river cleanup project.
- Join an Ocean/Fisheries Action Network

such as: Center for Marine Conservation Ocean Action Network (www.cmc-ocean.org), the Marine Fish Conservation Network (www.conservefish.org), SeaWeb (www.seaweb.org), or World Wildlife Fund Conservation Action Network (www.takeaction.worldwildlife.org).

Additional Resources

Films

- *Environmental Ethics: Examining Your Connection to the Environment and Your Community*, The Video Project, 2005, www.videoproject.com. This 62 minute documentary profiles a diverse group of courageous Goldman Environmental Prize winners who have made it their duty to protect their local environment. Includes protection of ocean fisheries. Download an accompanying study guide at: www.envethics.org.

Books

- *State of the World*, World Watch Institute, New York, www.worldwatch.org.

Websites

- www.fao.org/fi – United Nations Food and Agriculture Organization (FAO) Fisheries Resource website.
- www.montereybayaquarium.org – The mission of the Monterey Bay Aquarium is to inspire conservation of the oceans.

Fishing Log

Ocean Name: _____

Fishers: _____

Record your group's catch and the amount of fish left in ocean after each season:

Season	Catch	Fish Left In Ocean
1		
2		

Briefly describe the status/health of your fishery:

_____

_____

Season	Catch	Fish Left In Ocean
3		
4		

Briefly describe the status or health of your fishery now:

_____

_____

_____

_____

How could you have made your fishing practices sustainable?

_____

_____

_____

What's Up With the GDP?

OVERVIEW

In this economics simulation, students graph changes in the personal incomes of different community residents and in the community's proportion of the Gross Domestic Product (GDP) following an oil spill. The lesson explores the effect of an environmental disaster on the GDP, and the accuracy of GDP as a measurement of a community's overall health.

INQUIRY/CRITICAL THINKING QUESTIONS

- How do we measure the economic, social, and environmental health and well-being of a community?
- What are the limitations of using the GDP to measure the health and well-being of a community?
- What are other ways we can measure progress?

OBJECTIVES

Students will:
- Graph and evaluate the change in personal income and proportion of the GDP of a fictional community before and after an environmental disaster
- Consider the appropriateness of GDP as a measurement of the overall health of a community
- Identify and discuss other indicators to measure a community's health and well-being

TIME REQUIRED: 1.5 - 2 hours

FTF Related Reading

- Intermediate: Chapter 7 from *Global Issues and Sustainable Solutions*
- Advanced: Unit 1, Chapter 2 and Unit 5 from *It's All Connected*

KEY ISSUES/CONCEPTS

- **Gross Domestic Product**
- **Community indicators**
- **Economic growth versus community well-being**

SUBJECT AREAS

- **Social Studies** (Geography, Economics, Global Studies)
- **Science** (Environmental)
- **Math**
- **Business/Finance**

NATIONAL STANDARDS CONSISTENCY

- **NCSS: 3, 5, 7, 10**
- **NSES: F, G**

GRADE LEVEL: 7–12

What's Up With the GDP?

Materials/Preparation

- Tape and scissors
- Handout: *Role Cards*, copy and cut as many as the table below indicates. One set of role cards is enough for a class of 30.
- Handout: *100-Dollar Bills*, copied and cut into strips (refer to amounts in table below:

for 20 students, 180 bills or 12 sheets; for 30 students, 270 bills or 18 sheets)
- Handout: *Income Graphs*, 1 per student
- Handout: *After Spill Cards*, copied and cut (refer to amounts in table below; 1 set of role cards is enough for a class of 30).

Community Roles	Percent of Community	A Class of 20 Students	A Class of 30 Students	Before Spill $100 Bills Per Student (total $$ per person)	After Spill $100 Bills Per Student (total $$ per person)
Oil Executive	5%	1	1	20 ($2,000)	+15 ($3,500)
Attorney	5%	1	2	15 ($1,500)	+15 ($3,500)
Doctor	5%	1	2	15 ($1,500)	+10 ($2,500)
Retail Business Owner	5%	1	2	10 ($1,000)	+5 ($1,500)
Environmental Technician	10%	2	3	10 ($1,000)	+5 ($1,500)
Oil Pipeline Worker	25%	5	7	10 ($1,000)	-3 ($700)
Service Worker	20%	4	6	5 ($500)	-2 ($300)
Commercial Fisher	25%	5	7	5 ($500)	-4 ($100)

© 2006 FACING THE FUTURE: PEOPLE AND THE PLANET www.facingthefuture.org

What's Up With the GDP?

Activity

Introduction

1. Begin by defining and discussing Gross Domestic Product (GDP): GDP is the total market value of the goods and services provided within a region's borders. Explain that GDP is often used as a primary means of measuring a nation's economic health. Tell the students that they are going to examine the applicability of GDP as a measurement of the overall health of a community and explore other possible indicators of a community's health and progress.

Steps

1. Read the following scenario to the class:

   You are a community of people living in the town of Salmon Bay, Alaska, located on the Pacific coast adjacent to Salmon Sound, an area containing an important ocean fishery. Salmon Bay's economy is based primarily on oil development, commercial fishing, and small retail/service businesses. The Majestic Oil Company's pipeline, carrying 2,000 gallons of oil per minute, runs through the town of Salmon Bay. Each of you will represent 1 of the following roles in the community: Majestic Oil Company chief executive officer, a doctor, an attorney, a business owner, an oil pipeline worker, an environmental technician, a commercial fisher, and a service worker (restaurant cooks and waiters, grocery store clerks, hotel workers, etc.).

2. Randomly assign roles (pass out role cards) and give each student his or her starting money as indicated in the table above (the oil executive gets 20 100-dollar bills, the doctors get 15, the retail business owners get 10, etc.).

3. Have students write their name on their role card.

4. Have each student tape his/her 100-dollar bills together to form a lengthwise strip and then tape their role card, with their name written on it, to the bottom of the strip.

5. Holding their strip of money, students line up in a row in order of shortest to longest strip, forming a human graph of income distribution in the town of Salmon Bay.

6. Have them tape the strips to the wall or chalkboard in the same order as step 5, keeping the bottom edges even to form a graph. Make sure role cards and student names are visible at the bottom of the strip.

7. Pass out the handout, *Income Graphs* and have students make a bar graph of "Individual Incomes in the Starting Economy" based on amounts from the main graph posted on the board.

8. Calculate the total income in the starting economy and write it in the space next to the graph.

9. Arrange students in groups based on their community roles (put all the fishers together, etc.). Group the CEO, attorney, doctor, and business owner together. If needed, subdivide the groups so each has no more than 5 students.

10. Read the following scenario:

    A pipeline worker accidentally runs a piece of heavy equipment into the pipeline, causing a severe rupture. The pipeline rupture is right next to an estuary that opens directly into the Salmon Sound fishery. Oil begins to flow out of the ruptured pipeline at the rate of 2,000 gallons per minute, directly into the estuary and into Salmon

What's Up With the GDP?

Sound. It takes Majestic Oil Company 4 hours to discover the damaged pipeline and stop the flow of oil. Officials from the Environmental Protection Agency (EPA) and the Department of Oil and Gas (DOG) arrive on site to assess the damage.

(Optional: Have students calculate how many gallons of oil are spilled.)

11. Ask the students to predict how this event will affect their personal income and Salmon Bay's overall proportion of the GDP.

12. One at a time and starting with the lowest economic group, give each group the *After Spill Card* that pertains to them, and have them read the card aloud to the class and follow the card's instructions. Some students will make more money and others will lose their money. Students either cut their dollars off the top of their strip or tape new dollars onto it, depending on what the card says.

13. Have students complete the bar graph of "Individual Incomes Post-Spill" and calculate the total post-spill income using the bottom graph on the handout.

14. Conclude with the following reflection questions.

Assessment Reflection Questions

For Intermediate and Advanced Students

- What happened to personal incomes and the GDP? Is this what you predicted would happen?
- What professions/vocations seem to benefit the most? Which suffer the most? Explain why.
- What happened to the health and well-being of the community?
- Do you think people in Salmon Bay were happier/better off before or after the oil spill?
- What happened to the health of the environment? What are some of the long-term consequences of the oil spill?
- What are some indicators in your community that you could look at to determine the health of your community?

For Advanced Students

- Is there a difference between well-being and progress? Explain.
- Did the GDP give an accurate picture of

© 2006 FACING THE FUTURE: PEOPLE AND THE PLANET   www.facingthefuture.org

What's Up With the GDP?

the community's overall health? If not, where did it fall short and why?

- What are some indicators besides GDP that could more accurately gauge the well-being of the Salmon Bay community (education levels, health, number of parks, air and water quality, etc.)?

Writing Connection

- Have the class design a new "Index of Progress" to measure advances or declines in the human condition. List the indicators they believe are important in measuring human progress. Include indicators of environmental, economic, physical, and social health. Rank these indicators in terms of importance, and determine how to measure them. Compare rankings on the class index to conventional measures such as the GDP, the stock market, or the Consumer Price Index.

Technology Connection

- Visit the "Redefining Progress" website at **www.rprogress.org** for information on the Genuine Progress Indicator (GPI) developed in 1995. The GPI starts with the same accounting framework as the GDP, but then makes some crucial distinctions: It adds in the economic contributions of household and volunteer work, but subtracts factors such as crime, pollution, and family breakdown. Explore how the GPI has performed compared to the GDP. What might lie behind that trend?

Action Projects

- Have students research the dominant industries or economic activities (those that generate the most income

or greatest number of jobs) in their community. List the benefits of this activity in one column and the negative impacts in another. Analyze the result, and propose policies to balance social, economic, and environmental concerns by writing letters to schools or local papers.

- Build community knowledge by working with elders to gather oral histories. Ask them about general trends as well as specifics about what has changed in regards to the local economic situation, equity, culture and traditions, and the environment. This information can be catalogued at the local library.

- Visit **www.facingthefuture.org** and click on **Take Action**, then **Fast Facts Quick Actions** for more information and action opportunities on related global economic issues.

Additional Resources

Websites

- **www.iisd.org** – The International Institute for Sustainable Development (IISD) website has background information and a directory of community-based projects that have developed and used alternative indicators of progress.

- **www.rprogress.org** – Redefining Progress (RP) works with a broad array of partners to shift the economy and public policy towards sustainability. They have developed the Genuine Progress Indicator, an alternative to the GDP for measuring progress.

© 2006 FACING THE FUTURE: PEOPLE AND THE PLANET   www.facingthefuture.org

WHAT'S UP WITH THE GDP? – Role Cards 1 of 2 (FOR A CLASS OF 30)

**Chief Executive Officer
Majestic Oil Company**

**Attorney
Salmon Bay Law Firm**

**Attorney
Salmon Bay Law Firm**

**Doctor
Salmon Bay Clinic**

**Doctor
Salmon Bay Clinic**

Retail Business Owner

Retail Business Owner

**Environmental
Technician**

**Environmental
Technician**

**Environmental
Technician**

Oil Pipeline Worker

Oil Pipeline Worker

Oil Pipeline Worker

Oil Pipeline Worker

Oil Pipeline Worker

© 2006 FACING THE FUTURE: PEOPLE AND THE PLANET   www.facingthefuture.org

WHAT'S UP WITH THE GDP? – Role Cards 2 of 2 (FOR A CLASS OF 30)

Oil Pipeline Worker

Oil Pipeline Worker

Service Worker
(restaurant, retail clerk, hotel worker)

Service Worker
(restaurant, retail clerk, hotel worker)

Service Worker
(restaurant, retail clerk, hotel worker)

Service Worker
(restaurant, retail clerk, hotel worker)

Service Worker
(restaurant, retail clerk, hotel worker)

Service Worker
(restaurant, retail clerk, hotel worker)

Commercial Fisher

Commercial Fisher

Commercial Fisher

Commercial Fisher

Commercial Fisher

Commercial Fisher

Commercial Fisher

© 2006 FACING THE FUTURE: PEOPLE AND THE PLANET   www.facingthefuture.org

WHAT'S UP WITH THE GDP? – After Spill Cards 1 of 2

Chief Executive Officer of Majestic Oil Company —

Majestic Oil Company will spend up to $2 million on cleanup operations and legal fees. We will hire the best law firm in town to fight any lawsuits. However, the company plans to raise the per-barrel price of our oil from $15 to $20 to pay these costs. Unfortunately, the company has decided that I must step down from my duties as CEO, but in honor of my many years of service, I have received a "golden handshake". The CEO earns $1,500.

Attorneys with Salmon Bay Law Firm —

We are pleased to announce that Majestic Oil Company has just hired the Salmon Bay Law Firm to defend it in a lawsuit filed by "Save Salmon Bay". Majestic Oil is willing to pay whatever it costs to win this pending lawsuit. We are working day and night on this case, and therefore our incomes double. Attorneys earn $1,500 each.

Doctors with Salmon Bay Clinic —

As a result of the oil spill, several Majestic Oil Company workers have been exposed to toxic fumes and require immediate medical attention. Salmon Bay's fresh water has also been contaminated, and many townspeople have come to the hospital complaining about headaches and stomach problems. Because of this increase in medical demand, our income increases by almost 70 percent. Doctors earn $1,000 each.

Retail Business Owners —

We are sorry to say that some oil workers and fishers are out of work and are now spending less at the grocery store, movie theaters, and gas stations. However, the good news is that hotels and restaurants have been very busy since the spill, as there are many officials in town reviewing and monitoring the cleanup operations. We are experiencing a 50 percent increase in business. Business owners earn $500 each.

WHAT'S UP WITH THE GDP? – After Spill Cards 2 of 2

Environmental Technicians —

The environmental technicians have started immediate oil-spill monitoring and cleanup operations. We are monitoring wildlife impacts, testing water quality, and starting oil cleanup procedures. We are very busy these days, and our incomes have increased by 50 percent. Each technician earns $500.

Oil Pipeline Workers —

Since the spill, regular operations on the pipeline have stopped and a few of us have been laid off, although some of us are working overtime on pipeline operations. Because of the spill, we also have medical costs from exposure to toxic fumes and contaminated water supplies. Our overall income is reduced by 30 percent. Each pipeline worker loses $300.

Service Workers —

Salmon Bay's commercial business is booming these days because there are so many government officials and news reporters here looking over the cleanup operations. However, we haven't been feeling too well since the spill because our water supply is now contaminated. We are spending our money on bottled fresh water and on doctor visits. Service workers each lose $200.

Commercial Fishers —

The Salmon Sound fishery has been wiped out by the oil spill. The oil dumped into the Sound killed most of the adult fish, and the fish breeding ground in the bay is devastated. There will be no fishing in this area for several years. We will have to take our fishing boats out of the Sound and look for fish in other areas. Each fisher loses $400.

ENGAGING STUDENTS THROUGH GLOBAL ISSUES
© 2006 FACING THE FUTURE: PEOPLE AND THE PLANET   www.facingthefuture.org

Individual Incomes in Starting Economy

	1	2	3	4	5	6	7	8	9	10	11	12	13	14	15	16	17	18	19	20	21	22	23	24	25	26	27	28	29	30
$3,500																														
$3,000																														
$2,500																														
$2,000																														
$1,500																														
$1,000																														
$500																														
$0																														
people in community	1	2	3	4	5	6	7	8	9	10	11	12	13	14	15	16	17	18	19	20	21	22	23	24	25	26	27	28	29	30

Total income: _____
(Sum of all incomes)

Individual Incomes Post Spill

	1	2	3	4	5	6	7	8	9	10	11	12	13	14	15	16	17	18	19	20	21	22	23	24	25	26	27	28	29	30
$3,500																														
$3,000																														
$2,500																														
$2,000																														
$1,500																														
$1,000																														
$500																														
$0																														
people in community	1	2	3	4	5	6	7	8	9	10	11	12	13	14	15	16	17	18	19	20	21	22	23	24	25	26	27	28	29	30

Total income: _____
(Sum of all incomes)

© 2006 FACING THE FUTURE: PEOPLE AND THE PLANET   www.facingthefuture.org

WHAT'S UP WITH THE GDP? –100 Dollar Bills

Livin' the Good Life?

OVERVIEW

Students develop indicators to measure quality of life and conduct a survey of peers and adults to obtain data for their indicators. They analyze the survey data using spreadsheet software and produce charts to demonstrate their results. Students compare their own performance as measured by the quality of life indicators against averages determined by the survey results.

INQUIRY/CRITICAL THINKING QUESTIONS

- How is quality of life measured?
- What are other ways to measure quality of life?
- How does the concept of what is necessary for a high quality life change over the course of our lives?

OBJECTIVES

Students will:
- Develop quality of life indicators
- Develop and administer a quality of life survey
- Analyze data and present the results
- Understand the connection between how quality of life is measured and global issues such as sustainability, inequality, poverty, and good governance

TIME REQUIRED: 3 hours*

*plus out of class time for data collection and entry

KEY ISSUES/CONCEPTS

- **Quality of life**
- **Community indicators**

SUBJECT AREAS

- **Social Studies**
  (Civics/Government, Economics, Global Studies, Contemporary World Problems)
- **Science** (Environmental)
- **Math**
- **Technology/Computers**
- **Business/Finance**

NATIONAL STANDARDS CONSISTENCY

- **NCSS: 1, 2, 3, 4, 9, 10**
- **NSES: F**

GRADE LEVEL: 9–12

FTF Related Reading

- Intermediate: Chapter 6 from *Global Issues and Sustainable Solutions*
- Advanced: Unit 4, Chapters 1, 2, 3, and 5 from *It's All Connected*

Materials/Preparation

- Overhead: *Quality of Life Categories*
- Overhead/Handout: *Quality of Life Survey* (you can download the survey form from **www.facingthefuture.org**)

Livin' the Good Life?

- Handout: *Excel Instruction Sheet*, 1 copy per student
- Students will need basic competency with spreadsheet applications (e.g. Microsoft Excel). You may need to review how to enter data and perform basic summing and averaging functions before beginning this exercise.

Activity – Day 1

Introduction

1. (Optional) Do a Sides Debate using 1 of the following prompts (see Sides Debate description on page 28):
   - "People who make more money have a better quality of life."
   - "The 40 hour work week should be reduced to 32 hours."
2. Ask the class, "If everyone in the world was "livin' the good life," what would we have in common?" OR "If everyone in the world had a high quality of life, how do you think the world might be different than it is today?" (Encourage students to think about quality of life as a positive concept, not just a lack of negative aspects. For example, the World Health Organization defines "health" as "a state of complete physical, mental and social well-being and not merely the absence of disease or infirmity.")

Steps

1. Ask the class to brainstorm general categories of things in their lives that are important to their quality of life. Start with 1 example such as "family".
2. Either use the categories that they come up with or display the overhead, *Quality of Life Categories*.

3. Give the class the following information and instructions:
   - You are going to develop indicators (measurements) to evaluate quality of life based on these categories. You will develop and administer a survey of peers and adults asking for data on the indicators you develop.
   - In groups of 2-3 students, each group will come up with an indicator for 1 of these broad quality of life categories either from the pre-prepared list or from the list created by the class.
   - The indicators must be **measurable in units of time or quantities** and should fit into the formula **Number of ____ per _____.** For example, if an important element of quality of life is Relaxation, how would you measure that (e.g. number of hours per week you do after-school activities; number of days you take a vacation per year)?
   - Consider how easy or difficult it will be for the people you survey to provide data for the indicators. For example, an indicator of Recreation could be the number of milliseconds a person spends playing sports every day, but not many people can tell you how many milliseconds they spend doing anything!
4. Break the class into groups of 2-3 students, and assign each group one of the quality of life categories. Tell the groups they will have about 10 minutes to come up with their indicator and write it on a piece of paper. Circulate around the groups and assist where necessary.
5. Have each group tell you the indicator they came up with and write it on a transparency of the survey. Check that the indicator is something measurable in units of time or

© 2006 FACING THE FUTURE: PEOPLE AND THE PLANET   www.facingthefuture.org

Livin' the Good Life?

quantity, and that a person being surveyed could provide an answer easily. Check that the indicator will fit into the formula **Number of ____ per _____**.

6. Explain to the whole class that you will create a final survey based on their indicators and then the students will survey peers and adults to assess their quality of life as defined by these indicators.

7. Show the transparency of the indicators and conclude Day 1 with the following reflection questions.

Assessment
Reflection Questions - – Day 1

For Intermediate and Advanced Students

• Why did you choose the indicator you did to define your quality of life category?

• Can you think of other indicators for the categories written on the transparency? (Note: Do not change the original indicators given by the groups, as you will use those indicators for the survey portion of the exercise. Be sure that the students do not attack each other's ideas; explain that there are many different ways to measure quality of life.)

• How do you think people might adjust their

lives to be in line with 1 or more of these indicators? (For example, if it was socially accepted that a quality of life measurement for Relaxation is the number of vacation days taken annually then people might adjust their balance between work and vacation time.)

Activity – Day 2
Materials/Preparation

• Download and save on your computer the *Quality of Life Survey* from **www.facingthefuture.org** (or make a copy or retype the handout *Quality of Life Survey*). Type in the students' indicators in the "Indicator" section of the survey form.

• Make 7 copies of the completed *Quality of Life Survey* for each student in the class (1 copy for each student to complete during class, and 6 for each student to administer outside of class). You may decide that students will conduct more or less than 6 surveys outside of class, but the quantity of surveys per student should remain an even number to ensure that survey data from their peers and adults is represented equally.

• Make 1 copy of the *Excel Instruction Sheet* handout for each student.

Steps

1. Tell the class that they are going to take

© 2006 FACING THE FUTURE: PEOPLE AND THE PLANET   www.facingthefuture.org

Livin' the Good Life?

a survey themselves and then administer the same survey to peers and adults in order to gather data for their quality of life indicators.

2. Explain that by collecting data, the class will be able to see the average performance in quality of life for their community, as well as determine how their personal quality of life compares against the community average.

3. Give each student 1 copy of the *Quality of Life Survey* you have prepared with their indicators and have them complete it in class. Tell them to be as accurate and honest as possible with the data they provide. Be sure they write their name on their survey, as you will be handing it back to them later.

4. Collect the surveys and tell the students they will get their surveys back later so they can compare their performance against the community average.

5. Pass out the remaining 6 surveys for each student and go over the *Survey and Excel Instructions*.

6. Tell the students to be aware of problems they may encounter when conducting their surveys that could make the data they collect less accurate. Typical issues to be aware of when conducting a survey include:
   - Are the people they are surveying being honest?
   - Are they surveying people in groups, instead of individually (people tend to adjust their answers based on what they hear their peers saying)?
   - Do people understand the questions?
   - Do people have enough information to give an accurate answer?

7. Ask the class to think of reasons why

inaccurate data could be harmful if it is used to make important decisions.

8. Give them about 2-4 days to conduct their surveys, enter the data in Excel, and turn in their Excel documents to you.

Activity – Day 3

Materials/Preparation

- Prior to class, cut and paste the data from the students' Excel sheets so that all the students' survey results are combined in 1 master sheet (you may want to give this task to a teacher assistant or a student).
- Calculate the average of the data for each indicator, combining the data for "Peer and Adult", "Peer only", and "Adult only" (i.e. add all numbers together for each indicator and divide by the total number of respondents).
- Print out a copy of the results and bring to class.
- Create and expand the following table on the board or overhead (or if you have access to an LCD projector you can display the actual Excel chart), including all of the survey indicators and the data from each set of respondents:

Indicator	Average Peer/ Adult	Average Peer	Average Adult
			.

Steps

1. Ask the students how their surveying went, and if they think the data they collected is accurate.

2. Ask if they noticed any significant differences between responses from peers and adults.

3. Tell the students that you have combined

© 2006 FACING THE FUTURE: PEOPLE AND THE PLANET   www.facingthefuture.org

Livin' the Good Life?

all of their data, and that you now have averages for their community's performance in each quality of life category. Ask them how they would determine the average, or explain how you obtained the averages.

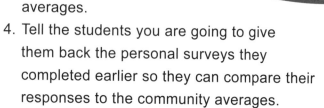

4. Tell the students you are going to give them back the personal surveys they completed earlier so they can compare their responses to the community averages.
5. Give each student his/her own *Quality of Life Survey*.
6. Have the students look at their personal surveys and compare their performance against the averages of the other survey respondents (adults and peers).
7. Bring the class together for reflection questions.

Assessment
Reflection Questions – Day 3
For Intermediate and Advanced Students

• Do you think this process accurately measures quality of life? What worked and what was difficult about the process?
• What was surprising about the results?
• What could you and/or other people do differently to change or improve your/their quality of life?
• How did the results of the class surveys compare to the community's averages?
• Are these indicators of quality of life sustainable? If everyone on the planet

measured well-being by these indicators, what would the impact be on the environment, the economy, and society?

For Advanced Students

• If this process was accepted as the right way to measure quality of life, should governments be responsible for guaranteeing people a basic level of quality of life?
• How is our government currently involved in guaranteeing basic quality of life (minimum wage, national parks, etc.)? Should they be more involved? Less involved?
• Would the indicators for quality of life be the same across this country? The world? For example, how might they differ between a wealthier country and a poorer country?
• How are international standards for quality of life determined?

Writing Connection

• Have students research an African cultural group, and write a brief paper explaining how they think this tribe might measure "the good life" in light of their values, economic system, spiritual beliefs, and geographic location. A list of African cultural groups, including basic background on geography, history, culture, and economics can be found at: **http://www. africaguide.com/culture/tribes/**. The students can compare and contrast their interpretation of the cultural group's good life with their own interpretation of the good life. They can use the indicators developed in class during the exercise, or create their own indicators.

Livin' the Good Life?

Students may need to conduct some additional web based research on the cultural group they choose to supplement the information found on this site.

Action Projects

- Have students write a "Quality of Life Report" for their local newspaper, based on the survey. Include the research methodology, results, and recommendations.
- Develop an "Alternative Holiday Catalog" with ideas for gifts that improve the quality of life of individuals in your local and global community. Distribute the catalogs at school events and in the community.
- Visit **www.facingthefuture.org** and click on **Take Action** for more information and action opportunities related to quality of life.

Additional Resources

Films

- *Affluenza*, 1997, 56 minutes; *Escape from Affluenza*, 1998, 56 minutes, John de Graaf, Bullfrog Films. Humorous documentary films on the history and effects of consumption and a growing movement to live simply and consume less. **www.bullfrogfilms.com**

- *Work and Time* (from "Reinventing the World" series), David Springbett and Heather MacAndrew, Bullfrog Films, 2000. This 50 minute documentary examines work and time as intertwined problems in our fast-forward lives. **www.bullfrogfilms.com**

Books

- *Take Back Your Time: Fighting Overwork and Time Poverty in America,* John de Graaf, Editor, Berrrett-Koehler Publishers, Inc., San Francisco, 2003. The official handbook of the national movement behind "Take Back Your Time Day"

Websites

- **www.yesmagazine.org** – Yes! Magazine's 2004 Summer Issue discusses what constitutes the good life according to a range of people including scientists, writers, sociologists, and religious leaders.

- **http://hdr.undp.org/statistics/** United Nations Development Program (UNDP) page on statistics and indicators.

- **http://www.who.int/substance_abuse/ research_tools/whoqolbref/en/** The World Health Organization's Quality of Life project uses a life assessment instrument to measure 26 broad areas, including physical health, psychological health, social relationships, and environment.

- **www.redefiningprogress.org** Redefining Progress is a leading organization in creating indicators that measure progress in the context of sustainable development.

- **www.timeday.org** – Home of the October 24th "Take Back Your Time Day".

- **www.sustainablemeasures.com** Sustainable Measures develops indicators that measure progress toward a sustainable economy, society and environment. Their website offers information and resources on sustainable indicators.

© 2006 FACING THE FUTURE: PEOPLE AND THE PLANET   www.facingthefuture.org

Lesson 22 Overhead:

Quality of Life Categories

Family

Recreation

Creative Pursuits

Work/Earning Money

Friends

Health

The Environment

Rest/Relaxation

Spiritual Pursuits

Volunteering/Helping Others

© 2006 FACING THE FUTURE: PEOPLE AND THE PLANET   www.facingthefuture.org

Quality of Life Survey

Survey Administered by (your name): _____

Person being surveyed is: ☐ **Peer (Age 18 or younger)**   ☐ **Adult (Older than 18)**

Quality of Life Category	Indicator
Family	Number of _____ per _____ Answer:
Recreation	Number of _____ per _____ Answer:
Creative Pursuits	Number of _____ per _____ Answer:
Work/Earning Money	Number of _____ per _____ Answer:
Friends	Number of _____ per _____ Answer:
Health	Number of _____ per _____ Answer:
The Environment	Number of _____ per _____ Answer:
Rest/Relaxation	Number of _____ per _____ Answer:
Spiritual Pursuits	Number of _____ per _____ Answer:
Volunteering/ Helping Others	Number of _____ per _____ Answer:

© 2006 FACING THE FUTURE: PEOPLE AND THE PLANET   www.facingthefuture.org

Lesson 22 Handout:
Survey and Excel Instructions for "Livin' the Good Life?"

Step 1 – Administer Quality of Life Survey:

- Each student will survey 3 different peers outside of this class (under the age of 18) and 3 different adults (e.g. parents, teachers, relatives, etc.) using the Quality of Life Survey developed by your class.
- Survey responders do not need to give their name, but you will need to check the "Peer" or "Adult" box on the survey form.
- Explain to the survey responders that your class has developed some quality of life indicators and that you would appreciate them taking 5 minutes of their time to answer some questions (Note: Be sure that they have not already been given the survey by another student in your class).
- While administering the surveys, be sure to keep the units of measurement constant for each indicator. If an indicator is "hours of sleep per day", make sure that hours per day is the measurement consistently used for that indicator, and not hours per week, per month, etc.
- If someone cannot answer a question, record that as N/A for "Not Available".
- Record their answers legibly, since you will need to type it into the Excel sheet later.

Step 2 – Create Excel Spreadsheet and Input Survey Data:

- Create an Excel document like the one in the example below and save it on your computer or on a disk.
- Enter the data from your surveys into the Excel spreadsheet. Enter peer or adult in the left hand column and their response under each category as shown in the example below. The sample data filled in below represents data from one surveyed peer and one surveyed adult (this data is just an example; the categories and indicators your class came up with may produce completely different kinds of numbers).
- If you have surveys with some unanswered indicators, DO NOT enter 0 in that category on the Excel sheet. Write N/A, like in the example under the "Creative Pursuits" category. Only use 0 if their answer is actually 0.

Quality of Life Data Entry Sheet [Your names]										
Respondent Type (Peer or Adult)	**Family**	**Rec.**	**Creative Pursuits**	**Work/ Earning Money**	**Friends**	**Health**	**The Environment**	**Rest/ Relax**	**Spiritual Pursuits**	**Volunteer/ Helping Others**
Peer	5	2	N/A	5	4	10	0	30	1	2
Adult	7	1	2	40	2	12	5	10	3	3
Adult										
Peer										

Step 3 – Submit Excel Spreadsheet:

- After you have entered all your data, save the spreadsheet and either e-mail or hand in a disk to your teacher.
- Be sure you include your name somewhere in the e-mail or written on the disk.

What's In The News?

OVERVIEW

In this media literacy activity, students use an "iceberg model" to analyze the global patterns and underlying structural causes that drive events in the news.

INQUIRY/CRITICAL THINKING QUESTIONS

- What are the economic, political, and social forces that drive the dramatic events we see reported in the news?
- How are news events connected to each other in terms of their underlying causes?
- What are some positive ways we can address the structural causes of many negative world events?

OBJECTIVES

Students will:
- Analyze several news articles using a model that helps identify the particular global patterns and economic, political, and social forces (i.e. structural causes) behind the story.
- Diagram the events, patterns, and underlying structures in a news article
- Identify connections among news articles
- Discuss structural solutions to address these events
- Write an article about the emerging patterns and underlying causes of a particular current event

TIME REQUIRED: 1–2 hours

KEY ISSUES/CONCEPTS

- **Newsworthy events, global patterns, and economic, political, and social structures**
- **Media literacy**

SUBJECT AREAS

- **Social Studies** (Geography, World History, World Cultures, U.S. History, Civics/Government, Economics, Global Studies, Contemporary World Problems)
- **Science** (Environmental)
- **Language Arts**
- **Journalism**

NATIONAL STANDARDS CONSISTENCY

- **NCSS:** 1, 2, 3, 4, 5, 6, 7, 8, 9
- **NSES:** A, C, F

GRADE LEVEL: 9–12

FTF Related Reading

- Intermediate: Chapter 9 from *Global Issues and Sustainable Solutions*
- Advanced: Unit 1, Chapter 3 and Unit 5, Chapter 4 from *It's All Connected*

Materials/Preparation

- 1 sample news article to model the activity
- Overhead: *Iceberg Model*
- A variety of news articles, 2 or 3 per group. Gather articles from the newspaper, magazines, and/or the Internet about significant events in the world (you can gather the articles yourself and/or have students bring in articles).
- Butcher paper, 1 sheet per group
- Marking pens, colored, 3–4 pens per group

What's In The News?

Activity

Introduction

1. Ask the students to define media literacy (the ability to read, analyze, evaluate, and produce communication in a variety of media forms such as television, print, radio, computers, etc.).

2. Tell them that they are going to explore an aspect of media literacy by analyzing some news articles using a tool called the "Iceberg Model".

Steps

1. Share with the class your sample news article about an important current event, such as a significant conflict, an environmental disaster, an economic situation, or a criminal activity.

2. Ask students to paraphrase the event depicted in the sample article.

3. Use the overhead, *Iceberg Model*, to lead a class discussion about the relationship between current events and the global patterns and underlying economic, political, and social forces that propel them to prominence in the news. Explain that what we read about most often in the news are **events**—the newsworthy, exciting, and dramatic things that happen in our world. *Events* in the news are like the tip of an iceberg. The visible part of an iceberg is

only about 10 percent of its total mass and the remaining 90 percent is underwater and never seen. However, it is this hidden 90 percent that the ocean currents act on and which determine the behavior of the iceberg's tip. Likewise, news events "at the tip of the iceberg" may be things such as war in the Middle East, crime in our community, or a massive flood in China. On the news, these events are witnessed as dramatic isolated incidents—the forces that create and shape them (what happens "underwater") are not often revealed.

When we notice the occurrence of similar events (wars or terrorist attacks in other parts of the world, or other extreme natural disasters such as earthquakes or a tsunami), we are seeing the emergence of a **pattern**. It may appear that more of these events are happening, or it may be that the media is reporting these events more often. For example, we might read a news article in the paper today about a local robbery (an event). Over the course of a year we may notice that there are several articles about robberies and other crimes committed in

What's In The News?

the same area of town (a pattern). Does this indicate that crime is up or just that we are hearing about it more frequently? Patterns underlie and act upon events, so they are shown just below the tip in the iceberg model.

Finally, deep beneath the surface are the **underlying structures** or **root causes** that drive the events and patterns—just as the underlying ice mass drives the tip of the iceberg. These underlying structures or causes can be economic, political, or social. For example, the underlying cause of the robberies and other crimes may have to do with the economics of the area. Perhaps schools in that area are unable to offer quality education or unemployment may be high. Underlying structural causes may be the growing gap between the rich and poor, or a lack of education, job opportunities, or other forces that preclude sustainable livelihoods. Are underlying structural causes such as these typically revealed in news stories? If not, what effect does this have on how we understand an event and how we perceive the people who are involved in the event?

4. Go back to the sample news article, and together with the students use the iceberg model to analyze it. Ask them, "Has this type of event been in the news before? Is it a recurring event? If so, can you identify a global pattern that is driving these events? What are some possible root causes of these patterns? For example, is the event related to poverty, lack of education and/or health care, or development practices that

are not environmentally sound? Does the article discuss some or all of these root causes?" If you use an article about a war in Africa, you might look for a discussion in the article about Africa's colonial past, arbitrary boundaries, population growth, the AIDS epidemic, environmental destruction, and poverty.

5. Before moving on, be sure students understand how to use the iceberg model to analyze a news article in terms of the events, emerging patterns, and underlying causes.

6. Arrange the class into groups of 3-4 students and give each group 2-3 different news articles, 1 sheet of butcher paper, and 1 set of pens.

7. In their groups, have the students read the articles, choose 1, and use the iceberg model to analyze the event and look for patterns and root causes. Have students discuss whether they have noticed other similar events in the news. Then have them brainstorm, discuss, and list on a separate piece of paper all of the root causes they can think of that might contribute to the event.

8. Have each group create an iceberg diagram of their news article by gluing or taping the article onto the top of the paper, listing and/or drawing the patterns they have noticed, and finally listing and/or drawing the underlying root causes. Their final diagram should have a shape similar to an iceberg with the news article at the top (the event), the pattern below, and the underlying causes at the bottom.

9. Have each group present their iceberg models to the class. Discuss how many

© 2006 FACING THE FUTURE: PEOPLE AND THE PLANET   www.facingthefuture.org

What's In The News?

of the events presented connect to each other through similar underlying causes. For example, wars, social unrest, and environmental damage are often closely linked by factors such as poverty, lack of education, and limited resources.

10. Have each group discuss structural solutions that could be implemented to address the root causes of events and patterns identified in their articles.

11. Conclude with the following reflection questions.

Assessment
Reflection Questions

For Intermediate and Advanced Students

• How did using the iceberg model to analyze the news articles help in your understanding of events, patterns, root causes, and their connections?

• How does the iceberg model fall short as an analysis tool? In other words, are there news stories and/or events that would not fit this model?

• What was the most surprising thing you found in your analysis?

• How could you use the iceberg model to improve your reading skills (reading for content versus understanding)?

• What can we do to address the underlying structural problems of the events and patterns you studied?

Lesson Extension

• The Iceberg Model is based on a "systems thinking" approach to problem solving, which looks at issues from a holistic, dynamic, interconnected, systemic perspective. Have students research systems thinking. A good place for links to system thinking resources

and information is Pegasus Communications at **www.pegasuscom.com**.

Writing/Technology Connection

• As a class or individually, students can do a media research project. There are several good media literacy sites on the web. Visit the *Independent Media Center* website at **www.indymedia.org** or the *Fairness and Accuracy in Reporting* website at **www.fair.org**.

Action Projects

• Have each group rewrite their article explaining the event, but also including the patterns and underlying structures. Students can publish their articles in the school paper or submit them to the news source that published the original article.

• Visit **www.facingthefuture.org** and click on **Take Action**, then **Fast Facts Quick Actions** for more information and action opportunities about global issues.

Additional Resources
Websites

• **www.indymedia.org** – The Independent Media Center is a network of collectively run media outlets for the creation of radical, accurate, and passionate telling of the truth.

• **www.fair.org** – Fairness and Accuracy in Reporting is a national media watch group working to invigorate the First Amendment by advocating for greater diversity in the press and by scrutinizing media practices that marginalize public interest, minority, and dissenting viewpoints.

© 2006 FACING THE FUTURE: PEOPLE AND THE PLANET www.facingthefuture.org

© 2006 FACING THE FUTURE: PEOPLE AND THE PLANET   www.facingthefuture.org

Lesson 23 Overhead:

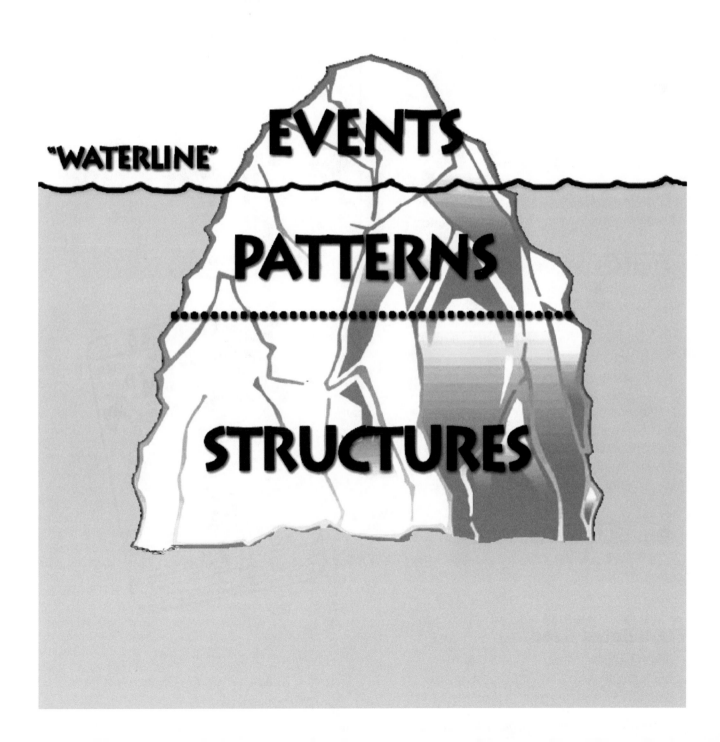

Are You Buying This?!

OVERVIEW

Students work in groups to create and present mock television commercials for products linked to unsustainable or unhealthy behavior. Students first present the commercial as it would typically be seen on television, and then present it again incorporating the product's negative impacts. A lesson extension has the students create a commercial advertising a new product or variation of their product that would mitigate the negative impacts.

INQUIRY/CRITICAL THINKING QUESTIONS

- How does advertising influence consumption?
- How does advertising shape a society's vision of "the good life"?
- Who bears responsibility for regulating the marketing and consumption of legal but harmful and/or unsustainable products?

OBJECTIVES

Students will:
- Recognize the connection between advertising, consumption choices and the unstated consequences of those choices
- Become critical consumers of marketing directed towards them and recognize tactics used by advertisers to influence their behavior
- Understand the power of advertising in selling U.S. values and ideals to foreign countries and cultures

TIME REQUIRED: 1 hour

KEY ISSUES/CONCEPTS

- **Media**
- **Consumerism**
- **Corporate responsibility**
- **Marketing**
- **Quality of life**

SUBJECT AREAS

- **Social Studies** (Global Studies, Contemporary World Problems)
- **Science** (Environmental)
- **Language Arts/Drama**
- **Journalism**
- **Business/Finance**
- **Health/Nutrition**

NATIONAL STANDARDS CONSISTENCY

- **NCSS: 1, 4, 7, 9**
- **NSES: F**

GRADE LEVEL: 6–12

FTF Related Reading

- Intermediate: Chapters 5 and 6 from *Global Issues and Sustainable Solutions*

- Advanced: Unit 3, Chapter 2 and 4; Unit 4, Chapter 2; Unit 5, Chapter 4 from *It's All Connected*

© 2006 FACING THE FUTURE: PEOPLE AND THE PLANET   www.facingthefuture.org

Are You Buying This?!

Materials/Preparation

- Handout: *Product and Consequence Cards*, make 1 double-sided front-to-back copy with "Products" on 1 side and "Consequences" on the other, and cut into individual cards
- Blank paper and color pens/pencils for creating props/signage

Activity

Introduction

1. (Optional) Do a Sides Debate using the following prompt (see sides debate description on page 28):

    "Only ads promoting healthy foods and activities should be allowed during television shows targeting children under the age of 8."

2. Ask the class if they have seen a television advertisement recently that made them really want to buy a product. Ask them if they remember how the ad presented the product. Was a celebrity promoting it? Did it feature people doing fun and exciting activities unrelated to the product? Were there attractive models involved?

3. Tell the class that in the first 9 months of 2004 alone, companies in the U.S. spent over $100 billion advertising their products. The average young person views over 40,000 television ads each year, plus thousands more in magazines, movies, billboards, and other outlets.

4. Explain that most ads leave out any negative consequences tied to consuming that product, and generally only include information on potential dangers if required to by law (like with some advertising for prescription drugs). Advertisers do not

Are You Buying This?!

discuss the impact of their products on the environment or unfair labor practices unless the product is being marketed as "eco-friendly" or "socially responsible".

5. Tell the class that they are going to try their talent at creating advertisements for products that are often marketed to U.S. citizens. However, not only will they have to create an ad that makes the product look good, they will also have to create an ad that focuses on the product's less glamorous side.

out in front of the class. One commercial will only focus on the attractive side of the product, and the other should only focus on the consequences. Students should use the same advertising technique for both ads. If they are using supermodels or extreme sports to sell the attractive side of the product, they should use supermodels and extreme sports to sell the consequences as well.

5. Tell the students that the ads have to be the same length as a regular television commercial, so each ad should not be longer than 1 minute.

6. After the groups put their ads together, have them present both commercials to the class, with the ad selling the attractive side of the product presented first.

7. Continue with the following lesson extension, or bring the class back together for reflection questions.

Steps

1. Break the class into groups of 4-5 students.
2. Tell the students that they are going to get a card with the product they are in charge of advertising. 1 side of the card has some attractive selling points for the product. The other side has some of the consequences of consuming that product.
3. Tell the students that in order to effectively sell their product, they have to decide:
   a. What is the demographic they are selling to? (who they think will buy this product)
   b. What is the advertising technique they will use? A celebrity? Humor? Will using the product make you smarter/sexier/cooler?
4. Tell the students they have 15-20 minutes to create 2 commercials that they will act

Lesson Extension

• Have students create a commercial advertising a new product or variation of their product that would mitigate its negative consequences.

© 2006 FACING THE FUTURE: PEOPLE AND THE PLANET   www.facingthefuture.org

Are You Buying This?!

Assessment
Reflection Questions

For Intermediate and Advanced Students

- When you were deciding how to sell your product, why did you choose the advertising techniques you used?
- Do you think these advertising techniques influence what you and your friends purchase?
- If you lived in a far away country, and your only knowledge of the U.S. came from watching U.S. commercials, what would you think were the most important values of our society?
- Do you think advertising should be regulated more or less than it is now? How so? What changes would you like to see?

For Advanced Students

- What could be some of the consequences if everyone in the world was exposed to the same amount of advertising that U.S. citizens are exposed to?

- Who should be most responsible for regulating what we consume – government, companies, or consumers?
- What could be some of the consequences – both positive and negative – if government decided to greatly restrict how much advertising we are exposed to each year?
- How does advertising influence a society's vision of "the good life"?

Writing Connection

- At home, have students analyze a commercial break during a program they typically watch. Have them record notes on each ad during the break, keeping an eye out for the following:
  - What was the product?
  - What was the brand?
  - What was the marketing technique?
  - What was the demographic the ad was targeting (women, teens, parents, the elderly)?

Instruct the students to pick out 1 of the products they recorded that might have consequences for their personal health and the health of the planet. Have the students research that product and write 1-2 paragraphs identifying how consuming that product could affect global issues such as health, the environment, and poverty.

Art Connection

- Have students develop a print ad for a product that is widely considered to be harmful to human health and well-being. The ad should focus on the negative consequences of consuming the product, and incorporate some of the imagery found in real print ads promoting the product. Possible topics are: cigarettes, beer, fast food, jumbo sized sodas, diet pills, etc.

Action Projects

- Have students research their favorite brand or company to learn about the company's environmental and social business practices. Students can then create an awareness campaign on campus or at shopping malls, etc. about environmentally and socially

Are You Buying This?!

responsible companies. Alternatively, they can develop a brochure for teenagers displaying environmentally- and socially-friendly businesses and products.

- Collect used cell phones and ink cartridges and send them to EcoPhones (**www.ecophones.com**). They will pay you for each cell phone and ink cartridge regardless of whether or not it works. Have students donate the money they make from the cell phone/ink cartridge drive to an organization of their choice.

- Have students do an experiment to reveal the influence commercialism has on consumer choices and consumption patterns. Bring in 2 pizzas from a name brand pizza company. Gather a group of students in the room, blindfold them, and feed each blindfolded person 1 slice of pizza, telling them it's fresh from the name brand company. Then feed the students a second, identical slice and tell them it's from a no-name company – Uncle Albert's Down Home Pizza, for example. Ask them which slice tasted better. See if the name brand pizza gets more votes than the non-name brand, even though both pizzas are made by the same company (adapted from **www.adbusters.com**).

- Visit **www.facingthefuture.org** and click on **Take Action**, then click **Fast Facts Quick Actions** for more information and action opportunities on consumption.

Additional Resources

Films

- *Affluenza*, 1997, 56 minutes; and *Escape from Affluenza*, 1998, 56 minutes, John de Graaf, Bullfrog Films. Humorous documentary films on the history and effects of consumption and a growing movement to live simply and consume less. **www.bullfrogfilms.com**

Books/Magazines

- *Fast Food Nation*, Eric Schlosser, Perennial, 2002. An exposé of the fast food industry with a large section focusing on how junk food is marketed to youth.

- *Adbusters Magazine*. A not-for-profit, reader-supported magazine concerned about the erosion of the physical and cultural environment by commercial forces. **www.adbusters.org**

Websites

- **www.commercialalert.org** – Focuses on campaigning to limit exposure to advertising and the effects of advertising and commercialism on kids' health.

- **www.marketingpower.com** – The American Marketing Association's website provides information on marketing, including history, best practices, and a code of ethics.

- **www.coopamerica.org** – Co-op America offers practical steps for using your consumer and investor power for social change.

© 2006 FACING THE FUTURE: PEOPLE AND THE PLANET   www.facingthefuture.org

Product Cards – (copy on front side)

The Ultra Behemoth Burger

- 4 beef patties, a full half-pound of meat!
- 6 slices of cheese
- 5 strips of smoked bacon
- Incredible low price of $1.99
- Available 24 hours a day

The Dominator XL SUV

- Over 12 feet long
- 4 wheel drive
- Fits 8 people comfortably
- Includes 6 disc CD player and TV sets in each seat
- Protects your family in case of an accident

Pine Valley Estates

- Magnificent all-wood dream homes
- Located in a quiet wooded area
- Over 4,000 square feet, plus 2 acres of private land
- Only a 30 minute drive from the city center

Super Clean Car Wash Foam

- Keeps your car shiny and new looking
- Protects your paint job from scratches
- Makes every car look expensive

Handi-Lunches

- A complete pre-packaged lunch for kids
- Saves you time preparing food
- Kids love the taste
- Includes healthy meats, cheeses, snacks, and a drink

Mega Cool Jeans

- Stylin'
- Very hip – worn by famous people
- Only $25 a pair

Consequence Cards – (copy on back side)

The Dominator XL SUV

- Global warming caused by fossil fuel pollution contributes to the extinction of species, loss of arable land, and destruction of natural habitats
- Destruction of the ozone layer caused by carbon emissions increases the risk of skin cancer

The Ultra Behemoth Burger

- It takes about 12,000 gallons of water to produce 1 beef patty
- Nearly 59 million U.S. citizens (about 20%) are obese
- Annual healthcare costs for a person with diabetes is about $13,000 (4 times the cost for a non-diabetic)

Super Clean Car Wash Foam

- Washing your car at home puts hazardous chemicals into streams, rivers, and oceans
- Runoff from car wash soap contaminates fish we eat and kills plants
- Frequent car washing wastes hundreds of gallons of water

Pine Valley Estates

- Over a 5 year period, 6 million acres of farmland in the U.S. were paved over for homes
- About half of the Earth's forests have already been destroyed
- Deforested areas suffer from flooding, mudslides, and lack of biodiversity

Mega Cool Jeans

- Sewn in a sweatshop by 12 year olds who work 16 hour days and are not paid minimum wage
- Workers do not have time to go to school, so they stay poor forever
- Made from non-organic cotton, which is one of the crops most heavily sprayed with toxic chemicals

Handi-Lunches

- Each food item is wrapped in non-recyclable plastic, producing huge amounts of trash that end up in landfills
- In 2001, the U.S. threw away over 250 million tons of garbage into landfills and incinerators

Life: The Long and Short of It

OVERVIEW

Students compare life expectancy (a common indicator of good health) among several countries and discuss possible explanations for the differences. They also examine the connection between per capita expenditures on health care and life expectancy.

INQUIRY/CRITICAL THINKING QUESTIONS

- Why do people in some countries live longer than people in other countries?
- What factors contribute to long life expectancy?

OBJECTIVES

Students will:
- Identify the many factors that affect life expectancy
- Compare life expectancy rates for a variety of countries

TIME REQUIRED: 15-30 minutes

(15 for main activity and 15 for optional extension)

KEY ISSUES/CONCEPTS

- **Life expectancy**
- **Global health**
- **Factors affecting average life expectancy**

SUBJECT AREAS

- **Social Studies** (Geography, Economics, Global Studies, Contemporary World Problems)
- **Science** (Life)
- **Math**
- **Health/Nutrition**

NATIONAL STANDARDS CONSISTENCY

- **NCSS: 3, 8, 9, 10**
- **NSES: A, C, E, F**

GRADE LEVEL: 6–11

FTF Related Reading

- Intermediate: Chapter 7 from *Global Issues and Sustainable Solutions*
- Advanced: Unit 5, Chapters 5, 6, and 7 from *It's All Connected*

Materials/Preparation

- Handout: *Life Expectancy Country Cards*, 1 card per student (if you do not use all 30 cards, be sure that you still include a range of life expectancies in the ones you do use)
- 8.5 x 11 sheets of blank paper, 1 per student
- (Optional) Handout/Overhead: *Top 30 Countries for Life Expectancy*, 1 per student, or make an overhead

Activity

Introduction

1. Begin by asking the class why they think people in some countries live longer than people in other countries.
2. Ask students to define life expectancy. Life expectancy is the average number of years, for an entire population, that an individual born today would be expected to live if current mortality rates continued (i.e. how long individuals in a certain population are expected to live if the conditions affecting life do not change).

Life: The Long and Short of It

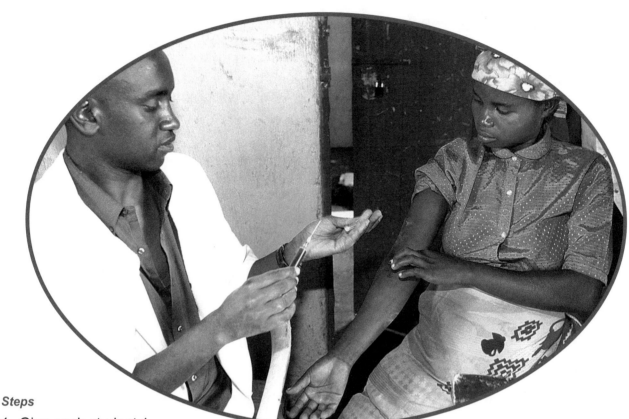

Steps

1. Give each student 1
   Life Expectancy Country Card
   and 1 blank 8.5 x 11 sheet of paper.

2. Have students transfer the information on their card to the blank paper so it is large enough for the class to read.

3. Tell students to look at their *Life Expectancy Country Card* and then stand in a line in order of longest to shortest life expectancy as you ask: Is there anyone expected to live to be over 80? Over 70? Over 60? Over 50? Over 40? Over 30? Have students form a half-circle so all country cards are visible to the rest of the class and/or have them read aloud their country and life expectancy.

4. (Optional) Have students identify their country on a map.

5. Either continue with the following lesson extension or conclude with the reflection questions below.

Lesson Extension

1. Give each student, or show as an overhead, *Top 30 Countries for Life Expectancy*.

2. Have students review the information and answer the following questions:
   - Why do you think someone in Japan is likely to live almost 5 years longer than someone in Cuba?
   - Why do you think the U.S. is 29th?
   - Now look at the amount of money spent per person, per year on health care. Who spends the most? Who spends the least?
   - Why might Cuba be in the top 30 if they only spend $236 per person, per year on health care?
   - Why might Cuba be almost tied with the U.S. for life expectancy if the U.S. spends more than 22 times the amount of money that Cuba spends on health care?

3. Conclude with the following reflection questions.

© 2006 FACING THE FUTURE: PEOPLE AND THE PLANET www.facingthefuture.org

Life: The Long and Short of It

Assessment
Reflection Questions

For Intermediate and Advanced Students
- Why do you think there is such a large gap in life expectancy between countries (total range is from 32 to 82 years)?
- Do you think life expectancy is a good way to measure health?

For Advanced Students
- Identify some possible characteristics of the countries with long, mid-range, and short life expectancies.
- If we only look at life expectancy as an indicator of a country's health, what other information might we be missing?

Writing Connection
- Have students write a 1 page description of their country that offers a possible explanation for its average life expectancy.

Math/Technology Connection
- Have students produce a life expectancy graph using the data on their cards to compare countries. Alternatively, have them use the Internet site, Nationmaster, at **www.nationmaster.com** to produce graphs and tables of country statistics.

Action Projects
- Have students research and then do an awareness raising campaign for the United Nations 8 Millennium Development Goals (MDGs), which aim to improve the lives of people living in extreme poverty. The MDGs form a blueprint agreed to by all the world's countries and all the world's leading development institutions. Visit **http://www. un.org/millenniumgoals/** to learn more about the MDGs.

- Visit **www.facingthefuture.org** and click on **Take Action**, then click **Fast Facts Quick Actions** for more information and action opportunities on HIV/AIDS, reproductive health, and women and girls.

Additional Resources
Films
- *Rx for Survival: A Global Health Challenge*, PBS, 2006, 360 minutes. From vaccines to antibiotics, clean water to nutrition, bioterror threats to the HIV/AIDS pandemic, this 6-part series tells the stories of global health champions and the communities they strive to protect.

Books
- *Mountains Beyond Mountains*, Tracy Kidder, Random House, 2003. A true story of Paul Farmer, a doctor who sets out to diagnose and cure infectious diseases and to bring the lifesaving tools of modern medicine to people in Haiti.

Websites
- **http://hdr.undp.org** – The Human Development Report (HDR), a project of the United Nations Development Program (UNDP), provides data and statistics on human development, including life expectancy and literacy rates.

- **www.prb.org** – Population Reference Bureau's website with extensive country data.

- **www.pih.org** – Partners In Health is a non-profit organization promoting global health.

© 2006 FACING THE FUTURE: PEOPLE AND THE PLANET   www.facingthefuture.org

Life Expectancy Country Cards

(source: UNDP 2005)

Japan 82 years	**Canada** 80 years	**Norway** 79.4 years
Costa Rica 78.2 years	**United States** 77.4 years	**Cuba** 77.3 years
Mexico 75.1 years	**Sri Lanka** 74 years	**Venezuela** 72.9 years
Hungary 72.7 years	**China** 71.6 years	**Jamaica** 70.8 years
Vietnam 70.5 years	**Thailand** 70.0 years	**Peru** 70 years
Nicaragua 69.7 years	**Turkey** 68.7 years	**Uzbekistan** 66.5 years
India 63.3 years	**Nepal** 61.6 years	**Yemen** 60.6 years
Cambodia 56.2 years	**Papua New Guinea** 55.3 years	**Haiti** 51.6 years
Kenya 47.2 years	**Niger** 44.4 years	**Chad** 43.6 years
Mozambique 41.9 years	**Malawi** 39.7 years	**Swaziland** 32.5 years

© 2006 FACING THE FUTURE: PEOPLE AND THE PLANET   www.facingthefuture.org

Top 30 Countries for Life Expectancy

(source: UNDP 2005)

	Country	Life Expectancy 2003 (years)	Health care expenditure per capita 2002 ($)
1	Japan	82.0	$2133
2	Hong Kong	81.6	$ (not available)
3	Iceland	80.7	$2802
4	Switzerland	80.5	$3446
5	Australia	80.3	$2699
6	Sweden	80.2	$2512
7	Italy	80.1	$2166
8	Canada	80.0	$2931
9	Israel	79.7	$1890
10	France	79.5	$2736
11	Spain	79.5	$1640
12	Norway	79.4	$3409
13	New Zealand	79.1	$1857
14	Austria	79.0	$2220
15	Belgium	78.9	$2515
16	Germany	78.7	$2817
17	Singapore	78.7	$1105
18	Cyprus	78.6	$883
19	Luxembourg	78.5	$3066
20	Finland	78.5	$1943
21	Netherlands	78.4	$2564
22	United Kingdom	78.4	$2160
23	Malta	78.4	$965
24	Greece	78.3	$1814
25	Costa Rica	78.2	$743
26	United Arab Emirates	78.0	$750
27	Chile	77.9	$642
28	Ireland	77.7	$2367
29	United States	77.4	$5274
30	Cuba	77.3	$236

Partners for Health

OVERVIEW

Students learn about the impact of today's most urgent global health issues (such as HIV/AIDS, malaria, and tuberculosis), and practical solutions to help address these issues. The activity concludes with an optional writing assignment in which students research and develop a proposal to address a particular global health issue.

INQUIRY/CRITICAL THINKING QUESTIONS

- What are some of the world's most pressing health issues?
- What are some of the root causes of global health issues?
- What can be done to improve global health?

OBJECTIVES

Students will:

- Understand the connection between poverty and poor health
- Understand how international organizations, NGOs, and local governments coordinate to address global health issues
- Learn how they can improve global health at the local level
- Understand the difference between *treating* and *preventing* global health issues

TIME REQUIRED: 1 hour

(includes assigning the writing project)

KEY ISSUES/CONCEPTS

- **Global health**
- **Interconnections**
- **International health aid organizations**

SUBJECT AREAS

- **Social Studies** (Global Studies, Economics, Civics/Government, Contemporary World Problems)
- **Science** (Life)
- **Health/Nutrition**

NATIONAL STANDARDS CONSISTENCY

- **NCSS: 3, 8, 9, 10**
- **NSES: A, C, E, F**

GRADE LEVEL: 9–11

FTF Related Reading

- Intermediate: Chapter 7 from *Global Issues and Sustainable Solutions*
- Advanced: Unit 5, Chapter 5 from *It's All Connected*

Materials/Preparation

- Handout: *Global Health Issue Cards*, make 1 copy and cut into individual cards
- Overhead: *Partners for Health Questions*
- Handout: *Essay Assignment: Advocate for a Healthy World*, 1 copy per student

© 2006 FACING THE FUTURE: PEOPLE AND THE PLANET   www.facingthefuture.org

Partners for Health

Activity

Introduction

1. Optional: Do a Sides Debate using the following prompts (see Sides Debate lesson, page 28):

- "The U.S. government should regulate the consumption of fast food for people under the age of 18."
- "The U.S. government should contribute more money to international health issues, such as combating HIV/AIDS, malaria, and malnutrition."

2. This exercise may be very difficult for students to do. The statistics are stark. It is easy to be overwhelmed by the immensity of some global health issues. It may be beneficial to start this exercise with a survey of recent initiatives aimed at improving global health. Talk about the Millennium Development Goals, Live 8, and some local non-profit organizations that are involved in helping people around the world. Emphasize that there is hope and that the students can make a difference.

Steps

1. Walk around the room and have each student randomly pick a *Global Health Issue Card.*

2. Explain to the students that each card has either a fact about the scope of a global health issue or a solution to that global health issue.

3. After everyone has picked a card, have each student read his or her card aloud, in random order.

4. Have students walk around the room and find their "partner" (the person who has the accompanying scope or solution to their global health issue).

5. Put up the overhead *Partners for Health Questions* and instruct the pairs of students to brainstorm answers to the questions for a few minutes. Have them write their answers on a sheet of paper.

6. After the students have completed the discussion questions, call on each pair to read their health issue fact and solution aloud (together) to the class.

7. Bring the class back together and conclude with the following reflection questions.

8. Have students do the Writing Connection described below.

Assessment
Reflection Questions

For Intermediate and Advanced Students

- Ask what they found most surprising, disturbing, and encouraging.
- Call on students to share their answers to the 3 questions.
- Write on the board any common trends that emerge from the students' answers that highlight the connection between health and other global issues (poverty, population, education, governance, environmental damage, etc.).

Writing Connection

- There is a website on each student's *Global Health Issue Card* that will lead him/her to an organization that is working on his/her particular global health issue, and is a good starting point for research. The purpose of this assignment is to help students learn about different organizations that are working on global health issues; articulate how global health issues impact other aspects of a country's well being; and articulate why global health should matter to policy makers. Give each student the *Advocate for a Healthy World* handout and go over it with them.

Partners for Health

Action Projects

- Help WaterPartners International bring safe, accessible drinking water to those who do not have it. Students will have an opportunity to make a difference in the lives of real people by adopting a Honduran community. For a detailed description of this and other service learning projects, visit **www.facingthefuture.org** and click on **Take Action**, and then **Service Learning Projects.**

- World AIDS Day takes place every year on December 1. Get your class involved with the following activities: Decorate trees, school buildings, classrooms, lampposts, or fences with red ribbons; Develop a pen pal exchange between students and persons affected in different cities and countries; Have your class organize a school-wide poster contest on the theme of the current year's World AIDS Day.

- Visit **www.facingthefuture.org** and click on **Take Action**, then **Fast Facts Quick Actions** for more information and action opportunities on HIV/AIDS, reproductive health, and women and girls.

Additional Resources

Films

- *Rx for Survival: A Global Health Challenge,* PBS, 2005, 360 minutes. From vaccines to antibiotics, clean water to nutrition, bioterror threats to the HIV/AIDS pandemic, this 6-part series tells the stories of global health champions and the communities they strive to protect.

- *Silent Killer: The Unfinished Campaign Against Hunger,* John DeGraaf, Bullfrog Films, **www.bullfrogfilms.com**, 2005, 57 minutes. Highlights promising attempts in Africa, and in South and Central America, to end world hunger.

- *Super Size Me,* Morgan Spurlock, 2004, 100 minutes. Spurlock documents his experiment to eat nothing but three McDonald's meals a day for 30 consecutive days, and provides an entertaining and disturbing narrative about American culture's trend toward obesity.

- *The Insider,* Michael Mann, 1999, 157 minutes. A true story of a man who decided to tell the world what the seven major tobacco companies knew about (and concealed) the dangers of their product.

Books

- *Fast Food Nation,* Eric Schlosser, Perennial, 2002. An exposé of the fast food industry and its agricultural, labor, and health impacts.

Partners for Health

- *Invisible Enemies: Stories of Infectious Disease,* Jeanette Farrell, Farrar, Straus and Giroux, 2005 (Revised Edition). In this young adult book, Farrell discusses seven infectious diseases (smallpox, leprosy, plague, tuberculosis, malaria, cholera, and AIDS), highlighting the causes, history of treatment, popular notions and fears about the disease, and the story of how breakthroughs came about.

- *Mountains Beyond Mountains,* Tracy Kidder, Random House, 2003. A true story of Paul Farmer, a doctor who sets out to diagnose and cure infectious diseases and bring the lifesaving tools of modern medicine to people in Haiti.

- *Smallpox: the Fight to Eradicate a Global Scourge,* David Koplow, University of California Press, 2003. An analysis of smallpox policy focusing on two major points: smallpox has killed millions of people over the millennia, and the eradication of naturally occurring smallpox from the world has been one of humankind's most amazing success stories.

Websites

- **www.who.int** – The World Health Organization is the United Nations specialized agency for health.

- **www.unicef.org** – United Nations Children's Fund includes information on children's health, education, equity, and protection around the world.

Example graph from the World Health Organization vaccine-preventable disease monitoring system, 2005 global summary

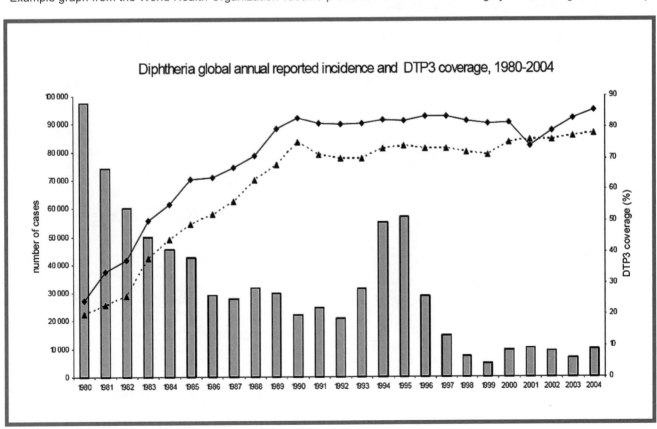

© 2006 FACING THE FUTURE: PEOPLE AND THE PLANET   www.facingthefuture.org

Global Health Issue Cards
1 of 3

In 2004, about 42 million people were living with HIV/AIDS world-wide and over 3 million people died from AIDS.

www.unaids.org

Providing condoms at 3 cents each and educating about sexual health can reduce the spread of HIV/AIDS.

www.unaids.org

About 2 million people die world-wide every year from Tuberculosis, a curable respiratory illness spread by coughing and sneezing.

www.who.int

Treating Tuberculosis with antibiotics costs about $10 per patient.

www.who.int

Three to four million people are infected with Hepatitis C each year, which severely damages the liver and can cause death.

www.who.int

Clean needles cost 5 cents each and can prevent millions of Hepatitis C infections.

www.who.int

Each year, 3 to 4 million people are infected with Hepatitis C, which severely damages the liver and can cause death.

www.who.int

Healthier eating and increased exercise can reduce the risk of Type 2 Diabetes by up to 60%.

www.cdc.gov

A child in Sub-Saharan Africa dies every 30 seconds from Malaria, an infection carried by mosquitoes.

http://mosquito.who.int

Mosquito netting with anti-Malaria insecticide costs around $3 and can reduce deaths in children by up to 20%.

www.who.int

Global Health Issue Cards

17% of deaths in children 5 years or younger worldwide are caused by preventable Diarrhea.

www.who.int

A village well can provide clean water for 1,200 people at a cost of 12 cents per person each year, preventing children from dying of Diarrhea.

www.chrf.org

Malnutrition contributes to more than 50% of all childhood deaths worldwide.

www.who.int

It costs 50 cents to help prevent Malnutrition in a child through Vitamin A supplements, which can save about 250,000 lives a year.

www.jsi.com

More than 500,000 people worldwide, mostly children, died of Measles in 2003.

www.who.int

Immunizing a child against Measles costs less than $1 per child.

www.who.int

In 2005, an estimated 6 million people worldwide suffered from Trachoma, the world's leading cause of preventable blindness.

www.trachoma.org

Basic surgery to prevent blindness by Trachoma costs less than $10 per patient.

www.sightsavers.org

Over 2 million women and girls in developing countries suffer from Fistula, a painful, preventable condition that occurs during childbirth.

www.endfistula.org

Providing family planning services to women could reduce birth related injuries such as Fistula by at least 20%.

www.endfistula.org

© 2006 FACING THE FUTURE: PEOPLE AND THE PLANET   www.facingthefuture.org

Global Health Issue Cards
3 of 3

Hookworm infects an estimated 1 billion people globally, causing severe dehydration and stunting children's growth.

www.cdc.gov

Anti-hookworm medicine costs as little as 3 cents per dose.

www.unicef.org

Indoor Air Pollution from cooking stoves causes over 1.5 million deaths in children under 5 in the developing world every year.

www.who.int

Cleaner and more efficient stoves, which significantly reduce indoor air pollution from cooking, can be produced for as little as $2 per stove.

www.care.ca

Every five seconds a child dies because she or he is hungry.

www.wfp.org

19 cents a day can feed a hungry child through a school lunch program.

www.wfp.org

Each year, over 17 million babies born to adolescent girls face almost twice the risk of dying during their first year of life than do babies born to adult women.

www.who.int

Education of girls and keeping them in school is a key solution to reducing adolescent pregnancy.

www.unicef.org

Half of those who smoke today - about 650 million people - will eventually die from tobacco.

www.who.int

Increasing taxes on cigarettes and preventing youth from smoking can significantly reduce deaths from tobacco.

www.who.int

© 2006 FACING THE FUTURE: PEOPLE AND THE PLANET   www.facingthefuture.org

Lesson 26 Overhead:

Partners for Health Questions

Discuss these questions with your partner and then write your answers on a piece of paper:

1. What might accelerate progress of this health solution?

2. What else do I know or want to know about this issue?

3. How is this health issue connected to other global issues?

Lesson 26 Handout:
Essay Assignment:
Advocate for a Healthy World

You are the leader of an organization that is working on improving global health. You have been invited to write a proposal explaining why it is important that world leaders act to address a global health issue your organization is working on. Your proposal will be sent to one or more Heads of State. You may address your letter to the U.S. Head of State and/ or the Head(s) of State of another country.

Instructions
- On the Global Health Issue Card you received in class, you will see a website address of an organization that is working on your assigned health issue. For this assignment, you will take the role as the leader of this organization.
- Go to that website and learn about the history of the organization and some of the programs it operates that address your global health issue. You may have to do some surfing around the organization's website to find the information you are looking for.
- Write your proposal to the Head of State of a country using the following format:

Salutation– Determine to which Head(s) of State you will write your proposal. What countries do you think should or could do something about this issue? You may write your proposal to one or more Head(s) of State.

Paragraph 1 – Briefly tell the Head(s) of State why you are writing them. Why is it urgent they read this proposal about your global health issue?

Paragraph 2 – Tell the Head(s) of State about the organization you lead. What does it do? How long has it been around? How big is it? Why is the organization effective and why should they listen to you? Establish your credibility.

Paragraph 3 – Explain to the Head(s) of State how this health issue has impacted other issues (for example: how has this health issue impacted peoples' ability to work, or go to school?). Be sure to include evidence of the scope and impact of the health issue.

Paragraph 4 – Tell the Head(s) of State what you want from them. What should they do to help address the global health issue? Address the issue of who is going to pay for it and how and why they should prioritize this problem (e.g. malaria) over others (e.g. HIV/AIDS, tuberculosis, malnutrition, etc.). Provide specific examples of your recommendations to them.

Paragraph 5 – Conclude your proposal by explaining to the Head(s) of State why addressing your global health issue is the right thing to do. Why is it their responsibility to respond to your proposal?

Three Faces of Governance

OVERVIEW

Students create a national energy policy via cooperation and negotiation among the 3 faces of governance: the *State* (Government), *Civic Organizations*, and the *Private Sector*. In groups representing each of these areas, students work to accomplish their individual policy goals while negotiating and forming coalitions with other groups to strengthen their overall energy policy. Policy proposals are presented and one plan is selected to become a national energy policy.

INQUIRY/CRITICAL THINKING QUESTIONS

- How are government policies determined and who has a say in creating policy?
- What considerations should be taken into account when developing energy policies?
- How are government policies connected to other global issues?

OBJECTIVES

Students will:
- Understand how the 3 parts of governance – the state (government), civic organizations, and the private sector – work together to create policy
- Experience the process of finding common interests and building coalitions with other organizations
- Recognize the difficult choices policy makers face in balancing the short- and long-term costs and benefits of their decisions
- Understand the role governance plays in other global issues

TIME REQUIRED: 1 hour

KEY ISSUES/CONCEPTS

- **Governance and its 3 faces: the state, civic organizations, and the private sector**
- **Civic engagement**
- **Sustainable policies**

SUBJECT AREAS

- **Social Studies**
  (Geography, Civics/Government, Economics, U.S. History, Global Studies, Contemporary World Problems)
- **Science**
  (Earth, Environmental, Physical)

NATIONAL STANDARDS CONSISTENCY

- **NCSS: 5, 6, 7, 8, 9, 10**
- **NSES: B, D, E, F**

GRADE LEVEL: 10–12

FTF Related Reading

- Intermediate: Chapter 6 and Chapter 8 from *Global Issues and Sustainable Solutions*

- Advanced: Unit 3, Chapters 4 and 5; Unit 6, Chapters 2, 3, 4, and 5 from *It's All Connected*

Three Faces of Governance

Vocabulary

- **Policy** – A plan of action for tackling political issues and is often initiated by a political party in government.

- **governance** – The exercise of economic, political, and administrative authority to manage a country's affairs at all levels. Governance is a process through which people and groups exercise their citizenship. There are 3 interconnected parts of governance: the state (government), the private sector, and civic organizations.

- **The State (Government)** – Includes elected officials, government agencies, and associated rules, regulations, laws, conventions, and policies of government at the local, state, and federal level.

- **Private Sector** – Business, companies, and professionals who trade products and services for income and profit.

- **Civic Organizations** – Community groups and non-governmental organizations (NGOs) that work on a broad range of issues that affect a community. The Sierra Club, Amnesty International, and the Boy Scouts of America are examples of civic organizations.

- **Coalition** – An organized group of people, often from different factions, in a community working toward a common goal. A coalition can have individual, group, institutional, community, and public policy goals.

- **Subsidy** – A direct (e.g. money) or indirect (e.g. tax break) payment from the government to businesses, citizens, or institutions to encourage something that the government believes is desirable.

Materials/Preparation

- Overhead: *Questions for Energy Policy*
- Handout: *Policy Position Cards*, 1 copy per class, cut into cards
- Handout: *Strategy Worksheet*, 8 copies per class (1 per group)
- 8 large (legal size) pieces of blank paper, and colored pens or pencils
- Blank name tags, 1 per student
- Prior to class, on paper, divide the students into groups as follows:

The State (Government)	Civic Organizations	Private Sector
President: Teacher	Friends of the Environment: 3-4 students	Coal industry: 3-4 students
Department of Environmental Protection: 2 students	Citizens for Economic Growth: 3-4 students	Nuclear power industry: 3-4 students
Department of Energy: 2 students	Rural Homeowners Association: 3-4 students	Wind power industry: 3-4 students

Activity

Introduction

1. (Optional) Do a Sides Debate to introduce this activity (see Sides Debate description on page 28)
   - "If a country holds elections to choose its leaders, that country is a democracy."
   - "Once people have elected their political leaders there is not much else they can do to participate in the governing of their country."

2. Go over the vocabulary words to the left.

© 2006 FACING THE FUTURE: PEOPLE AND THE PLANET   www.facingthefuture.org

Three Faces of Governance

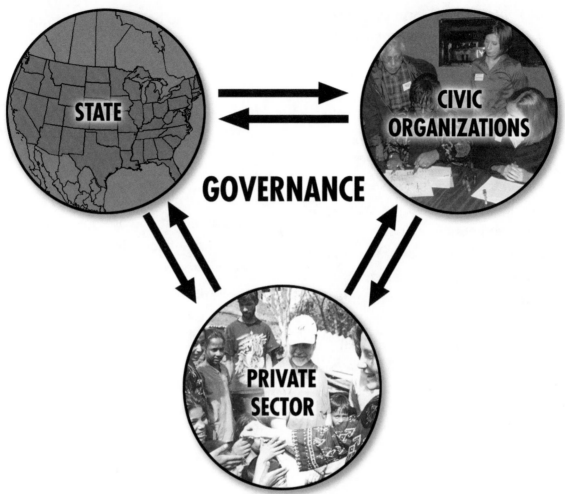

Steps

1. Tell the class they are going to draft a policy that will determine the future of the small country of Loma. Some of the students will represent the interests of the private sector, some of them will represent different civic organizations, and some will represent the state (government).

2. Arrange students into the 8 groups specified in the Materials/Preparation section above. Have each group assign a note-taker and a reporter.

3. Pass out to each group the *Policy Interest Cards* (1 per group), name tags, a large piece of paper, and pens. Have each student write the name of their group on a name tag and attach to their shirt.

4. Give groups about 5 minutes to create

a sign with a logo that represents their group. Have them tape the signs up in their group's area.

5. Begin by reading the following statement:

I'd like to welcome you and thank you for coming to this important meeting. As you may be aware, the population and economy of Loma is growing rapidly. As President, I have decided that we need a plan that will assure a steady supply of energy to sustain our growth. I have invited representatives from civic organizations and the private sector to participate in the planning process alongside my Department of Environmental Protection and Department of Energy. I hope the final plan that I select will address Loma's need for plentiful energy, while also considering

Three Faces of Governance

environmental and quality of life concerns. Your job today will be to recommend to me an energy plan for our country. I will give more consideration to a plan that includes the widest number of interests and points of view.

6. Show and go over the *Questions for Energy Policy* overhead. The position cards contain that group's position on each of the issues. However, these may be compromised during negotiations to produce an energy plan with broad support.

7. Pass out and go over the *Strategy Worksheet* (1 per group). Tell students this will be used to help them form their strategy, and to identify potential allies, obstacles, and points of negotiation.

8. Give them about 10 minutes to complete the worksheet. Circulate and help groups that are having difficulty.

9. Next, tell the students they will have 10 minutes to form coalitions with other groups that will agree to submit a plan together, and negotiate on the 4 issues required in the energy plan. Remind them that plans that are supported by more groups will get more consideration from you, especially plans that include a broad range of interests. They can belong to more than 1 coalition, and have their interests represented in more than 1 plan. They cannot talk to you directly during negotiations, but can discuss their ideas with the Department of Environmental Protection and Department of Energy.

10. Be sure to circulate during the exercise and make sure students are participating and reaching out to other groups to negotiate and form coalitions. Encourage students to speak with groups that would

not appear to be likely partners, and try to find 1 or 2 issues they might agree on. Encourage students in the government department groups to sit in on negotiations and get their interests heard as well. Do not let groups lobby you directly during the exercise. Tell them to talk to your government department staffers.

11. About 7-8 minutes through the exercise, announce that you are going to hold a cabinet meeting with your Department of Environmental Protection and Department of Energy. If there is anything the groups want to get across to the President, they should tell the department staffers right away.

12. Call over the students in the Department of Environmental Protection and Department of Energy groups and tell the rest of the groups to continue negotiating while you meet. Meet with the Department groups for 1-2 minutes and take notes on which groups they have spoken with, and their opinions on which groups they think have good ideas. You will reference this when making your final policy decision at the end of the exercise.

13. Call attention to the entire class and instruct groups to gather together in their coalitions, or get together with their original group if they did not form a coalition. If a group is part of more than 1 coalition, have them split their members between the coalitions.

14. Tell the coalitions (newly formed groups) that they now have about 5 minutes to finalize their plan and complete question #5 on their strategy worksheet, and choose a representative to present the plan.

© 2006 FACING THE FUTURE: PEOPLE AND THE PLANET   www.facingthefuture.org

Three Faces of Governance

15. Call the meeting to order and ask the representative from each coalition to present their plan, going through their proposal for each of the 4 issues on the Policy Position Cards. During the presentation, you may want to ask the group these questions:
    - What could be some of the negative side effects of the plan (e.g. pollution, high cost to consumers)?
    - Is this plan affordable?
    - Is this plan sustainable (i.e. will the plan meet the needs of people today and ensure that the needs of future generations will also be met? How does it affect the environment, the economy, and society?)?

16. After all the coalitions have presented, choose the plan to be submitted to the legislature and explain your reasoning behind the choice to the class. The following can be reasons for choosing a plan, and will also prompt a good follow up discussion:
    - The plan with the broadest support
    - The plan that seems most sustainable over time
    - The plan that can be implemented most quickly and inexpensively
    - The plan recommended by your Department staffers

17. Bring the class back together for reflection questions.

From Institute On Governance, *Governance Principles for Protected Areas 3*
Figure 1 illustrates four sectors of society, situated among citizens at large: business, the institutions of civil society (including the voluntary or not-for-profit sector), government and the media. A similar illustration for other countries could show a very different distribution of power. For example, the military or a political party (see figure 2) might occupy the largest part of the terrain. Government's role might be quite insignificant. In some settings, multinational corporations might play a dominant role.

Figure 1

Figure 2

Three Faces of Governance

Assessment
Reflection Questions

For Intermediate and Advanced Students

- Were you satisfied with the final decision that was made? Why or why not?
- Which part of Loma's population will benefit from this policy? Which will be burdened?
- Did you feel that other groups' opinions were listened to more than yours?
- Did you end up talking with any groups that you did not think you would have anything in common with at first?
- Which of the 4 issues/questions were most important to you? Why?
- Do you think the process you went through accurately reflects how policies are created today? Why or why not?
- Do governments have a responsibility to represent long-term interests (such as future environmental damage and impacts on future generations) when creating policies?

For Advanced Students

- Did you find yourself seriously compromising your interests so you would not be left out of a coalition? Were some members of the group more willing to compromise than others? How did you resolve differences within the group?
- What could be some of the consequences of a policy that is created without any input from either the private sector or civic organizations?
- What do you think groups can do to influence policy if they are left out of the formal planning process (e.g. sue in court, go to the media, arrange protests/rallies)?

- Do you feel that your real political representatives represent your concerns? Why or why not? What do you think you can do to get your interests heard by lawmakers?

Action Projects

- Organize a voter registration campaign. Even if you are not old enough to vote, you can send a message to others about the importance of voting by helping them register. Contact your local library, city hall, or your Secretary of State for information on voter registration.
- Research what is on the agenda at an upcoming city council meeting or public hearing. Learn about the issue and develop a position to present at the meeting.
- Visit **www.facingthefuture.org** and click on **Take Action**, then **Fast Facts Quick Actions** for more information and action opportunities pertaining to governance.

Additional Resources

Websites

- **www.iog.ca** – The Institute on Governance (IOG) is a non-profit organization founded to promote effective governance.

- **http://www.unescap.org/huset/gg/ governance.htm** – United Nations article titled, "What is Good Governance?"

- **http://magnet.undp.org/policy/ chapter1.htm#b** – This United Nations Development Program (UNDP) document discusses the relationship between good governance and sustainable human development.

© 2006 FACING THE FUTURE: PEOPLE AND THE PLANET   www.facingthefuture.org

Lesson 27 Overhead:

Questions for Energy Policy

- How will energy be produced?

- Where will energy production facilities be located?

- What should be done about pollution from the energy source?

- How will the energy facility be paid for?

Three Faces of Governance Policy Position Cards

Department of Environmental Protection
- Energy should be produced in the way that is least harmful to the environment
- Energy facilities should be located away from water sources and natural habitats
- Energy facilities should be state regulated to prevent pollution
- Coal and nuclear industries should pay the costs of developing their facilities, but the government should give subsidies to wind power, since it is less harmful to the environment

Department of Energy
- Energy should be produced in the most affordable and quickest way possible
- Energy facilities should be located in both rural and urban areas
- The energy industry should voluntarily agree to pollute as little as possible
- Energy facilities that can produce the most power quickly and cheaply – primarily coal burning plants – are more likely to be subsidized by the government

Friends of the Environment
- Energy should be produced in a way that is least harmful to the environment
- Energy facilities that generate pollution should be located away from water sources and should not destroy natural habitats
- The energy industry should be heavily regulated by the state to prevent pollution
- The government should offer subsidies to the wind power industry and not offer any subsidies to the coal and nuclear industries

Citizens for Economic Growth
- Energy should be produced in a way that is most affordable for businesses and consumers
- Energy facilities should be located wherever land is most affordable
- The energy industry should voluntarily agree to pollute as little as possible
- Energy facilities should pay for themselves, but some government subsidies are acceptable if they lead to cheap and plentiful energy for consumers and businesses

Rural Homeowners Association
- Energy should be produced in a way that is low-cost to rural families and does not heavily damage our land
- Facilities should be located in or near cities since they use more energy
- There should be some pollution regulation, but it should not overburden the industry unnecessarily
- Rural landowners should not have to pay increased taxes for energy facilities since urban people will be using more of it

Coal Power Industry
- Coal is cheap, quick, efficient, and because of new technology, it does not produce much pollution
- We want to locate plants wherever it is most cost effective and provides enough space to build our facility
- We want to self-regulate our pollution - we don't need the state to regulate us
- We would like government subsidies, but can get by without them if we are allowed to produce the bulk of Loma's energy

Wind Power Industry
- Wind power is the cleanest energy source and the most sustainable
- We need to build plants in flat rural areas where there is a lot of wind
- We do not produce pollution, so we do not need to be regulated by the state
- We will need some government subsidies to build our facilities; however, once the facility is constructed it will generate a long-term inexpensive source of energy

Nuclear Power Industry
- Nuclear power is a clean and reliable source of energy. As coal reserves begin to run out, nuclear power is the best long-term energy solution
- We need to build our reactors in rural areas that are near water sources and open space
- We will accept some routine safety checks, but we do not need state regulation for pollution prevention because we will build our facility to the highest standards
- We need government subsidies to build our plants and dispose of and store our waste

© 2006 FACING THE FUTURE: PEOPLE AND THE PLANET   www.facingthefuture.org

Lesson 27 Handout:
Strategy Worksheet for Three Faces of Governance

Four Issues facing Loma's Energy Policy
- How will energy be produced?
- Where will energy production facilities be located?
- What should be done about pollution from the energy source?
- How will the energy facility be paid for?

Group members: _____

_____

Name of your organization/entity: _____

1. Your Position: Read your *position card* and discuss the 4 questions above.
You should be able to answer each question based on the position stated on the card.

2. Potential Allies
Which other groups do you think share a similar view of what Loma's energy policy should be?
Are there groups that may agree with you on some but not all 4 issues of the energy policy?

_____

3. Potential Obstacles
Which groups may have different views than you on what Loma's energy policy should be?

_____

4. Prioritize Objectives
Of the 4 issues in the energy policy, rank them from 1 (being most important and non-negotiable) to 4 (being least important and willing to compromise on).

1. _____   **2.** _____

3. _____   **4.** _____

5. Final Plan (complete this after the negotiations)

With what group/s have you formed a coalition? _____

   1. How will energy be produced? _____

   2. Where will energy production facilities be located? _____

   3. What should be done about pollution from the energy source? _____

   4. How will the energy facility be paid for? _____

Taxes: Choices and Trade-offs

OVERVIEW

In this federal tax simulation lesson, students representing "special interest groups" discuss, recommend, and lobby for a budget allocation for federal tax spending. Interest groups include military, education, housing, healthcare, social security, and the environment. The exercise continues over consecutive years in which taxes are lowered and raised.

INQUIRY/CRITICAL THINKING QUESTIONS

- How are federal taxes spent and what role do special interest groups have in influencing this process?
- What are some of the trade-offs when taxes are raised, lowered, or reallocated?
- What role do citizens have in influencing the allocation of tax dollars?

OBJECTIVES

Students will:
- Identify major spending categories for the federal government
- Recognize the role that special interest groups and citizens play in the federal budget process
- Understand the tradeoffs involved in funding and cutting government programs

TIME REQUIRED: 1 hour

KEY ISSUES/CONCEPTS

- **Taxes**
- **Budgeting**
- **Government expenditures**
- **Costs, benefits, and trade-offs**

SUBJECT AREAS

- **Social Studies**
  (Economics, U.S. History)
- **Science** (Environmental)
- **Business/Finance**
- **Math**

NATIONAL STANDARDS CONSISTENCY

- **NCSS: 5, 6, 10**
- **NSES: F**

GRADE LEVEL: 7–11

FTF Related Reading

- Intermediate: Chapter 8 from *Global Issues and Sustainable Solutions*
- Advanced: Unit 6, Chapter 4, 5, and 6 from *It's All Connected*

Materials/Preparation

- Handout: *Special Interest Cards*, copy and cut into 6 cards (1 per group of 3-4 students)
- Handout/Overhead: *Tax Worksheet*, make 1 copy per group of 3-4 students and make 1 overhead

© 2006 FACING THE FUTURE: PEOPLE AND THE PLANET   www.facingthefuture.org

Taxes: *Choices and Trade-offs*

Activity

Introduction

1. (Optional) Do a Sides Debate using the statement below (see Sides Debate lesson on page 28)

   "Taxes are good for the health of a country."

2. Tell the class that they are going to do an activity in which they take on the role of special interest groups who will recommend a federal budget allocation to you, the President of the fictional country of Paradise. Tell them that the federal budget is a statement of the federal government's planned spending and anticipated income for the upcoming year.

3. Ask students to define *taxes* (i.e. money paid to the government by individuals and businesses in exchange for government services). You might also need to define social security. (i.e. a government insurance program that provides income and health benefits to retirees and others. Benefits paid are based on the monetary contribution an individual makes during his or her lifetime.)

Steps

1. Arrange the class into 6 groups of 3-4 students and have each group randomly draw a *Special Interest Card*.

2. Give the groups several minutes to "take on" their roles by reading, discussing, and completing the information on their identity card.

3. Give each group a copy of the *Tax Worksheet* and go over it with them using an overhead.

4. Begin the Year 1 budget cycle, which has a budget of $25 million. Instruct groups to discuss and then pencil in a recommended dollar amount for their interest area on the *Tax Worksheet.*

5. Call the class to order to begin the Year 1 budget negotiations. Call on each special interest group 1 at a time and have them describe who they are, their specific objectives, and why they care about their issue. Have them tell you their recommended budget amount for their area of interest. As groups give you their recommendations, begin filling out the *Tax Worksheet* overhead (there is a strong likelihood you will change the final allocations, so use an erasable overhead pen).

6. If the recommended budget exceeds $25 million (which is likely given that the Year 1

Taxes: Choices and Trade-offs

budget will not meet the basic needs of all special interest groups), have the groups begin lobbying you for their interest area. Have the interest groups debate the merits of their recommended budget amounts to help reveal the complexity and importance of all issues at stake.

7. Based on the interest groups' input, debate, and pressure, you will now make a final decision on the Year 1 budget allocation.

8. Give groups a few minutes to respond and share with the class the question on the worksheet: "Briefly describe some of the implications of the Year 1 budget allocation. What spending areas might be negatively and positively affected?"

9. Begin the Year 2 budget cycle. Announce that due to pressure from *Paradise Citizens Against Taxation*, you have authorized a tax cut of 20% so the total budget for Year 2 has been reduced to $20 million. Each tax paying

citizen (65,000 working adults) in Paradise will get a $75.00 tax refund this year!

10. Repeat the budget allocation steps for Year 2 with students recommending and lobbying for a proposed budget for their interest area. As President, you will decide on the final budget for Year 2. Students will respond to the questions on the worksheet.

11. Begin the Year 3 budget cycle. Announce that due to pressure from *Paradise Citizens for Greater Public Services*, there has been a 50% tax increase to help address some of the budget shortfalls from the previous year, so the Year 3 budget total is $30 million. Each tax paying citizen (65,000 working adults) in Paradise will pay an additional $150.00 in taxes this year.

12. Repeat the budget allocation steps for Year 3.

13. Conclude with the following reflection questions.

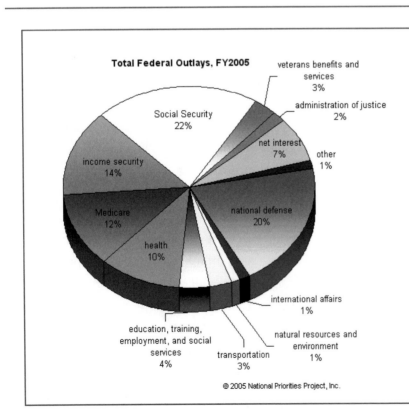

Total Federal Outlays, FY2005

veterans benefits and services 3%

administration of justice 2%

Social Security 22%

net interest 7%

other 1%

income security 14%

national defense 20%

Medicare 12%

health 10%

international affairs 1%

education, training, employment, and social services 4%

transportation 3%

natural resources and environment 1%

Source: Office of Management and Budget, Budget of the U.S. Government, FY2006, Mid-Session Review.

© 2005 National Priorities Project, Inc.

© 2006 FACING THE FUTURE: PEOPLE AND THE PLANET   www.facingthefuture.org

Taxes: Choices and Trade-offs

Assessment
Reflection Questions

For Intermediate and Advanced Students

- What were some of the trade-offs when the budget was cut and when it was increased?
- Why are interest groups important? What role do interest groups play in shaping government policy? Why might an interest group form?
- What are some reasons a person might support a tax increase? What are some reasons a person might support a tax decrease?
- How might political factors influence allocation of the federal budget?
- How are federal taxes connected to global issues?

For Advanced Students

- How is the perspective of an interest group different from the perspective of the President when debating allocation of the federal budget?
- What trade-offs did your interest group have to make? How might these trade-offs impact people and the planet in the real world?
- If you were the President and were faced with the decision to raise taxes or cut government programs, which position would you choose and why?

Action Projects

- During campaign season, candidates are often willing to get involved in the community, so try inviting a candidate to your classroom to share their views on taxes. Encourage students to volunteer for a campaign of their choice.
- Research the concept of "progressive taxation" and national and international initiatives that advocate using taxes as a way to finance social development and alleviate global poverty. For a list of resources to help students get started, visit http://www.stampoutpoverty.org/?lid=520

- Visit www.facingthefuture.org and click on **Take Action**, then **Fast Facts Quick Actions** for other action project ideas related to taxes.

Additional Resources

Films

- *Economics* (from "Reinventing the World" series), David Springbett and Heather MacAndrew, Bullfrog Films, 2000. This 50 minute documentary examines the modern economic system and its purported benefits to global society.

Books

- *The Ultimate Field Guide to the U.S. Economy,* Heintz, Folbre, and the Center for Popular Economics, The New Press, 2000. A humorous guide to economic life in America.

- *Tax Shift,* Alan Thein Durning and Yoram Bauman, Northwest Environment Watch, 1998. A blueprint for shifting taxes from the things we want more of (pay checks and enterprise) to the things we want less of (pollution and resource depletion). Available in full-text download at http://www.northwestwatch.org/publications/Tax_Shift.pdf

Websites

- www.whitehouse.gov – U.S. government website where you can find, read, and download the federal budget.

- www.nationalpriorities.org –The National Priorities Project is a nonpartisan and nonprofit organization that offers citizen and community groups tools and resources to shape federal budget and policy priorities that promote social and economic justice.

- www.taxpolicycenter.org – The Tax Policy Center is a joint venture of the Urban Institute and Brookings Institution and is comprised of nationally recognized experts in tax, budget, and social policy.

© 2006 FACING THE FUTURE: PEOPLE AND THE PLANET   www.facingthefuture.org

Special Interest Cards for *Taxes: Choices and Trade-offs*

You represent **Paradise Veterans for Military Strength**, a group of war veterans who support increasing military funding to protect the country from terrorists. You estimate $7 million needs to go into the Defense budget just to meet the basic defense needs of your country.

Discuss the specific objectives of your interest group.
Why does your interest group care about this issue?

You represent members of the **Paradise Association of Teacher Educators**. You are devoted to the education of all young people in the country of Paradise. You need $4 million in the Education budget to meet basic education needs in your country.

Discuss the specific objectives of your interest group.
Why does your interest group care about this issue?

You represent members of the **Paradise Coalition for Universal Healthcare**. You lobby your government to establish a universal healthcare system to provide quality and affordable healthcare for everyone. You need $5 million in the Healthcare budget to meet basic healthcare needs in your country.

Discuss the specific objectives of your interest group.
Why does your interest group care about this issue?

You represent the **Paradise Affordable Housing Corporation**. You collaborate with local and national governmental agencies in setting public policy and priorities for more affordable housing. You need $3 million in the Housing budget to meet basic low income housing needs in your country.

Discuss the specific objectives of your interest group.
Why does your interest group care about this issue?

You represent members of the **Paradise Association of Retired Persons**. You are concerned with quality of life issues for senior citizens. You need $5 million in the Social Security budget to meet basic social security needs in your country.

Discuss the specific objectives of your interest group.
Why does your interest group care about this issue?

You represent members of the **Paradise Environmental Network**, the largest environmental organization in the country. You work together to protect and promote the responsible use of the Earth's ecosystems and resources. You need $4 million in the Environment budget to meet basic environmental needs in your country.

Discuss the specific objectives of your interest group.
Why does your interest group care about this issue?

© 2006 FACING THE FUTURE: PEOPLE AND THE PLANET   www.facingthefuture.org

Lesson 28 Handout:
Tax Worksheet for *Taxes: Choices and Trade-offs*

Names:_____

You are members of the Special Interest Group_____
in the country of Paradise.

Paradise is a small country with the following vital statistics:
- Total population: 100,000
- School-age kids: (20%) 20,000
- Working adults: (65%) 65,000
- Senior citizens (15%) 15,000
- Wealthy class: (20%) 20,000
- Middle class: (50%) 50,000
- Poor: (30%) 30,000
- Total land area: 8,000 sq miles (about the size of New Jersey or the country of El Salvador)
- Natural areas/wildlands (mountains, lakes, rivers, etc.): 2000 square miles

	Total Budget	Federal Tax Spending					
		Military & Defense 1 million = 100 soldiers trained and supplied	**Education** 1 million = 5,000 students reached	**Healthcare** 1 million = Healthcare for 7,000 school-age kids and senior citizens	**Housing** 1 million = Housing assistance for 10,000 poor people	**Social Security** 1 million = Retirement for 3,000 senior citizens	**Environment** 1 million = 500 square miles of natural land preservation
Year 1	$25 million						
Briefly describe some of the implications of the Year 1 budget allocation. Which spending areas might be negatively and positively affected?							
Year 2 Tax Cut of 20%	$20 million						
Briefly describe some of the implications of the Year 2 budget allocation. Which spending areas might be negatively and positively affected?							
Year 3 Tax Increase of 50%	$30 million						
Briefly describe some of the implications of the Year 3 budget allocation. Which spending areas might be negatively and positively affected?							

Take a Step for Equity

(Adapted from "The World Sits Down to Dinner," created by Torkin Wakefield. Statistics were also gathered from the United Nations Development Program (UNDP) and Oxfam America's "Hunger Banquet".)

OVERVIEW

Students are randomly assigned an economic class, and then hear poverty and wealth statistics describing their economic class as they step forward in a line. Ultimately, a distance is created between the wealthiest and the poorest illustrating the economic gap between the rich and poor. Students then brainstorm and discuss ways to alleviate poverty and hunger.

INQUIRY/CRITICAL THINKING QUESTIONS

- How are resources distributed throughout the world?
- What are the factors contributing to the inequitable distribution of resources?
- What steps can be taken to alleviate hunger and poverty?

OBJECTIVES

Students will:
- Experience what it feels like to be part of a specific economic class
- Consider social, environmental, and economic impacts of poverty and scarcity
- Consider and write about ways to help alleviate poverty and create a just and sustainable world

TIME REQUIRED: 15–30 minutes

KEY ISSUES/CONCEPTS

- **Poverty and scarcity**
- **Economic class**
- **Structural solutions**

SUBJECT AREAS

- **Social Studies** (Geography, Economics, Global Studies, Contemporary World Problems)
- **Science** (Environmental)

NATIONAL STANDARDS CONSISTENCY

- **NCSS:** 3, 4, 5, 7, 9
- **NSES: F**

GRADE LEVEL: 7–12

FTF Related Reading

- Intermediate: Chapter 5 from *Global Issues and Sustainable Solutions*
- Advanced: Unit 4, Chapter 5 and Unit 6, Chapter 6 from *It's All Connected*

Materials/Preparation

- Construction paper, card stock or tickets in 4 colors, 1 card/ticket per student (see Table on next page for card color and distribution)
- Teacher master: *Take a Step for Equity—Readings*

© 2006 FACING THE FUTURE: PEOPLE AND THE PLANET   www.facingthefuture.org

Take a Step for Equity

- Clear a large space in the room so that students can stand in a line in the back of the class and step about 25 feet forward
- Prepare/gather enough colored cards or tickets so that you have 1 for each student in accordance with the guidelines in the Table below:

Economic Class	% World Population	# of students and card color for a class of 20	# of students and card color for a class of 30
Wealthiest	20% (1.2 billion)	4 blue	6 blue
Middle Income	35% (2.1 billion)	7 red	11 red
Working Poor	25% (1.6 billion)	5 yellow	7 yellow
Poorest of the Poor	20% (1.2 billion)	4 white	6 white

Activity

Introduction

1. Ask students what percentage of the people living on Earth do they think are poor. What percentage do they think are rich? Have them write down their estimates and hold on to them for later.

Steps

1. Have each student randomly select 1 of the colored cards.
2. Have students line up at the back of the class facing forward.
3. Stand in front of the class and tell them, "Today, by random chance in the lottery, you now belong to a temporary economic class. Although there are more than 6 billion people living on this planet together, we are separated by our diverse fortunes and are divided by economic groups. Some of us are rich or

poor by the circumstances of our behavior or opportunities, others by our birth."

4. Read aloud to the class from the teacher master *Take a Step for Equity—Readings*. Be dramatic in your reading, pause often, and make eye contact with the students. Each economic class will be directed to step forward before hearing the description of their class. Students in the wealthiest group will end up farthest away from those in the "poorest of the poor" group.

5. Conclude with a discussion, using the following reflection questions (Note: The information in this lesson may be difficult for many students to hear, and therefore it is important to focus on the positive opportunities for change, as outlined in the Action Projects section below).

Assessment
Reflection Questions

For Intermediate and Advanced Students

- How did it feel to be in your economic class?
- Look back at the predictions you made before this activity. Were you surprised to learn what percentage of the world's people are poor? Middle class? Wealthy? Do you think people should work to change the statistics or do you think there is not any way to change the situation?
- What questions do you have about hunger and/or poverty?
- What are some causes of hunger and poverty?

For Advanced Students

- How are poverty and hunger connected to other global issues such as population growth, environmental degradation, discrimination, and conflict?

Take a Step for Equity

- What are some of the social, environmental, and potential security consequences of poverty?
- What do you think some solutions are to these issues?

Writing Connection

- Have students write a diary entry of "A day in the life of [a person in their randomly assigned economic class]." Ask them to write a detailed entry of their day. Prompts may include: When I wake up; Where I live; A description of my surroundings; What I have for breakfast, lunch, and dinner; Details about my work; How much money I get paid; What my family is doing; How I feel; and What I am thinking about.

Action Projects

- Organize a "Hunger Banquet" to build awareness and raise money to alleviate global poverty. A Hunger Banquet can be done with just your class (e.g. for lunch one day), with parents, or as a school/community event. The Hunger Banquet is a project of Oxfam America. For a detailed description of this project, visit **www.facingthefuture.org** and click on **Take Action**, and then **Service Learning Projects**.
- Do *Take a Step for Equity* at a school assembly. Have students present web search information and perform skits about poverty, highlighting the actions that can be taken to help alleviate poverty and hunger in their community and in the world.
- Students can research laws or policies that adversely affect the poor in their state or country and then write letters to their elected officials about changes they would like to see.

- Do a "Heifer International" service learning project in which students raise money to buy farm animals for poor families to help them become more self-sufficient. For a detailed description of this project, visit **www.facingthefuture.org** and click on **Take Action**, then **Service Learning Projects**.

Additional Resources

Films

- *Small Fortunes: Microcredit and the Future of Poverty,* Sterling van Wagenen, 2005, 60 minutes. This documentary describes the impact that microcredit is having throughout the world through the stories of twelve microentrepreneurs living in Bangladesh, India, Kenya, Peru, The Philippines, and the United States. Microcredit luminaries and experts describe how microcredit is a powerful tool in fighting poverty and provide insights into the issues confronting the microcredit movement.

Websites

- http://www.un.org/millenniumgoals/ – The United Nations developed 8 Millennium Development Goals which range from halving extreme poverty to halting the spread of HIV/AIDS and providing universal primary education, all by the target date of 2015. This blueprint has been agreed to by all the world's countries and leading development institutions.

- www.un.org/cyberschoolbus – United Nations Cyber School Bus website includes articles and information on poverty.

© 2006 FACING THE FUTURE: PEOPLE AND THE PLANET   www.facingthefuture.org

Take a Step for Equity Readings - Page 1

(Statistics from the United Nations Development Program (UNDP) and Oxfam America)

The Poorest of the Poor

Those of you with white cards please take one step forward. You are the world's poorest of the poor. There are about 1.2 billion of you. You are 20 percent of the world's population and you live on less than one U.S.- equivalent dollar a day. Seventy percent of you are women and girls.

You own virtually nothing. You live in a train station in India and on top of a garbage dump in Guatemala City. You are a girl in Zambia orphaned at age two when your parents died of AIDS. You are an Afghan farmer living through three years of drought, famine, and war. You tend to die young, whether from disease or a hidden land mine. You don't go to school, nor do you go to the doctor when you are sick.

You and your family spend your entire day trying to feed yourselves. You're always hungry. About 24,000 of you die every day from hunger or hunger-related causes. That's one person every 3.6 seconds. Three-fourths of these deaths are children under the age of five. Sixteen billion dollars a year could meet the basic food needs of all of the world's poor.

Many of you could have a sustainable livelihood. Programs promoting education, access to health care, and support of democratic governments could all help to break the cycle of poverty in the world.

Everyone else please take two steps forward.

The Working Poor

Now the working poor, those of you with yellow cards, take one step forward. You represent about 25 percent of the world's people, and you live on less than two U.S. equivalent dollars a day. You are the factory workers and farm laborers of the world. You make sport shoes in Vietnam, jeans in Mexico, and designer dresses in El Salvador. You produce the goods and services that are used by those wealthier than you.

You own the simplest possessions—one or maybe two changes of clothes, and a few household items. You have no savings. In case of illnesses, accidents, and bad luck, you have no safety net. While there are exceptions, generally there are few opportunities for you to move up the economic ladder. In spite of the hardships you face, many of you live with great dignity: You often have close connections to family and to the land.

The remaining people, those with the blue and red cards, take two steps forward.

Take a Step for Equity Readings - Page 2

(Statistics from the United Nations Development Program (UNDP) and Oxfam America)

The Middle Income People

Now, the middle-income people with the red cards take a step forward. You represent 35 percent of the world's people. You are an industrious, hard-working group. You are striving to move up the economic ladder, to be part of the wealthy group. You have possessions – most of you own a television; some of you own a car. Many of you have been to school, some have a high school education, and a few of you have been to college. A handful of you may even have some savings. You occasionally eat at restaurants, although more often you eat fast food because you are on the run, working hard, and trying to stay on top.

You are in a position to make changes in the world. Because of your numbers and status in the world's workforce, you have the power to change some things. You can do this by supporting policies that help the poor and provide for better working conditions. You can choose to spend your money on products from socially responsible companies. You can be a strong advocate for people with less than yourselves.

The Wealthy

Now, those of you with the blue cards take three steps forward. You represent 20 percent of the world's population but you control about 86 percent of the world's resources. You own homes and cars and have closets full of clothes and shoes. Many of you fly around the world for business trips and exotic vacations. You have a diet rich in meat, dairy products, fresh vegetables, and fruit. Since most of you exceed your daily requirement of calories, you sometimes face health problems such as heart disease, diabetes, and obesity; however, you have access to the best health care in the world.

Even among the wealthy there are the richest. One of you please take two more steps forward to represent the three richest people in the world. Your combined net worth is more than 115 billion dollars. You have more wealth than the 48 poorest countries.

The wealthy have many opportunities to make a difference in the world. You can choose to buy from companies that are socially responsible, and you can reduce your consumption by choosing to use less. Because of your education, money, and resources, you have great power to help others. You have connections; you can gather networks of people. When you set your mind to something, you can make it happen.

© 2006 FACING THE FUTURE: PEOPLE AND THE PLANET   www.facingthefuture.org

Take a Step for Equity Readings - Page 3

(Statistics from the United Nations Development Program (UNDP) and Oxfam America)

Everyone

That's all of us. We live in a world where a few have a lot and many have very little. The world today produces enough food to supply everyone on Earth with about 2,700 calories each day. In the United States alone, 34.6 million people are hungry or don't have a secure source of food. Twenty-six million people could be fed if the amount of edible food wasted in the United States each day was reduced by one-third.

The roots of hunger and poverty lie in the inequity of access to education, resources, and power. The results are illiteracy, illness, and powerlessness. But it doesn't have to be that way. The first step starts with imagining a world without hunger, poverty, environmental destruction, and deadly conflict; then we can work toward a just and sustainable future for all.

Shop Till You Drop?

OVERVIEW

In this simulation, students experience how resources are distributed and used by different people based on access to wealth. Students discuss and work toward personal and structural solutions to address the environmental impacts of resource consumption, and to help alleviate poverty.

INQUIRY/CRITICAL THINKING QUESTIONS

- What are the choices that people with relatively little access to wealth/income can make compared to people with relatively high access?
- What are the impacts of each of those choices and decisions?
- What personal choices can we make to help reduce some of these impacts, and what actions can we take to help alleviate poverty?

OBJECTIVES

Students will:
- Determine and explain purchasing/consumption choices
- Compare different purchasing/consumption choices and their social and environmental effects
- Describe how relative affluence and high consumption patterns relate to environmental degradation
- Discuss and begin to implement personal choices they can make to reduce environmental impacts as well as develop and implement an action plan to help alleviate poverty

TIME REQUIRED: 1 hour

KEY ISSUES/CONCEPTS

- **Equity, poverty, and scarcity**
- **Consumption patterns**
- **Environmental resources**

SUBJECT AREAS

- **Social Studies** (Geography, Economics, Global Studies, Contemporary World Problems)
- **Science** (Environmental, Life)
- **Math**
- **Health/Nutrition**

NATIONAL STANDARDS CONSISTENCY

- **NCSS: 1, 2, 3**
- **NSES: C, F**

GRADE LEVEL: 6–12

FTF Related Reading

- Intermediate: Chapters 4 & 6 from *Global Issues and Sustainable Solutions*
- Advanced: Units 3 & 5 from *It's All Connected*

© 2006 FACING THE FUTURE: PEOPLE AND THE PLANET www.facingthefuture.org

Shop Till You Drop?

Materials/Preparation

- Handout: *Global Mall Dollars*, 1 card per student (there are 6 cards per sheet)
- Handout: *Global Mall Items*, 1 sheet per student
- (Optional) Teacher master: *Global Mall Impacts*, 1 copy as teacher reference
- Butcher paper, 1 sheet per group
- Marking pens, 2–3 pens for each group
- Make enough copies of the *Global Mall Dollars* sheet so that there is 1 card for each student. (Each sheet has 3 $200 cards, 2 $1,000 cards, and 1 $2,500 card to reflect income distribution around the world. Therefore, more students will end up with $200 cards and $1,000 cards than $2,500 cards.) Cut the sheets along the dotted lines and fold each card so the amount is not visible.

Activity

Introduction

1. Have the class brainstorm human needs (food, water, energy, clothing, health care, etc.).
2. Tell the students that today, as global citizens, they will have a chance to shop for these needs at the "Global Mall". The Global Mall sells all of the resources that humans depend on to live, as well as some "nonessential" items.

Steps

1. Pass out the handout, *Global Mall Items*, which lists the items available. Tell students they can select items from the list to purchase with their *Global Mall Dollars*, but that they must first meet their basic needs by selecting items from the categories of food, water, and fuel, and only then can they buy any of the other items.
2. Pass around a basket with the *Global Mall Dollars* and instruct each student to take 1 card and not show it to anyone.
3. Instruct students to write the items they purchase on the lines on their card (or on the back), along with the cost of each item (be sure they do this part of the activity individually).
4. While students are making their purchasing choices, you should keep the pressure on to instill a sense of urgency. Ask, "Who's done shopping?" Say, "The mall is closing soon!" Students with $200 *Global Mall Dollars* will likely finish much sooner than those with $1,000 and $2,500.
5. When students finish their shopping, have them break into 3 groups, putting students with the same dollar amounts ($200, $1,000, $2,500) together (there will be more students with $200; if necessary, subdivide groups so you have between 3 and 5 students per group).
6. In their groups, have students share and compare what they chose to purchase, and why. Ask them to discuss anything they could not afford to purchase and how not having those items might affect their lives.
7. Have each group report to the class on the decisions they made and the impact that these decisions would have on their lives.

Shop Till You Drop

8. You can choose to stop the lesson here and conclude with the reflection questions below, or continue with the following part of the activity.

9. Give each group a large sheet of paper and some pens, and ask students to list 3-5 items that members of their group purchased. Have them create 2 columns titled "Social Impacts" (effects of the choices on people) and "Environmental Impacts". For each item listed, have groups write all of the impacts they can think of, positive or negative, for each category. Give them the following example: "If your group chose 'Firewood Gathering', you might list such Social Impacts as women and children spending their time gathering wood rather than going to school, harvesting food, cooking, or engaging in recreation activities. Environmental Impacts might include deforestation, habitat destruction, and soil erosion."

10. Circulate among the groups and suggest impacts they might not have considered. Use the handout *Global Resource Mall Impacts* as a teacher reference.

11. Have each group present and discuss their findings with the class.

12. Conclude with the following reflection questions.

Assessment
Reflection Questions

For Intermediate and Advanced Students

- How did it feel to have more or less money and options than other people in the class? How did it feel to see what you could and could not afford at the Global Mall?
- How many of you could not afford education? What would your lives be like if you could not go to school?
- How would it feel to have to choose between food and health care?
- How many of you have ever been very sick or gone to a hospital or had friends and family who have? What would your life be like now if you had been unable to get medical care?
- What is the effect on people when a small group is consuming the majority of resources?
- What were the impacts caused by people with fewer Global Mall Dollars, and what were the impacts caused by people with more Global Mall Dollars?
- What are some specific examples of how to reduce the social or environmental harm of some choices? What are 3 things that every one of us could do in the next week to lessen our environmental impact?

For Advanced Students

- How do poverty and wealth afford people different options? Discuss the fact that roughly one-fifth of all people worldwide survive on less than $1 (U.S.) a day – how does this limit their choices, and what are the environmental, social, and global security implications of this?
- When you were choosing what to buy, did you think about the environmental impact? For those of you in the lowest income range, did you have a choice about the environmental

© 2006 FACING THE FUTURE: PEOPLE AND THE PLANET   www.facingthefuture.org

Shop Till You Drop?

impact you produced? If not, how did it feel to not have a choice?

- How is this activity like the real world?
- Which income group from this activity is most prevalent in our country?

Lesson Extension

- Assign each group a family from the book, *Material World*, by Peter Menzel. Have the students analyze what that family owns and brainstorm the relative impact of those items. Have them create a graph of the relative wealth and consumption of each family measured against their environmental and social impacts.

Writing Connection

- Students write and illustrate a short story about a family who has the same budget as they did in the activity. Have them include details about the family's life, choices, impacts, and solutions.

Math Connection

- Have students create a monthly budget for a family of 4 based on an annual income of $18,850, which is the average annual poverty threshold in the U.S. for a family this size. Have students take into account expenses such as housing, food, clothing, medical, insurance, transportation, etc. They can research local organizations in their community that may be able to help meet the needs of this family.

Action Projects

- Throw a "BeadWear Party" at your school through the BeadforLife project. BeadforLife is an organization that fights poverty by employing very poor women in Uganda to make beautiful jewelry out of recycled paper. This project provides you with the opportunity to help women feed their children and send them to school by selling their products, while at the same time educating yourself and your friends, parents, and community about Uganda and the plight of poor people around the world. For a detailed description of this

and other service learning projects, visit **www.facingthefuture.org**, click on **Take Action** and then **Service Learning Projects**.

- Contact your local chapter of Habitat for Humanity to find out how you can help alleviate homelessness in your community. Habitat for Humanity builds simple, decent, and safe homes both in the U.S. and around the world that low-income families can afford to buy. For more information, visit **www.habitat.org**.
- Visit **www.facingthefuture.org** and click on **Take Action**, then **Fast Facts Quick Actions** for more information and action opportunities on poverty, consumption and other connected global issues.

Additional Resources

Books

- *Plan B: Rescuing a Planet Under Stress and a Civilization in Trouble,* Lester Brown, W.W. Norton & Company, New York, 2003. Brown calls for a worldwide mobilization to stabilize population and climate before they spiral out of control. It provides a plan for sustaining economic progress worldwide.

Websites

- **www.netaid.org** – NetAid is a non-profit organization that educates, inspires, and empowers young people to fight global poverty.

- **www.gbmna.org** – The mission of the Green Belt Movement International is to empower individuals worldwide to protect the environment and to promote good governance and cultures of peace.

- **www.undp.org** – The United Nations Development Program (UNDP) is the UN's global development network organization advocating for change and connecting countries to knowledge, experience, and resources to help people build a better life.

Global Mall Items

Food	Rice and beans once or twice a day	Beans, vegetables, and rice daily, plus meat/dairy about once a month	A variety of fast foods 3 times a day, such as hamburger, chicken sandwich, tacos, French fries, soda, and ice cream	High quality food 3 times a day, including eggs, meat, fish, fresh vegetables, fresh imported fruit, bread, milk, imported cheese, chocolate, and other desserts
	$75	**$150**	**$300**	**$500**
Water	Untreated water collected from a lake and carried 2 miles by women and children	Untreated water collected from the village well 9 months a year, and from a river the other 3 months	Purified water brought by government trucks every week	Indoor plumbing with hot and cold running water, showers, and bathtubs
	No cost	**$75**	**$200**	**$400**
Heat / Fuel	Firewood cut from local forest, sometimes hours away; work done mostly by children	Coal purchased in the market and used for cooking and heating	Oil used for gasoline, cooking, and heating	Solar panels using the sun's energy to heat home and water; natural gas for cooking
	No cost	**$125**	**$300**	**$700**
Education	Crowded school 1 hour away through grade 5 (free, but you must buy a uniform to attend)	Elementary, middle school, and high school located in the local village	K-12 education with college an option for most people	Graduate degree preparing people for professions such as doctor, lawyer, professor
	$50	**$125**	**$400**	**$900**
Health Care	Walk or be carried 10 hours to the nearest village clinic, where they have a dozen medicines	Good medical care available in a city 1 hour away by bus	High-quality health care and hospital anytime you are sick and for yearly checkups	High quality health care, including elective surgery such as knee repair and cosmetic and laser eye surgery
	$75	**$200**	**$500**	**$700**
Luxury Items	Radio running on batteries	Small color television in your house	Refrigerator and air conditioning in your house	Hawaii surf vacation, airline ticket, and hotel
	$50	**$150**	**$350**	**$700**

© 2006 FACING THE FUTURE: PEOPLE AND THE PLANET   www.facingthefuture.org

Global Mall Impacts

Food	**Rice and beans** Environmental: locally grown, no pesticides Social: lack of essential vitamins results in more malnutrition	**Beans, veggies, meat** Environmental: may be locally grown/raised, may include some pesticide use Social: better nutritional value	**Fast foods** Environmental: beef production means high water/feed use, deforestation Social: convenient, but unhealthy, high fat related to heart disease	**High quality food** Environmental: beef production, imports use more energy, chemicals, pollution Social: healthy but cash crops take away from staple food production
Water	**Untreated water** Environmental: use of lake, stream water degrades habitat Social: disease, death, poverty (time spent away from school, work, etc.)	**Village well** Environmental: high use degrades aquifer Social: disease, death, poverty	**Water trucked in** Environmental: truck uses fuel, pollution, global warming Social: less disease, more convenient	**Indoor plumbing** Environmental: energy use, metal, and plastic for pipes Social: fast, easy, safe, convenient
Heat / Fuel	**Firewood** Environmental: deforestation, global warming, desertification Social: poverty (time away from school, work, food production), smoke linked to lung disease	**Coal** Environmental: air pollution, mining Social: easier to use than firewood, but may result in lung disease if cooking area is not ventilated, miners susceptible to lung disease	**Oil/Gas** Environmental: oil drilling, spills, pipeline impacts, pollution, loss of habitat, global warming Social: convenient, but results in dependency on oil/gas supplies	**Solar panels** Environmental: clean renewable source Social: convenient, expensive to install but saves money in the long run, no health risks
Education	**School: 1-hour walk** Environmental: lack of education related to population growth Social: illiteracy, few job skills, poverty	**School in village** Environmental: educated people have resources and knowledge to protect environment Social: allows access to jobs, money, health care	**K-12 education** Environmental: better able to protect resources, but may consume more Social: better jobs, higher income, health care, quality of life	**Graduate school** Environmental: better able to protect resources, but high level of consumption Social: better jobs, quality of life, but may be more prone to stress
Health Care	**Clinic 10 hours away** Environmental: high mortality linked to high birth rates, population growth impacts environment Social: illness, death, disease transmission, poverty	**Medical care 1 hr away** Environmental: low mortality linked to lower birth rates Social: less disease, lower mortality, may not get treatment except in critical situation	**Hospital** Environmental: low mortality linked to lower birth rates Social: less illness, disease, etc., but with high financial cost	**Elective surgery** Environmental: may use many resources, medicine, equipment Social: cure non-life threatening problems, increase quality of life and social status
Luxury Items	**Radio** Environmental: energy, batteries toxic to soil Social: access to information, enjoyable	**Color TV** Environmental: energy resources to manufacture Social: entertainment, access to information	**Refrigerator** Environmental: global warming, resources to manufacture, energy Social: better health, fresh food	**Surf vacation** Environmental: air travel contributes to global warming, heavy use of resources Social: lower stress, enjoyable, but expensive

Global Mall Dollars

$200
Global Mall Dollars

ITEM   COST

_____   _____

_____   _____

_____   _____

$200
Global Mall Dollars

ITEM   COST

_____   _____

_____   _____

_____   _____

$200
Global Mall Dollars

ITEM   COST

_____   _____

_____   _____

_____   _____

$1,000
Global Mall Dollars

ITEM   COST

_____   _____

_____   _____

_____   _____

$1,000
Global Mall Dollars

ITEM   COST

_____   _____

_____   _____

_____   _____

$2,500
Global Mall Dollars

ITEM   COST

_____   _____

_____   _____

_____   _____

Let Them Eat Cake

OVERVIEW

Cutting and distributing pieces of cake, which represent shares of natural resources that students must negotiate and allocate, illustrates the inequitable distribution of resources around the world and the interconnectedness of human economic and social activities and resource scarcity.

INQUIRY/CRITICAL THINKING QUESTIONS

- What are some consequences of the unequal distribution of resources around the world?
- What feelings and behaviors result from such inequity?
- What can we do to make resource distribution around the world more fair and just?

OBJECTIVES

Students will:
- Experience an inequitable distribution of resources
- Consider, write about, and discuss the connection between resource distribution and hunger issues, and the underlying connections to human economic, environmental, and social activities

TIME REQUIRED: 1 hour

KEY ISSUES/CONCEPTS

- **Resource distribution**
- **Consumption patterns**
- **Environmental and structural scarcity**

SUBJECT AREAS

- **Social Studies** (Geography, Economics, Global Studies, Contemporary World Problems)
- **Science** (Environmental)
- **Math**

NATIONAL STANDARDS CONSISTENCY

- **NCSS: 3, 7, 9**
- **NSES: C, F**

GRADE LEVEL: 5–11

FTF Related Reading

- Intermediate: Chapter 5 from *Global Issues and Sustainable Solutions*
- Advanced: Unit 6 Chapter 6 and 7 from *It's All Connected*

Let Them Eat Cake

Materials/Preparation

- A delicious cake, pie, or other baked item that can be cut into wedges
- Plates, napkins, and forks, 1 per student
- Spatula (or knife) to cut and serve the cake
- Overhead: *Sharing the Cake – Divided by World Population*
- Overhead: *Sharing the Cake – Divided by Per Capita GNI in PPP*
- During the activity you will divide the class into groups according to the table below:

For a class of 20 form groups of	For a class of 30 form groups of	Representing	% of Earth's Population
3	4	Africa	14%
1	2	U.S. & Canada	5%
2	3	Latin America	9%
2	4	Europe	12%
12	17	Asia	60%

Activity

Introduction

1. (Optional) Do a Sides Debate using the statement below (see Sides Debate lesson on page 28)

    "The United States contributes more wealth and products to the world market, so therefore has the right to use more of the world's resources."

Steps

1. Show the cake to the class and explain that you have brought it for them to share. (You might set the cake out in front of the class a while before you start the activity to pique the students' interest.)
2. Ask the class if you should invite the class next door to join you in eating the cake. If the students say no, ask them why not.

Explain that this represents the concept of environmental scarcity, in which there is just not enough of a particular resource for everyone who wants or needs it. In this case, if the class next door came over, there would be less cake per person.

3. Tell them that instead of inviting the class next door, you will divide the cake for this class to share. Ask them to imagine that they represent all the people on the planet. Put up the overhead *Sharing the Cake—Divided by World Population*, showing how the cake would be cut if it were divided based on population. Physically separate the class into the groups as indicated in the table above.
4. Ask each region how they feel about this distribution. (This distribution equally divides the cake among each region and represents the "fairest" distribution.)

© 2006 FACING THE FUTURE: PEOPLE AND THE PLANET www.facingthefuture.org

Let Them Eat Cake

5. Tell the class that instead of dividing it by population you will divide the cake to represent how resources are actually distributed in the world, based on per capita Gross National Income (GNI) adjusted for purchasing power parity (PPP). Put up the overhead, *Sharing the Cake Divided by Per Capita GNI in PPP*.

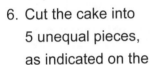

6. Cut the cake into 5 unequal pieces, as indicated on the overhead, and distribute the pieces to each "region". Be sure to hold up each piece so the class can see how much each region will get.

7. Ask each region how they feel about their share of the cake. Ask Asia and Africa how they are going to divide the cake among their population. Will they try to divide their very small piece equally among the group or will 1 or 2 people decide to eat all of it? (Some students will likely begin eating the cake, while others may get agitated. Allow some stress to develop.)

8. Ask each region what they are going to do about the situation. Some may choose to migrate to U.S./Canada and take their cake. You might see discrimination (only some people can have the cake), conflict (fighting over the cake), or "brain-drain" (only our "friends" – those with professional degrees or education – from another region can come over and share our piece of the cake). Make

sure there is enough time for everyone to experience the feeling of having very little or of having more than everyone else.

9. Explain that this unequal distribution of cake is an example of "structural scarcity," in that there may be enough of the resource to go around but it is not distributed fairly.

10. Conclude with the following reflection questions.

Assessment Reflection Questions

For Intermediate and Advanced Students

- How did it feel when you saw how much other groups got? How did you divide the cake within your group? Did you do anything to get more cake, or give any away?

- How does this activity relate to the real world?

- How would this have been different if you were really hungry and hadn't eaten much, or anything, for a couple of days?

- What are real examples of people trying to "get more cake"? Point out that there is also unequal distribution within countries, and brainstorm 10 cases of unequal distribution in your community, state, or country.

- Have the students brainstorm ways they could personally address the inequitable distribution of resources. Examples include: reduce, reuse, and recycle resources; buy energy-efficient and sustainable products; volunteer at nonprofit organizations working toward social justice; and talk about this issue with friends and family.

Let Them Eat Cake

For Advanced Students

- How could a comfortable and fulfilling lifestyle be provided for all the world's people? If this does not seem possible, what are some of the potential consequences of continued and increasing inequity between individuals and nations?

- What are some of the ethical, social, and security implications of this inequity? Do you see examples of that occurring today? If so, what consequences are evident, and where? What underlies them?

- Discuss the differences between emergency solutions and structural solutions (food aid vs. job creation).

Writing Connection

- Have students create a poverty zine (magazine) about local and global poverty. Assign each student 1 page in the zine and have them research and write about poverty in a specific country and a group or organization that is working to alleviate poverty there.

Action Projects

- Have students prepare and present a lunchtime forum at your school to increase awareness about the global distribution of resources and what youth can do to get involved in making a difference.

- Organize a "Hunger Banquet" to build awareness and raise money to alleviate global poverty. A Hunger Banquet can be held with just your class (e.g. for lunch one day), with parents, or as a school/community event. The Hunger Banquet is a project of Oxfam America. For a detailed description of this project, visit **www.facingthefuture. org** and click on **Take Action**, then **Service Learning Projects**.

- Do "Heifer International", a Service Learning Project in which students raise money to buy farm animals for poor families to help them become more self-sufficient. For a detailed description of this project, visit **www. facingthefuture.org** and click on **Take Action**, then **Service Learning Projects**.

Additional Resources

Books

- *Plan B: Rescuing a Planet Under Stress and a Civilization in Trouble*, Lester Brown, W.W. Norton & Company, New York, 2003. Brown calls for a worldwide mobilization to stabilize population and climate before they spiral out of control. It provides a plan for sustaining economic progress worldwide.

- *State of the World* [current year], World Watch Institute, New York, **www.worldwatch.org**.

Websites

- **http://www.un.org/millenniumgoals/** The United Nations developed 8 Millennium Development Goals which range from halving extreme poverty to halting the spread of HIV/AIDS and providing universal primary education, all by the target date of 2015. This blueprint has been agreed to by all the world's countries and leading development institutions.

- **http://www.unfpa.org** – The United Nations Population Fund (UNFPA) is an international development agency that supports countries in using population data for policies and programmes to reduce poverty, to prevent HIV/AIDS, and to promote reproductive health and dignity and respect for women and girls

- **www.oxfamamerica.org** – Oxfam America is an international development and relief agency committed to developing lasting solutions to poverty, hunger, and social justice.

© 2006 FACING THE FUTURE: PEOPLE AND THE PLANET www.facingthefuture.org

ENGAGING STUDENTS THROUGH GLOBAL ISSUES
© 2006 FACING THE FUTURE: PEOPLE AND THE PLANET   www.facingthefuture.org

Sharing the Cake
Divided by World Population

(data from 2005 World Population Data Sheet of the Population Reference Bureau)

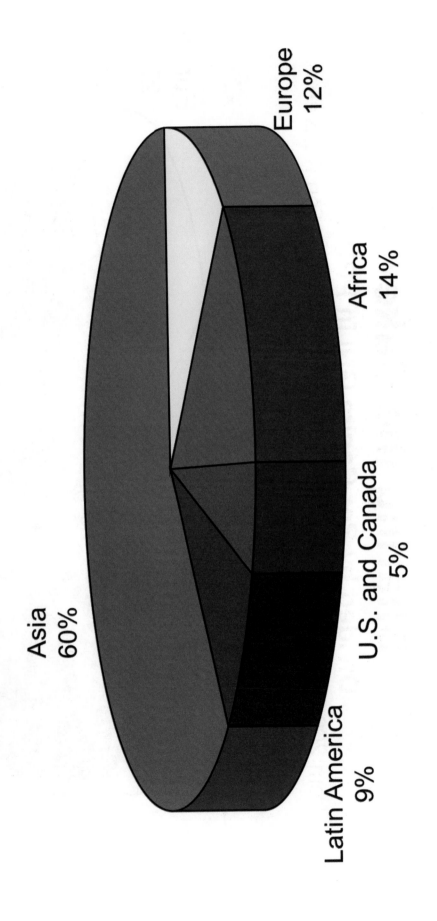

Asia
60%

Latin America
9%

U.S. and Canada
5%

Africa
14%

Europe
12%

ENGAGING STUDENTS THROUGH GLOBAL ISSUES
© 2006 FACING THE FUTURE: PEOPLE AND THE PLANET   www.facingthefuture.org

Sharing the Cake

Divided by Per Capita GNI in PPP

(data from 2005 World Population Data Sheet of the Population Reference

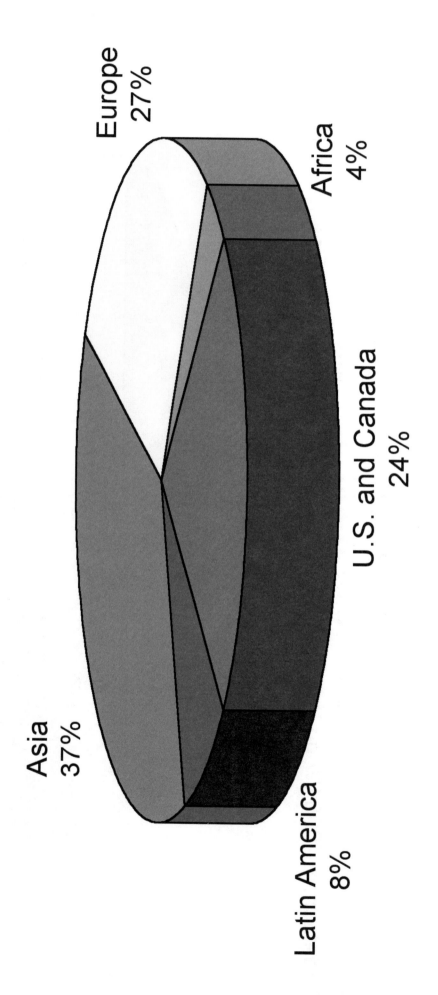

Europe
27%

Africa
4%

U.S. and Canada
24%

Latin America
8%

Asia
37%

Everyone Does Better When Women Do Better

(Lesson developed by Andra DeVoght, MPH)

OVERVIEW

Students enact the roles of citizens and government representatives from various countries at a "town meeting" forum. Citizens address their local government representative with concerns about the status of women and girls in their country and potential solutions. With input from the citizens, the leaders prioritize the concerns voiced at the meeting and decide on the most effective way to take action to improve the situation in each of the countries.

INQUIRY/CRITICAL THINKING QUESTIONS

- What does it take to make a population healthy?
- Why is women's health so important for everyone?
- What are the root causes of a population's poor health?
- Which solutions address the root causes of a population's poor health?

OBJECTIVES

Students will:
- Brainstorm indicators of the health and well-being of women and girls around the world
- Research facts about the demographics and status of people in a given country
- Give a verbal presentation of the situation in a given country
- Prioritize the needs of each country in order to develop an effective plan of action

TIME REQUIRED: 2 hours

KEY ISSUES/CONCEPTS

- **Status of women's/girls' health and human rights**
- **Measuring a population's health**
- **Connection between health and human rights**
- **Prioritizing solutions to global health issues**

SUBJECT AREAS

- **Social Studies** (Economics, Geography, Global Studies, Contemporary World Problems)
- **Science** (Life)
- **Health**
- **Math**

NATIONAL STANDARDS CONSISTENCY

- **NCSS: 3, 5, 6, 9, 10**
- **NSES: C, F**

GRADE LEVEL: 7–11

FTF Related Reading

- Intermediate: Chapter 7 from *Global Issues and Sustainable Solutions*

- Advanced: Unit 5, Chapters 5, 6, 7, and 8 from *It's All Connected*

Everyone Does Better
When Women Do Better

Materials/Preparation

- Handout/Overhead: *Vocabulary and Country Profile*, 1 per student
- Handout: *Town Meeting Role Cards*, 1 sheet per 5 students, 1 card per student. Each group will represent a different country (3-6 countries depending on class size) with 5 identities per group
- Handout: *Strategy Worksheet*, 1 per student

- Population Reference Bureau's *2005 World Population Data Sheet* and *2005 Women of Our World* download at **www.prb.org**, 1 hard copy per group or Internet access for each group
- From the table below, select the country groups that students will represent. Include at least 1 country from each category of development.

Category I: Low Development	Category II: Medium Development	Category III: High Development
Pakistan	China	Argentina
Ethiopia	India	Sweden
Kenya	Brazil	Mexico

Activity - Day 1

Introduction

1. (Optional) Do a Sides Debate using 1 of the statements below (see Sides Debate lesson, page 28)

    "As a country, we should spend more money on education and less on health care."

2. Discuss the following questions with the whole class:
    - How can you tell if women and girls around the world are doing well? Brainstorm a list with the class and record it for reference later in the lesson.
    - What would you measure? (e.g. life expectancy, infant mortality rate, literacy rates, HIV/AIDS rates, teen birth rates, number of women in poverty)
    - Why are these things important?

3. Go over the vocabulary words using the Handout/Overhead, *Vocabulary and Country Profile*.

Steps

1. Divide the class into country groups of 5 students and assign each group a country from the list above.

2. Hand out 1 role card to each student and have them write the name of their country in the first blank line on their role card.

3. Pass out PRB's 2005 World Population Data Sheet and 2005 Women of Our World (or have students access the reports online) and have students individually use the reports to fill in the blanks for their role.

4. In their country groups, students begin their town meetings. Give the following

© 2006 FACING THE FUTURE: PEOPLE AND THE PLANET   www.facingthefuture.org

Everyone Does Better When Women Do Better

instructions:

- All country groups will hold their meetings at the same time.
- The students representing citizens (teacher, farmer, nurse, and parent) will sit facing the government representative.
- The government representative will begin the meeting by introducing him/herself and sharing some facts about the country by reading the role card aloud to the group of citizens.
- The citizens will take turns reading their character role card aloud to the group.
- The government representative will take notes on the *Country Profile Sheet*, recording the facts that the citizens share.

5. Bring the class back together for reflection questions.

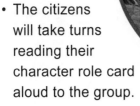

Assessment
Reflection Questions

For Intermediate and Advanced Students

- Have the students discuss the differences between the low, medium, and high development countries. Which countries seem to be doing well? Which countries are not doing well?
- What are the strengths and weaknesses of your assigned country?
- Are there differences between how men and women are doing? If so, what do you think is the cause of these differences?

Activity - Day 2

Steps

1. Have students return to their country groups to discuss the concerns brought to the table in the last meeting. Give each student 1 *Strategy Worksheet* and give the students about 10 minutes to complete steps 1 and 2. Referring to the *Country Profile Sheet*, students will discuss the questions on the Strategy Worksheet in their group, and individually list solutions to improve the health and well-being of their country.

2. Give students 10 minutes to complete step 3 of the *Strategy Worksheet*. Their country has been granted 10 million dollars to improve the health and well-being of all citizens. The government official will be making the final decision, but the citizens will be able to offer input. Students will write a brief synopsis of what they would like to spend the money on, why they chose to spend it that way, and what they think the result will be.

3. Bring the class together and have the government representative from each group announce his/her decision to the citizens.

4. Give citizens 1 minute each to voice their opinion about the decision. They can support or criticize the government official, but they must offer a thoughtful explanation for their views.

Everyone Does Better When Women Do Better

5. The government representatives can either change their decision based on the input from the community members or they can adhere to their original decision.

6. Conclude with the following reflection questions.

Assessment
Reflection Questions

For Intermediate and Advanced Students

- Were you satisfied with the decision made by your country's government representative?
- How well did the government representative represent everyone's views?
- How can citizens be involved in creating a healthy community?

For Advanced Students

- If a country is doing well, how do you know if everyone is doing well? Is it possible that there might be a group of people who are not represented by the country's averages?
- Why do some people say that everyone does better when women do better? Do you agree or disagree with this statement?

Writing Connection

- Have students prepare a report to present to the class about the situation in their assigned country and their solutions. This can be in the form of a poster presentation, a speech, a press release, or other interactive method.

Math/Technology Connection

- Students can make tables and graphs of the data found in the 2 PRB reports. Alternatively, have them use the Internet site, *Nationmaster* at **www.nationmaster.com** to produce graphs and tables of country statistics.

Action Projects

- Have students review the United Nations Millennium Development Goals for women at **www.un.org/millenniumgoals/** and develop an awareness raising and action project to help meet these goals.
- Students can write and illustrate books about women's issues both locally and globally. Sell the books as a fundraiser to raise money for an organization working to provide access to education for girls around the world such as NetAid at **www.netaid.org**.
- Visit **www.facingthefuture.org**, click on **Take Action**, and click **Fast Facts and Quick Actions** for information and action opportunities on issues pertaining to women and girls.

Additional Resources

Films

- *Iron Jawed Angels,* Katja von Garnier, 2003. A feature length film about women's right to vote. **www.iron-jawed-angels.com**

Websites

- **www.unifem.org** – UNIFEM, the United Nations Development Fund for Women, provides financial and technical assistance to innovative programs and strategies fostering women's empowerment and gender equality.

- **www.awid.org** – The Association for Women's Rights in Development is an international membership organization connecting, informing and mobilizing people and organizations committed to achieving gender equality, sustainable development, and women's human rights.

© 2006 FACING THE FUTURE: PEOPLE AND THE PLANET www.facingthefuture.org

Lesson 32 Handout:
Everyone Does Better When Women Do Better
Vocabulary and Country Profile

life expectancy at birth – the average number of years a newborn can expect to live under current conditions.

infant mortality rate – the annual number of deaths of infants under the age of 1 per 1,000 live births.

total fertility rate – the average number of children a woman would have under current conditions.

literacy rate – the percent of people who can both read and write a short simple statement about his or her everyday life.

births attended by skilled personnel – the percent of births attended by doctors, nurses, or midwives.

access to safe drinking water – the percent of the population with access to 20 liters of drinking water per person per day from a source within 1 kilometer of the dwelling.

percent of population living on less than $2 per day – the percent of the population with average consumption expenditures less than $2.15 per day measured in 1993; currencies across countries are adjusted to reflect their purchasing power.

women as percent of non-farm wage earners – women's paid employment in the non-agricultural sector as a percent of total non-agricultural employees.

Country Profile for: _____

Population	
Life expectancy	
% of population living on less than $2 per day	
% of government seats held by women	
Total fertility rate	
Infant mortality rate	
% of women attended by a skilled person when giving birth	
% of population living with HIV/AIDS	
% of population living with HIV/AIDS that are women	
% of population without access to safe drinking water	
% of girls enrolled in secondary education	
% of girls who are literate	
% of women working in jobs other than farming	

Additional notes: _____

_____

_____

_____

Lesson 32 Handout:
Town Meeting Role Cards

I am a school teacher in _____ . I should live to be about _____ years old. In my country, _____ % of girls are enrolled in secondary education and _____ % of girls are literate. **Both boys and girls / mostly boys / mostly girls** get to go to school. Girls who have the chance to go to school are better able to take care of themselves and their families.

I am **very proud of / satisfied with / very concerned about** the well-being of the people in my country.

I am a parent of 2 children in _____ . The fertility rate in my country is _____. I have **fewer / about the same number / more** children than most women. I should live to be about _____ years old. In my country, _____ infants per 1,000 will die before they turn one. _____% of women are attended by a skilled person when they give birth. When the infant mortality rate is high, parents are likely to have more children. When women do not have skilled help during childbirth, the mother's or baby's health is at risk.

I am **very proud of / satisfied with / very concerned about** the well-being of the people in my country.

I am a farm worker in _____ . I should live to be about _____ years old. In my country, _____ % of women are working in jobs other than farming. Although farming is an important part of life, in most countries farmers earn little to no money. If women are not allowed to work for fair wages then they are more likely to end up in poverty. This makes it more difficult for them to take care of their families. In my country, **men / women** have most of the wage earning jobs.

I am **very proud of / satisfied with / very concerned about** the well-being of the people in my country.

I work as a nurse in _____ . I should live to be about _____ years old. In my country, _____ % of the people live with HIV/AIDS. Of those people, _____% are women. More **men / women** have HIV/AIDS. _____ % of people have access to safe drinking water. Without access to safe drinking water, people – especially infants – can become very sick.

I am **very proud of / satisfied with / very concerned about** the well-being of the people in my country.

I am a member of the government of _____ . I should live to be about _____ years old. In my country, _____ % of government seats are held by women and _____% are held by men. Our population is _____, and of that population, _____% of the people live on less than $2 per day. It is well known that poverty is connected to poor health.

I am **very proud of / satisfied with / very concerned about** the well-being of the people in my country.

© 2006 FACING THE FUTURE: PEOPLE AND THE PLANET   www.facingthefuture.org

Lesson 32 Handout:
Strategy Worksheet

1. In your country group, discuss the following questions. Refer to the Country Profile notes and your role cards.
   - Which issue(s) have the greatest effect on the whole country?
   - Which issue(s) might be the cause of some of the other issues?
   - What are some solutions that would improve the situation in your country?
   - Which solution do you think is best? Why?
   - Which solutions should be tackled first?
   - Are there some solutions that might have a positive effect on more than 1 problem?

2. Individually, list in order of priority 3-5 solutions you would like to see implemented to improve the health and well-being of your country.

   _____

   _____

   _____

   _____

   _____

3. Now imagine that your country has been granted $10 million to spend on improving the health and well-being of all citizens. From the perspective of your role, take about 10 minutes to write a brief synopsis of **how** you think the money should be spent, **why** you would choose to spend it that way and what you think the **result** will be (you may use the back of this paper or another sheet of paper to write your synopsis).

   _____

   _____

   _____

   _____

   _____

   _____

   _____

   _____

What's Debt Got to Do With It?

OVERVIEW

Students model the impact of debt on the social and economic health of developing countries. Working in "very poor country" groups, students choose how to allocate limited funds to different sectors of their country's economy. The groups take on loans to help their country develop and experience what happens when their funds are diverted to debt repayment and away from investment.

INQUIRY/CRITICAL THINKING QUESTIONS

- How do poor countries plan and allocate for sustainable development?
- How does debt contribute to the cycle of poverty in developing countries?
- Should donor nations consider forgiving debt?

OBJECTIVES

Students will:
- Experience how to budget for development with limited funds
- Understand the impact of debt on a poor country's budget
- Understand how debt contributes to a cycle of poverty
- Be introduced to the concept of micro-credit and its growing role as a tool for poverty alleviation

TIME REQUIRED: 1 hour

KEY ISSUES/CONCEPTS

- **Budgeting and debt**
- **International debt relief**
- **International lender organizations**
- **Poverty cycle**

SUBJECT AREAS

- **Social Studies** (Economics, Civics/Government, Global Studies, Contemporary World Problems)
- **Science** (Environmental)
- **Business/Finance**
- **Math**

NATIONAL STANDARDS CONSISTENCY

- **NCSS: 3, 5, 6, 9, 10**
- **NSES: F**

GRADE LEVEL: 8–11

FTF Related Reading

- Intermediate: Chapter 5 from *Global Issues and Sustainable Solutions*
- Advanced: Unit 6, Chapter 6 and 7 from *It's All Connected*

Materials/Preparation

- Poker chips (9 chips per group of 3-4 students)
- Handout/Overhead, *Debt Vocabulary and Facts About Developing World Debt*, 1 copy

per student or 1 overhead
- Handout, *Resource Allocation Sheet*, 1 copy for every 3-4 students

Activity

Introduction

1. (Optional) Do a Sides Debate using the following prompt (see Sides Debate description on page 28):
    "Poor countries should have their debts forgiven."

What's Debt Got to Do With It?

2. (Optional) Ask students if they have ever bought something with a credit card. Ask how many of them (or their parents) have ever made a partial payment on their card. Tell them that if this is the case, they have accrued debt and paid interest on their credit card loan. Give this example: They buy a computer for $2000 using their credit card with an 18 percent interest rate. If they make a minimum payment of $50 per month, it will take 5 years to pay for their computer and they will have paid $1077 in interest for a total of $3077.

3. Write on the board or overhead: "$40,000 per person" and "$660 per person". Tell the class that these 2 amounts (in U.S. dollar equivalents) represent the annual average amount of money earned per person in 2 different countries. This is the total Gross National Income (GNI), or all the money that is generated in that country divided by the country's total population. These numbers represent a very wealthy country (U.S.) and a very poor country (Burundi). Ask the students what they think might be some of the implications of this difference. Ask what they think very poor countries do to meet the needs of their people. How can a poor country get the money it needs? Students may or may not raise the issue of borrowing money.

4. Go over the vocabulary list either as an overhead or handout.

Steps

1. Tell the class that they will work in small groups, with each group representing a poor country (like Burundi) of about 8 million people with very few resources. In order for their country to survive, they must

take out loans to invest in their country's health care, education, and infrastructure (e.g. roads, water projects, hospitals). However, the loans must be paid back with interest (Note to teacher: There are other areas in which countries spend money, such as military defense; however, the 3 areas of health care, education, and infrastructure were chosen for this activity because they are essential elements of a country's development).

2. Show the *Resource Allocation Sheet* and tell the class that they will be allocating their funds using this sheet. Go over the 4 areas where they can allocate funds.

3. Break the class into groups of 3-4 students. Give each group one copy of the *Resource Allocation Sheet* and have them choose a name for their country and write their own names on the sheet.

4. YEAR 1: Tell the class that they will begin in year 1 and the starting budget of their country is $600 million dollars. This includes some past loans that the country must pay back. They will receive 6 poker chips each worth $100 million. Pass out 6 chips to each group.

5. Tell them that since the countries must pay back their loans, $200 million (2 of the poker chips) must be placed in the Debt section on the *Resource Allocation Sheet.* The groups must decide where to invest the remaining $400 million (4 poker chips). Give them a few minutes to decide where they will allocate the 4 remaining poker chips and have them place those chips in the section indicated on the allocation sheet. Have them fill out the year 1 lines, indicating how much they allocated in each sector.

What's Debt Got to Do With It?

6. YEAR 2: Tell the class that it is now year 2 and the International Monetary Fund and the World Bank have agreed to give their country another loan (at a lower interest rate) to help with their debt and invest in their country's development. Each country will receive $300 million dollars (3 additional chips) and can move $100 million dollars (1 chip) currently in the Debt section to another sector on the *Resource Allocation Sheet*. However, they will have to pay back this new loan in a few years, along with interest. Hand out 3 additional poker chips to each group, and give students a few minutes to allocate those chips and the chip from the Debt section. Have them fill out the year 2 lines.

7. YEAR 3: Tell the class that it is now year 3, and while their country's economy has improved a bit, it has not grown nearly enough to pay off all their loans and interest. To pay off the loans, they must move more of their budget to the Debt section or they will not be able to borrow any more money in the future. Tell the groups to select $300 million (3 poker chips) currently invested in Health, Education, and/or Infrastructure, and move them to the Debt section. Have them fill out the year 3 lines.

8. YEAR 4: It is now year 4 and unfortunately they are falling further into debt. They must therefore move another 300 million (3 poker chips) into the Debt section and fill out the year 4 lines.

9. YEAR 5: Tell the class it is now the 5th year of their country's budget, and the IMF, World Bank, and other lenders have agreed to grant their country debt relief. The groups can take all the money (chips) in the Debt section and allocate them to other sectors on the *Resource Allocation Sheet*. Since this relief is permanent, they will not have to move any money back to the Debt section. Give the groups a few minutes to complete their final reallocation of money (chips) and fill out the Year 5 lines.

10. Bring the class back together for reflection questions.

Assessment Reflection Questions

For Intermediate and Advanced Students

- What happened in years 3 and 4 when you had to allocate most of your budget to debt? How did your country's debt affect other areas of development?
- How does investment in health, education, and/or infrastructure contribute to a poor country's development?
- When you did not have to put money in the Debt section, where did you choose to invest it and why?
- Had you wished there was another budget area to choose from? Instead of taking money only from Health, Education, or Infrastructure, can you think of another budget area to cut?
- Do you think it is fair that your country should have to pay back loans and interest even if there is no money for schools or medicine? What about the countries that gave you the money – is it fair that they do not get paid back?

For Advanced Students

- If you were to divert money from another

© 2006 FACING THE FUTURE: PEOPLE AND THE PLANET   www.facingthefuture.org

ENGAGING STUDENTS THROUGH GLOBAL ISSUES
WHAT'S DEBT GOT TO DO WITH IT?

LESSON
33

What's Debt Got to Do With It?

area not represented on the sheet, what would the consequences be? What deleterious social effects might have been avoided?

- Who do you think bears more responsibility for the debt cycle in this exercise – the IMF and World Bank for giving the loan and charging interest, or the government of the country for taking out the loan and spending the money?

- If it turned out that your government mismanaged the loan and invested in the wrong things, should your country still receive debt relief?

- Often a country accepting an IMF loan must give up control of resources like electricity, oil, and telephone lines to private companies, including companies from outside the country. Do you think this makes sense? Why do you think the IMF would make this a condition of the loan?

- Should donors be responsible for ensuring their loans are not used for projects that destroy the environment or hurt people? What if the project will generate a lot of money for a poor country, but will also cause heavy environmental and/or social damage?

- What do you think are the root causes of debt in the developing world? How could the legacy of colonialism be connected to developing world countries' debt? (Note: An Internet search for "developing world debt legacy of colonialism" will bring up some interesting resources on this topic).

- How might this cycle of debt actually benefit rich countries? (Note: According to some development

experts, the IMF, World Bank, and governments of rich countries are implicated in perpetuating the cycle of poverty in heavily indebted countries. The theory goes that when increasing debt payment and falling rates of foreign aid are coupled with the takeover of natural resources, the very poorest of the world effectively help to make rich countries richer).

Technology/Writing Connection

- Have students go to the World Resources Institute Earth Trends website at www.earthtrends.wri.org, click on "Economics, Business, and the Environment", then click on "Maps" and open the map labeled "Debt: Present value of debt as a percent of GNI 2002". Have them choose one of the countries with a debt value of 50 percent or greater and research other indicators of that country on the World Resources website where there are several maps and a large database of country statistics. Students can then write and present a "briefing paper" about their chosen country's economic, social, and environmental health, and make a recommendation to the IMF and World Bank about whether they should make further loans and/or offer debt relief for current loans.

Accounting/Business Connection

- To help students understand that debt is not limited to developing countries only, and that developed countries also incur debt, have students research the total debt of their country and the percentage of GDP that goes to foreign aid. An Internet search for "[country] total debt" is a good place to start the research.

What's Debt Got to Do With It?

Action Projects

- Microcredit is the extension of small loans to people who are too poor to qualify for traditional bank loans. In developing countries especially, microcredit enables very poor people to engage in income generating self-employment projects. Have students organize a "Penny Challenge" at your school to support a microcredit organization. Each penny is worth a point, and the team that gets the most points wins. Bills or coins other than pennies count as negative points (a quarter is –25 points) and can be put in the other team's container, thus decreasing your competitor's total points but increasing the total money raised. Display the pennies in large clear containers so that people can watch the money pile up. Try guys against girls, grades competing against each other, or classrooms racing to have the most points. The winning team gets to decide which microcredit organization they will donate money to.

- Choose a movie that addresses developing (or developed) country debt and that will inspire conversation and debate around the issue. Invite fellow classmates, friends, family, neighbors, etc. to join you for a night at the movies. Host the event at your school or community center and ask each person for a donation at the door. This is a great way to spread the word about the issue, discuss what can be done to help, and raise money. Donate the money you raise to an organization working on building awareness and action around debt relief like Jubilee USA Network: www.jubileeusa.org.

- For more information and action opportunities on poverty alleviation, visit www.facingthefuture.org, click on **Take Action** then **Fast Facts Quick Actions**.

Additional Resources

Films

- *The Debt Police*, Steve Bradshaw, Bullfrog Films, 2000, 24 minutes. Documentary film about Uganda's search for external debt relief and fight against internal corruption.

- *Life and Debt*, Directed by Stephanie Black, 2001, 80 minutes. A feature-length documentary that addresses the impact of the international lending organizations and current globalization policies on a developing country.

Websites

- **www.live8live.com** – Website of the Live 8 concert series that campaigned for debt relief and poverty alleviation in the summer of 2005.

- **www.imf.org** – International Monetary Fund includes information on their Heavily Indebted Poor Countries (HIPC) Initiative.

- **www.worldbank.org** – Click on "FAQs" on the home page, then click on "Debt Relief" for extensive information on the debt relief debate, along with an explanation of the World Bank's position against forgiving all debt.

- **www.earthtrends.wri.org** – World Resources Institute's on-line collection of environmental, social, and economic trends, including statistical, graphic, and analytical data in easily accessible formats.

© 2006 FACING THE FUTURE: PEOPLE AND THE PLANET   www.facingthefuture.org

Lesson 33 Handout:
Debt Vocabulary

debt – Money that is owed to a person or organization.

debtor – A person, company, or country owing debt.

creditor – An entity to whom debt is owed.

developing world debt – (also called Third World debt) – The debt of a developing country owed to outside creditors.

developing world debt relief – The partial or total forgiveness of debt, or the slowing or stopping of debt growth, owed by developing world countries.

International Monetary Fund – An international organization of 184 countries whose primary function is to provide temporary loans to poor countries. Money loaned from the IMF can only be used to help a country balance its budget.

World Bank – An independent specialized agency of the United Nations that provides loans and grants to poor countries. Money loaned and granted from the World Bank can be used for development projects.

Facts about Developing World Debt

For every US$1 received in aid, the world's most impoverished countries repay $13 on old debts. (Foreign Policy in Focus, Nov 2001)

Debt payments for loan-strapped countries are nearly three times the amount spent on healthcare. Per capita annual spending is US$22 on debt, $14 on education, and $8 on healthcare. (Global Treatment Access Campaign)

Africa is burdened with an unmanageable debt, which is hampering the continent's economic growth. Every African man, woman, and child owes US$357 to Northern creditors, despite the fact that millions live in abject poverty earning around 27 cents a day. (**www.afrodad.org**)

Lesson 33 Handout:

Resource Allocation Sheet

Name of Country: _____

Students in group: _____

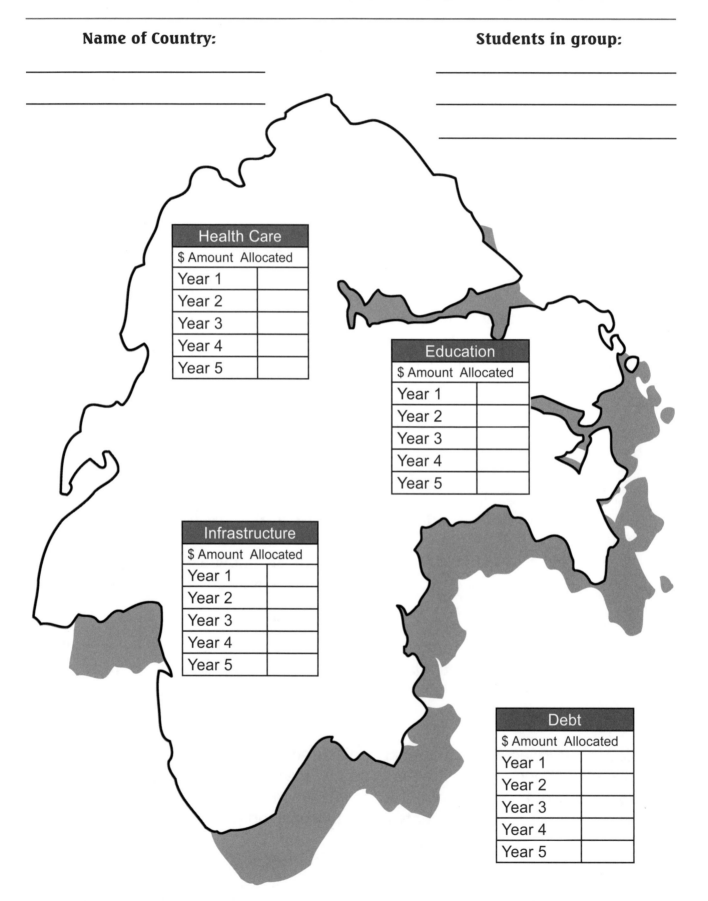

Health Care	
$ Amount Allocated	
Year 1	
Year 2	
Year 3	
Year 4	
Year 5	

Education	
$ Amount Allocated	
Year 1	
Year 2	
Year 3	
Year 4	
Year 5	

Infrastructure	
$ Amount Allocated	
Year 1	
Year 2	
Year 3	
Year 4	
Year 5	

Debt	
$ Amount Allocated	
Year 1	
Year 2	
Year 3	
Year 4	
Year 5	

Microcredit for Sustainable Development

OVERVIEW

Students research a developing country and then apply for a $100 microcredit grant to start a small business, as if they were a person living in that country. A business plan and an illustrated poster are presented to a "sustainable development panel of experts" (students) who determine whether or not the business plan is economically, socially, and environmentally sustainable.

INQUIRY/CRITICAL THINKING QUESTIONS

- What are some structural causes of poverty?
- What is sustainable development?
- What is microcredit and how can it help alleviate poverty?

OBJECTIVES

Students will:
- Conduct Internet research on a developing country
- Prepare a microcredit business plan as if they were a person living in that country
- Evaluate their peers' business plans
- Understand how structural solutions can help alleviate poverty

TIME REQUIRED: 2 hours

plus out-of-class time for research and poster preparation

KEY ISSUES/CONCEPTS

- **Sustainable development**
- **Microcredit**
- **Structural solutions**

SUBJECT AREAS

- **Social Studies** (World History, World Cultures, Geography, Economics, Global Studies, Civics/Government, Contemporary World Problems)
- **Science** (Environmental, Life)
- **Business/Finance**
- **Math**

NATIONAL STANDARDS CONSISTENCY

- **NCSS: 1, 3, 5, 7, 8, 9, 10**
- **NSES: C, E, F**

GRADE LEVEL: 9–12

FTF Related Reading

- Intermediate: Chapter 9 from *Global Issues and Sustainable Solutions*
- Advanced: Unit 6, Chapter 6 and 7 from *It's All Connected*

Vocabulary

- **Sustainability** – Meeting current needs without limiting the ability of future generations to meet their needs.
- **Sustainable Development** – Practices in areas such as agriculture, economic development, health care, and

Microcredit for Sustainable Development

education that lead to economic, social, and human progress, are locally appropriate, and meet the needs of current generations without limiting the ability of future generations to meet their needs.

- **Structural Solution** – A solution to a critical problem, such as poverty, that addresses the underlying causes of the problem. Structural solutions often require action by governments or large institutions.
- **Microcredit** – The business or policy of making small loans or grants to poor people for entrepreneurial (business) projects.

Materials/Preparation

- Overhead: *Sample Microcredit Business Plan*
- Handout: *Grant Application*, 1 copy per student
- Handout: *Microcredit Business Plan Presentation*
- Internet access for each student (or students can do their research out of class)

Activity – Day 1

Introduction

1. Write this quote on the board or overhead and have students do a freewrite on it:
   "Give a man a fish and he'll eat for a day, teach him how to fish and he'll eat forever."
   Have students share their thoughts on the quote. What does it mean? What might fish represent? To what global issues might this quote apply?

2. Review the vocabulary words, if necessary.

Steps

1. Show students the *Sample Microcredit Business Plan* and ask if they can figure out what it is. After students have shared their ideas, explain that this is an actual application from a person in India who applied for a microcredit grant from Trickle Up, a micro-granting organization that gives extremely poor people $100 grants to start a business.

2. Tell students that they are going to research a developing world country and, as if they were a person living in that country, they are going to apply for a microcredit grant to start a small business.

3. Go over the assignment sheet, *Microcredit Business Plan Presentation*. This assignment includes Internet research, a business application, and a poster presentation.

4. Pass out the *Microcredit Business Plan Application* and go over it with them. (You can either have students do this assignment individually or they can work in small groups of 2-3).

5. Give students assignment deadlines when they will be required to bring their poster and business applications to class. They will need a few days of outside class time to complete their research, paper, poster, and business application. Alternatively, you can have the students do some of the work in class if they have in-class Internet access and poster supplies.

© 2006 FACING THE FUTURE: PEOPLE AND THE PLANET   www.facingthefuture.org

Microcredit for Sustainable Development

Activity - Day 2 & 3

Steps

1. On Day 2 (and 3, if necessary) students present their posters and business plans to a panel of experts that include a **microcredit funder**, an **environmentalist**, and a **community activist**.

2. Go over the panelist instructions on the assignment sheet. Each student will have a chance to present his/her business plan and serve on the panel.

3. Call on 3 students to take the role of a panelist for each plan presented. Pass out the role cards and give them a few minutes to review their roles.

4. The panel will listen to the applicant's presentation, ask questions, and then assign points (as indicated in the assignment sheet) to the business proposal.

5. Proposals receiving a minimum of 15 points will be granted a microcredit grant. Those that do not receive the minimum points will have a chance to revise their plan until they receive the grant.

6. Conclude with the following reflection questions.

Assessment
Reflection Questions

For Intermediate and Advanced Students

• How do you think it would feel if your life was like the person you represented in your business plan?

• What business would you start if you were given a microcredit grant?

• Does this process of micro-granting seem like it works well as a way to alleviate poverty?

• What can you do personally to help alleviate poverty?

For Advanced Students

• What do you think might be potential flaws or problems associated with microcredit?

• What are other ways to alleviate poverty aside from microcredit?

Action Projects

• Do a "Trickle-Up" Service Learning Project in which students raise money to provide small business grants for poor people in developing countries. For a detailed description of this and other service learning projects, visit **www.facingthefuture.org** and click on **Take Action** and then click on **Service Learning Projects**.

• Organize a "Penny Challenge" at your school to support a microcredit organization. Each

Microcredit for Sustainable Development

penny is worth a point, and the team that gets the most points wins. Bills or coins other than pennies count as negative points (a quarter is –25 points) and can be put in the other team's container thus decreasing your competitor's total points, but increasing the total money raised! Display the pennies in large clear containers so that people can watch the money pile up. Try guys against girls, grades competing against each other, or classrooms racing to have the most points. The winning team gets to decide which microcredit organization they will donate money to.

- Throw a "BeadWear Party" at your school through the BeadforLife project. BeadforLife is an organization that fights poverty by employing very poor women in Uganda to make beautiful jewelry out of recycled paper. This project gives students the opportunity to help women feed their children and send them to school by selling their products, while at the same time educating yourself and your friends, parents and community about Uganda and the plight of poor people around the world. For a detailed description of this and other service learning projects, visit www.facingthefuture.org and click on **Take Action** and then **Service Learning Projects**.

Additional Resources

Films

- *Credit Where Credit is Due,* Ashley Bruce, Bullfrog Films, 2000, 24 minutes, www.bullfrogfilms.com. This documentary film recounts how taking out a loan revolutionized the lives of village women Jahanara, Bilkis, Nargis, Minara, Majeda and Shonda – not only increasing their incomes but also helping

to improve their health and the health of their children.

- *Small Fortunes: Microcredit and the Future of Poverty,* Sterling van Wagenen, 2005, 60 minutes. This documentary describes the impact that microcredit is having throughout the world through the stories of twelve microentrepreneurs living in Bangladesh, India, Kenya, Peru, The Philippines, and the United States. Microcredit luminaries and experts describe how microcredit is a powerful tool in fighting poverty and provide insights into the issues confronting the microcredit movement.

Websites

- **www.grameenfoundation.org** Grameen Foundation USA is a global nonprofit organization that combines microfinance, new technologies, and innovation to empower the world's poorest people to escape poverty.

- **www.trickleup.org** – The Trickle Up Program's mission is to help the lowest income people worldwide take the first step out of poverty by providing conditional seed capital and business training essential to the launch of a small business.

- **www.globalpartnerships.org** – Global Partnerships is an innovative leader in the fight against poverty around the world through microlending programs to help the poor help themselves, the development and sharing of model programs that offer sustainable solutions to poverty, and through the Initiative for Global Development.

Lesson 34 Overhead:

TRICKLE UP PROGRAM BUSINESS PLAN | 1999 |

PLEASE PRINT

Date : **01** / **11** / **99**
day month year

Business No. **IND** / **KSRA** / **143** / **99**

Initial Check Number : **935317**

Our Country's currency is the : **Rupees** _____ The exchange rate is **42·00** = US $1. Please provide figures in local currency

PRODUCT

1. What is your product or service? **CYCLE REPAIRING SHOP**
2. Where is your product sold?   ☑ In the market   ☐ Door to door   ☑ At Home   ☐ Other
3. What is the name of your business? _____

COSTS

4. What do you need to start or expand your business? (List only items that last a long time, such as equipment and tools.)

Items	Cost
MACHINE TOOLS	800
One - Time Costs : No. 4 Total =	**800**

COSTS

5. What do you need to buy to keep your business going each month? (List items such as raw materials, rent transportation, animal feed.)

Items	Cost / Month
BYCYCLE PART, TYRE-TUBE ETC.	1300
Monthly Operating Costs : No. 5 Total =	**1300**

6. Add No. 4 and No. 5 for total cost for 6 month of operations : **800** + **1300** = **2100**
     No. 4 Total   No. 5 Total   Total Cost 1st MO.

MEETING THE COSTS

7. What will you bring to the business?
8. What will others contribute?
9. What will you buy with Trickle Up $50 ?
10. Total resources available : (add 7,8,9)

Items (cash/tools/materials)	Cost
MACHENIC TOOLS, AIR PUMP etc.	800
CYCLE . PARTS, TYRE, TUBE	1300
One - Time Costs : No. 4 Total =	**2100**

11. Are the total resources available (No. 10) greater than or equal to your total costs for the 1st month (No.6)? ☑ Yes ☐ No.
     If yes, please answer the rest of the questions. If no, you should reconsider your business plan.

PROFITS

12. How much money do you think you can make in SALES in month?
     Please refer to Worksheet calculations.

     3500
     TOTAL SALES

13. What are your COSTS 6 months (No. 5)?

     1380
     TOTAL OPERATING COSTS

14. (a) Your 6 Months PROFIT is **3500** – **1300** =
          Sales (No.12)   COSTS (No.13)

     2200
     TOTAL PROFIT

     (b) What will your PROFIT be in three months (No. 14a X 3) = **6600**
          The Trickle Up Business Report is based on sales in a 3-month period

15. How will you use your profits? Check all that apply.

     (a) Reinvestment ☑ Buy tools/equipment   ☑ Buy raw materials/merchandise   ☑ For savings

     (b) ☑ For family/personal use

ENGAGING STUDENTS THROUGH GLOBAL ISSUES

© 2006 FACING THE FUTURE: PEOPLE AND THE PLANET   www.facingthefuture.org

Microcredit Business Plan Application - Page 1
(adapted with permission from Trickle Up)

PLEASE PRINT

Country: _____

Our country's currency is the: _____ The exchange rate is _____ = US $1. (Provide figures in local currency)

PRODUCT

1. What is your product or service? _____

2. Where is your product sold? ☐ In the market   ☐ Door to door   ☐ At Home   ☐ Other

3. What is the name of your business? _____

COSTS

4. What do you need to start or expand your business? (List only items that last a long time, such as equipment and tools.)

Items	Cost
One-Time Costs: No. 4 Total =	

5. What do you need to buy to keep your business going each month? (List items such as raw materials, rent, transportation, animal feed.)

Items	Cost/Month
Monthly Operating Costs: No. 5 Total =	

6. Add No. 4 and No. 5 for total cost for first month of operations: _____ + _____ = _____

No. 4 Total   No. 5 Total   TOTAL COST 1ST MO.

MEETING THE COSTS

7. What will you bring to the business?

8. What will others contribute?

9. What will you buy with the $50?

Items (cash/tools/materials)	Cost
Investment: No. 10 Total =	

10. Total resources available: **(7, 8, 9)**

11. Are the total funds available **(No. 10)** greater than or equal to your total costs for the 1st month **(No. 6)**? ☐ Yes ☐ No
    If yes, please answer the rest of the questions. If no, you should reconsider your business plan.

Microcredit Business Plan Application - Page 2

PROFITS

12. How much money do you think you can make in sales in 1 month?

_____
MONTHLY SALES

13. What are your costs each month (from No. 5)?

_____
MONTHLY OPERATING COSTS

14. (a) Your monthly profit is _____ - _____

Sales (No. 12)   Costs (No. 13)

= _____
MONTHLY PROFIT

(b) What will your profit be in 3 months (No. 14a x 3)?
The Business Report is based on sales in a 3-month period

= _____
PROFIT FOR 3 MONTHS

15. How will you use your profits? Check all that apply.
(a) Reinvestment: ❏ Buy tools/equipment   ❏ Buy raw materials/merchandise
(b) ❏ For family/personal use   ❏ For savings

16. Does your business involve? (check all that apply)
❏ growing crops   ❏ raising animals   ❏ Food processing or making something
❏ Services   ❏ Buying and selling ONLY
❏ Other (please describe): _____

17. How will you use the $50 grant? ❏ To start a new business   ❏ To expand an existing business

18. Will this be your main source of money? ❏ Yes   ❏ No

19. Is this a family business? ❏ Yes   ❏ No

20. How many people work in the business? _____ Of these, _____ are female, and _____ are male.

21. Is your business in a (check one) ❏ Rural area ❏ Urban area or ❏ Semi-urban/Suburban area?

LONG TERM GOALS

22. How will your business plan affect structural change and help to alter the cycle of poverty for you and your family?

23. How will the business plan be environmentally sustainable?

24. How will the business plan be socially and culturally sustainable?

I apply for a Conditional Grant of US$100 for this business. I have read and agree to the following conditions:
1. I will start a profit-making enterprise that generates continuing income;
2. If this plan is approved, the microcredit funder will make an immediate payment of $50 in the form of a conditional grant;
3. I will save or reinvest at least 20% of our profit in the business;
4. Each person in the business will work at least 250 hours within the first 3 months;
5. The final $50 payment will be made only if our business is continuing and if we submit a Business Report within 12 months, showing that the conditions of the grant have been met.

Signature _____

Lesson 34 Handout:

Research and Microcredit Business Plan Presentation - Page 1

The project consists of 3 parts:

- **Internet Research** – Research and take notes on a developing country, focusing on its economic situation
- **Microcredit Business Plan** – Prepare a Microcredit Business Plan and apply for a $100 microcredit grant as if you were a person living in that country
- **Poster Presentation** – Present your Microcredit Business Plan to a panel of experts who will decide if your plan is economically, environmentally, and socially sustainable

Internet Research

Choose a developing region or country and identify an economic challenge there. For example, in India an economic focus could be farmers whose topsoil has eroded away. Research the following questions about your country and take notes:

- **What is the essential geography and demographics of the country?** (physical geography, such as climate and topography, and vital statistics of population density, GDP, per capita income, infant mortality, and other key quality-of-life indicators for the region)
- **What are the economic challenges and effects of long-term poverty in the region?**

Some good websites to start your research:

United Nations Development Program: **www.undp.org**
CIA Factsheets: **http://www.cia.gov/cia/publications/factbook/index.html**
World Resources Institute: **www.wri.org**
Population Reference Bureau: **www.prb.org**

Microcredit Business Plan

As you conduct the research, think about what sort of business plan you will offer as a solution to pressing economic challenges. Then, as if you were a local person from that region, complete a *Microcredit Business Plan* for a $100 grant. Your plan should be underlined convincing and underlined promising in terms of the realities of the region and economy, as well as in terms of the hypothetical person that you portray as the business owner. In completing the application, you will address these questions:

- **Product:** What is a realistic product or service? Consider local resources, market, and skills.
- **Costs:** What are realistic one-time and on-going monthly costs?
- **Meeting the Costs:** What will the owner's monetary and capital investment be? What other financial resources will they need?
- **Profits:** Calculate and project monthly profit and 3 month profit.
- **Long Term Goals:** How will the plan affect structural change and help alter the cycle of poverty for the owner? His/her family? What are the environmental impacts of the proposed business? How will the business plan affect the local and regional culture?

Poster Presentation

You will present your *Microcredit Business Plan* in the form of a poster session before a 3-person committee representing different interests, including a **Microcredit Funder**, **Environmentalist**, and **Community Activist**.

- Your poster must include a business logo and other visual aids, such as a map, graph, table, diagram, flow chart, timeline, photographs, and drawings. Think about what type of business logo and visual aids will make your proposal more convincing and promising.
- When presenting your plan, be confident, knowledgeable, audible, clear, and organized.
- The committee will vote for or against funding your plan based on how factually convincing and how promising the proposal is in terms of **structural change/poverty alleviation, economic feasibility, environmental sustainability,** and **effect on society and culture.**

Lesson 34 Handout:
Research and Microcredit Business Plan Presentation - Page 2

Panel of Experts

Each of you will also serve on the panel representing one of the 3 experts: **Microcredit Funder**, **Environmentalist**, and **Community Activist**. As an expert, you will analyze the business plan for its economic, environmental, and social sustainability.

- Read your panel role carefully.
- During the presentation, listen carefully, pay close attention, and take notes.
- After the applicant presents his/her proposal you may ask questions from the perspective of your role.
- Without conferring with fellow panel members, rate the plan for each of the 2 categories listed in the rubric below.
- Converse and debate with the other panelists. You may ask panel members any clarifying question, but may disagree with their rating only if you can cite clear evidence why they should change their rating.
- Present to the applicant the final (total from all 3 panelists) rating.

A Total Final Rating of 15 is Required for Plan Approval			
Category	**3 Points**	**2 Points**	**1 Point**
Is the plan **convincing**? Does it rely on accurate information and include details that are relevant to **your** area of concern?	Very well researched, with thorough consideration of background information	Reasonably well researched, contains most, but not all relevant background information	Poorly or incompletely researched, lack of convincing background information
Is the plan **promising**? Does it offer positive change for your area of concern?	Not only sensible, but offers exciting promise and does not contain significant obstacles	Offers significant promise, but some obstacles remain	Seems completely unrealistic and does not offer realistic promise
Your Assigned Points			
Total Points (From all 3 panelists)			

Lesson 34 Handout:
Microcredit for Sustainable Development Panel Roles

Role: Microcredit Funder

You work for a nonprofit microcredit organization that grants money for microenterprises. Your job is to make sure their money is well spent. You must be rational in sorting out which plans deserve funding and which plans do not merit your limited financial resources. You are concerned with the success and longevity of microenterprises – as are your contributors!

Your primary concern is that your nonprofit organization's microcredit grants go only to microenterprises that offer <u>convincing evidence</u> and <u>promising hope</u>.

Initially and over time, will the plan alter the cyclical and structural nature of poverty for the business owner, community, and region?

Role: Community Activist

You work for a local organization devoted to the integrity of regional culture and the promotion of democratic citizenship. You oppose the negative effects of modernization and globalization. You are passionate about preserving local culture – traditions, arts, and language. While you are concerned about poverty, you are unwilling to sacrifice quality-of-life for 1 individual's short-term economic gain.

Your primary concern is that the microenterprise offers convincing evidence and promises that it will preserve and advance culture and democracy.

Initially and over time, will the microenterprise offer genuine progress, enhance local culture, and promote democracy for the business owner, community, and region?

Role: Environmentalist

You work for a large international nonprofit organization that is devoted to monitoring and preventing environmental degradation. Your job survival depends on how carefully you attend to possible environmental consequences of the microenterprises. You must be critical and creative in anticipating environmental effects of the microenterprise.

Your primary concern is that the microenterprise offers convincing evidence and promises that it will be ecologically sustainable. The plan should not be approved simply because it seems to be financially viable or meets the personal needs of the business owner.

Initially and over time, will the environmental impact (ecological footprint) of the microenterprise be acceptable for the business owner, community, and region?

To Fight or Not to Fight?

OVERVIEW

Students examine a variety of international and intra-national conflicts through a role-playing activity. They learn to identify the roots of conflict, how to separate positions from interests in a conflict, and experience mediating a conflict.

INQUIRY/CRITICAL THINKING QUESTIONS

- What are the sources of conflict?
- How are these sources of conflict connected to global issues?
- How can outsiders (e.g. mediators) help resolve conflicts?

OBJECTIVES

Students will:
- Understand the roots of conflict
- Learn to separate positions from interests
- Analyze conflicts from multiple perspectives

TIME REQUIRED: 1 hour

KEY ISSUES/CONCEPTS

- **International and intra-national conflict**
- **Scarcity**
- **Positions and interests**
- **Conflict mediation**

SUBJECT AREAS

- **Social Studies** (World History, World Cultures, Geography, Economics, Civics/Government, Global Studies, Contemporary World Problems)
- **Science** (Environmental)

NATIONAL STANDARDS CONSISTENCY

- **NCSS: 1, 3, 5, 6, 7, 9, 10**
- **NSES: F**

GRADE LEVEL: 9–12

FTF Related Reading

- Intermediate: Chapter 7 from *Global Issues and Sustainable Solutions*
- Advanced: Unit 6, Chapter 8 from *It's All Connected*

Materials/Preparation

- Handout: *Conflict Scenarios*, 3 copies per 15 students (scenarios for each group are arranged in strips of 3, so each student in a group will get 1 strip)
- Handout: *Conflict Resolution Worksheet*, 2 copies per student (copy the handout on both sides of a single sheet of paper)

Activity

Introduction

1. Ask students to think of a conflict situation they have experienced recently. It could be a disagreement with family, friends, teachers, etc. Take a few minutes to have the students think of (or write about) 1 or more conflicts they have had.

2. Ask for a volunteer to share his/her conflict situation with the class.

3. While they are explaining the conflict, write the basic elements of it on the board or overhead, breaking out the conflict as follows:
   - Who were the parties involved in the conflict?
   - Why did the student think he/she was right? This is their Position. Explain how to identify a position by writing the following terms common to position statements on the board: "It's my right to ...", "I've always done it this way", "It's my responsibility/job to...", "My beliefs teach me that ...".
   - What was the conflict about? This is the student's Interest. Did the student want something he/she could not have; was it an argument based on different values, etc.

To Fight or Not to Fight?

4. Tell the class they are going to role-play conflicts that take place around the world. Some of these conflicts arise from people competing for a scarce resource, and others from differences in culture, religion, and ethnic identity.

Steps

1. Read aloud 1 conflict scenario from the *Conflict Scenarios* handout and then walk students through the *Conflict Resolution Worksheet*, having them identify the parties involved, each party's position (why they think they're right), and each party's interests (what they want).

2. Lead the class in brainstorming how the conflict might be resolved, focusing on the *interests* they identified for each party.

3. Tell the class they are going to repeat this process in small groups. Explain that each group will work on 3 scenarios. For each scenario, 2 students will take opposing sides in the conflict, and 1 student will act as a *mediator*. The mediator will keep track of time during the exercise, and can suggest resolutions to the conflict if the 2 sides reach an impasse during negotiations. The mediator's job is to objectively help both sides reach a resolution through empathy and compromise – without giving up their vital interests.

4. Explain that for each scenario, the 2 students taking opposing sides in the conflict will have 2 minutes to read their scenario and fill out their *Conflict Resolution Worksheet*. They will have 3 minutes to present their positions and interests to the other side and try to reach an agreement. Be sure to emphasize that students will not be graded based on reaching an agreement. Some scenarios may not have resolutions. Students should keep in mind that they are representing an entire group or country in this negotiation, and that it is the student's duty to represent his/her best interests. Therefore, they should think carefully before agreeing to a solution.

5. Arrange the class into groups of 3 and give each group 3 strips with the same 3 conflict scenarios. Give each student 2 (or 1 double-sided copy) *Conflict Resolution Worksheets*.

6. Have each student number off from 1-3. Number 1 will mediate scenario 1, number 2 will mediate scenario 2, and number 3 will mediate scenario 3. For each scenario, the mediator will assign the other 2 students to a side.

7. Have students begin role-playing each of their conflict scenarios, starting with scenario 1 and continuing until they finish the third scenario on their strip. Circulate around the room listening and helping as students work through their scenarios.

8. After each group has completed its 3 scenarios (approximately 20 minutes), bring the class back together for reflection questions.

Assessment
Reflection Questions

For Intermediate and Advanced Students

- How many of you reached a solution to at least one of the scenarios you role-played? (If time permits, have students briefly summarize one of their scenarios).

- Did you have to give up something you wanted in order to reach a solution, or did you find a solution that gave both sides everything they wanted (met everyone's interests)?

© 2006 FACING THE FUTURE: PEOPLE AND THE PLANET   www.facingthefuture.org

To Fight or Not to Fight?

- Did you think the mediator in your group was fair, or did you feel the mediator was favoring the other side? Did you trust the mediator?
- Do you think the solutions you reached are sustainable (i.e. meet present human, economic and environmental needs without compromising the ability of future generations to meet these needs) or do you think there will be another conflict around the same issue in the future?

For Advanced Students

- What are some solutions that could be more sustainable? Do you think these sustainable solutions can happen without help from an outside party or entity? If you think a sustainable solution requires outside help, who should provide it?
- Do you think the solution you arrived at might cause new issues to arise, such as making a resource scarcer, or alienating some people you either represented in negotiations or others who were not directly represented?
- Which scenarios did you find more difficult to solve: conflicts over resources or conflicts over values, religion, and ethnicity? Were you willing to give up some of your values for a solution? Conflicts over core values and identity issues are often intractable. It is often impossible to move beyond discussing positions to discussing interests, since any concession is perceived as a renouncement of your core values and a "win" for an enemy.
- How does conflict resolution differ between international and intra-national issues?

Writing and Media Connections

- Watch a film in class that explores the roots and human impacts of conflicts. During the movie, have the class write down the positions and interests they hear identified in the film. Several good film recommendations can be found at **http://www.mediate.org/resources.htm**, which includes listings that focus on disputes over resources, land use, and other global issues.

To Fight or Not to Fight?

- Have students identify a conflict situation in the news, research the roots of that conflict, and write an essay outlining the history of the conflict, the positions and interests, and one potential sustainable solution to the conflict.

Drama Connection

- Have each group of 3 students choose 1 conflict from the scenarios they discussed. Then ask them to prepare a skit in which they act out the different sides of the conflict and express the opposing positions and interests to the class. Afterwards, have the class brainstorm ways to help solve the group's conflict.

Action Projects

- Have students find and join their nearest PeaceJam affiliate, an international organization that connects students with the inspiring stories and personalities of leading Nobel Peace Laureates. Through the program, students create a PeacePlan to engage with their local community. For a detailed description of this and other service learning projects, visit **www.facingthefuture.org** and click on **Take Action**, then **Service Learning Projects**.
- Plan activities and events in support of the UN's International Peace Day (September 21st). The Jane Goodall Institute provides

Life Cycle of a Conflict

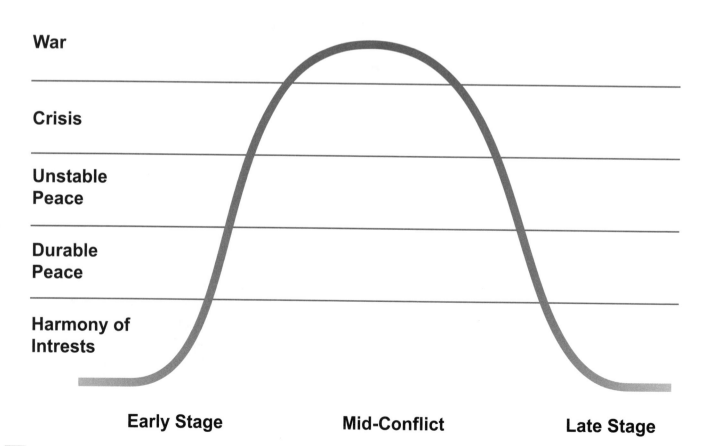

War

Crisis

Unstable Peace

Durable Peace

Harmony of Intrests

Early Stage   **Mid-Conflict**   **Late Stage**

© 2006 FACING THE FUTURE: PEOPLE AND THE PLANET   www.facingthefuture.org

To Fight or Not to Fight?

instructions on making Peace Doves for the occasion, sending out press releases, and much more. To learn how, visit **www.janegoodall.org**

- Have students create skits to perform at a school-wide assembly or for other schools in the community in which they role-play peer mediation techniques for common disagreements at school.
- For more information and action opportunities on peace and conflict, visit **www.facingthefuture.org**, click on **Take Action**, then **Fast Facts Quick Actions**.

Additional Resources

Films

- *Long Night's Journey Into Day: South Africa's Search for Truth and Reconciliation,* Frances Reid and Deborah Hoffman, 2000, 94 minutes. The film looks at South Africa's Truth and Reconciliation Commission, which examined crimes perpetrated during the apartheid era.

- *Prelude to Kosovo,* John Michalczyk, 1999, 52 minutes. Shot on location in Serbia, Croatia, and Bosnia, this documentary film investigates the ideology of "ethnic cleansing" and the massacres resulting from a nationalist quest for political, cultural, and religious domination.

- *Peace of Mind,* Mark Landsman, 1999, 56 minutes. A portrait of the Middle East conflict as seen by Palestinian and Israeli teenagers who meet at a peace camp in Maine and are then asked to document their experiences after they return to their homes.

- *Regret to Inform: A Journey in Search of Truth,* Barbara Sonneborn, 1998, 72 minutes.

The story of an American woman's journey to find the place her husband was killed in Vietnam becomes interwoven with that of her translator and guide, a war survivor with her own story.

- *Voices in War Time,* Rick King, 2005, 74 minutes. A feature-length documentary that delves into the experience of war through powerful images and the words of poets, both unknown and world-renowned.

Books

- *All Quiet on the Western Front,* Erich Maria Remarque, Little, Brown, and Company, 1929. Remarque's novel, set in World War I, centers around the changes wrought by the war on one young German soldier.

- *Earth and Ashes, Atiq Rahimi,* Harcourt Inc., 2000 (English translation 2002). Set in Afghanistan, this short, lyrical novel tells the story of loss and human perseverance during the Soviet invasion of Afghanistan.

- *Things Fall Apart,* Chinua Achebe, 1958. Achebe's novel portrays Nigerian tribal life before and after the coming of colonialism.

Websites

- **www.v4.crinfo.org** – The Conflict Resolution Information Source.

- **www.beyondintractability.org** Information on interest-based negotiation.

© 2006 FACING THE FUTURE: PEOPLE AND THE PLANET www.facingthefuture.org   © 2006 FACING THE FUTURE: PEOPLE AND THE PLANET www.facingthefuture.org

To Fight or Not to Fight? Conflict Scenarios - Page 1

(Note: Each group of 3 students will need 3 strips with the same 3 scenarios. There are 5 strips, enough for 15 students. If you have more than 15 students, repeat the scenarios in different groups.)

Scenario 1: Grazing vs. Farming
Sides: Farmers and Ranchers

Soyland is a small country with a growing population. There is very little land left that is suitable for growing crops by **Farmers**. That same small amount of land is also used by **Ranchers** to graze their cows. The cows use a lot of land, but they can be sold for more money than the crops can be sold for. The people of Soyland rely on the crops grown by Farmers for food, and the Farmers rely on selling crops to support themselves.

Scenario 2: International Water Rights
Sides: Electra and Foodville

A large river runs through two countries. In the past, the two countries have taken the same amount of water from the river. Now, **Electra** needs electricity and wants to build a dam on the river. Farmers in **Foodville** depend on water from the river to grow crops. If the dam is built, Foodville will have less water than before, and some farmers may not be able to produce as many crops.

Scenario 3: Forced Co-existence
Sides: Corats and Lemaks

The people of the country of Bursia are divided into two ethnic groups: **Corats** and **Lemaks**. For many years, a much larger country strictly controlled Bursia and kept the Corats and Lemaks from fighting. Recently, the larger country collapsed. Now the Corats want to rule all of Bursia, since they believe it has always belonged to them. The Lemaks want to split Bursia in half and form their own country without Corats living there. The Corats do not want this, because most of the natural resources are in the area of Bursia that Lemaks want for their new country.

© 2006 FACING THE FUTURE: PEOPLE AND THE PLANET   www.facingthefuture.org

To Fight or Not to Fight? Conflict Scenarios - Page 2

(Note: Each group of 3 students will need 3 strips with the same 3 scenarios. There are 5 strips,
enough for 15 students. If you have more than 15 students, repeat the scenarios in different groups.)

Scenario 1: Not in My Backyard!
Sides: Capital City and Smithville

Capital City is a growing metropolis that produces tons of garbage every week.
Recently their landfill used for their garbage became full, and city officials began
searching for a new site to put the garbage. The efficient option was to dump garbage
in an area near the small community of *Smithville*. Other options exist, but they
will cost much more and may result in more taxes – slowing Capital City's growth.
Smithville doesn't want to take Capital City's garbage. Capital City is prepared to
compensate residents of Smithville for having the garbage dump located near their
community.

Scenario 2: Water for Peace
Sides: Drylandia and Dustytown

Drylandia and *Dustytown* have been at war for many years. Drylandia captured and
has controlled a piece of Dustytown's territory for a long part of the war. In recent
peace negotiations, Dustytown has offered to stop fighting if Drylandia will give back
the piece of Dustytown's territory it controls. Drylandia would like to stop fighting, but
the piece of territory it controls contains a large aquifer, which Drylandia relies on to
provide its country with fresh water. The region the two countries are located in is
very dry, and fresh water is scarce.

Scenario 3: Family Planning
Sides: Government and Elders

The population of the country of Alagura has grown rapidly for the past 50 years, and
this has put a huge strain on Alagura's limited resources. Recently, the *Government*
of Alagura decided to offer free family planning services, in the hope of slowing
population growth. The plan immediately met resistance from a group of powerful
Elders, who believe it is against the deepest values of Alagurans to prevent people
from bringing more life into the world. Many Alagurans look to the Elders for moral
and ethical guidance, and many also rely on the Elders for help with food and
education for their children when times are tough.

To Fight or Not to Fight? Conflict Scenarios - Page 3

(Note: Each group of 3 students will need 3 strips with the same 3 scenarios. There are 5 strips, enough for 15 students. If you have more than 15 students, repeat the scenarios in different groups.)

Scenario 1: Right to Nuclear Power?
Sides: Ralcun and Celari

Ralcun and **Celari** share a border and have a history of fighting. The two countries have not fought a war for many years, but a recent announcement by Ralcun has raised tensions. Ralcun announced it intends to build a nuclear power plant for producing energy. Ralcun claims it has the right to build a nuclear power plant for peaceful purposes. Celari fears that Ralcun intends to use the plant to produce weapons. Celari has threatened to go to war with Ralcun if it continues with its plans to build a nuclear power plant.

Scenario 2: The Forest
Sides: Villagers and Tourism Company

In the country of Tropicio, there is a forest the **Villagers** depend on for fuel to cook their food and heat their homes. The local **Tourism Company** leads trips into the forest, where visitors come to see the rare trees and animals that live there. As the population of the village grows and people collect more and more wood for fuel, the forest is disappearing at a rapid rate. The Tourism Company is worried that the forest will soon be destroyed.

Scenario 3: Ethnicity and Power
Sides: Thalas and Zalas

The country of Izkara is populated by two ethnic groups: **Thalas** (the minority) and **Zalas** (the majority). Izkara has been ruled by its military for many years. Nearly all members of the military are from the minority Thalas ethnic group. Recently, the majority Zalas ethnic group has pressured the military government to step down, and asked for elections to be held. If fair elections are held, the Zalas will almost certainly come to power, since they are the majority. The Zalas have made it clear that if elections are not held soon, they will take up arms and fight a civil war against the military.

To Fight or Not to Fight? Conflict Scenarios - Page 4

(Note: Each group of 3 students will need 3 strips with the same 3 scenarios. There are 5 strips, enough for 15 students. If you have more than 15 students, repeat the scenarios in different groups.)

Scenario 1: Who Controls the Oil?
Sides: Residents and Government

Oil was recently discovered in a poor area of the country of Garanga. The **Residents** of the poor area were excited at first, since they expected money from the oil to help them achieve better lives. But after months went by, the Residents discovered that the money was going to the Garangan **Government**, which was not spending any of it on improving the lives of the Residents. Instead, the Government invested the money in Garanga's more wealthy areas in the city. Additionally, since the oil drilling began, water and air in the poor area have become more polluted. The Residents have threatened to start attacking the oil operations if they are not given money from the oil sales.

Scenario 2: Growing Pains
Sides: Burbists and Densers

More and more people have moved to Capital City looking for jobs, and soon there will not be enough housing for everyone to live there. **Burbists** want to build homes outside of Capital City, which they think is too noisy and dangerous. Many landowners are willing to sell their land to them to build on. **Densers** want to build taller apartment buildings within Capital City, and keep the land outside in its natural state. The Burbists, who give large amounts of money to provide services to the people of Capital City, recently threatened to move to another state if they are not allowed to build their homes where they want.

Scenario 3: A Holy Site
Sides: Plantians and Journeyans

The Temple of the Saint is located on top of a hill in a city holy to two religions. The **Plantians** believe that this site is where their prophet rested before walking up a stairway to heaven. The **Journeyans** believe this same site is where their ancient king saw a wheel in the sky that kept burning. The Plantians control the holy city but many Journeyans live there. Over the years, relations between the two religions have grown increasingly hostile. It is now so bad that both religions believe it is an insult to their values if the other side even sets foot in the Temple of the Saint. This tension recently led to violence when worshippers from the Journeyans and Plantians tried to enter the Temple at the same time.

© 2006 FACING THE FUTURE: PEOPLE AND THE PLANET   www.facingthefuture.org   © 2006 FACING THE FUTURE: PEOPLE AND THE PLANET   www.facingthefuture.org

To Fight or Not to Fight? Conflict Scenarios - Page 5

(Note: Each group of 3 students will need 3 strips with the same 3 scenarios. There are 5 strips, enough for 15 students. If you have more than 15 students, repeat the scenarios in different groups.)

Scenario 1: Who Owns the Forest?
Sides: Tribespeople and Government

The **Tribespeople** of Arborlandia have lived in the Big Forest for hundreds of years. Arborlandia is a poor country, and recently the **Government** decided that in order to raise money, it would start heavy logging in the Big Forest and sell the wood to people in the North. The Tribespeople have refused to leave the Big Forest, since it is their home and they do not believe the Government has the right to make them leave. The Government believes that selling wood from the Big Forest will bring in much needed income, which it will use to pay off debts and provide services to thousands of people in Arborlandia. The Government is willing to pay the Tribespeople some money to move out of the Big Forest.

Scenario 2: Intra-national Water Rights
Sides: Farmers and Fisherfolk

Farmers in the Country of Aguaville depend heavily on the Blue River for water for their crops, which they sell to support their families. **Fisherfolk** in Aguaville also depend on the Blue River for fish, which they sell to support their families. Due to a long period of dry weather, there is increasingly less water in the Blue River. With the Blue River running low, the Aguaville Fisherfolk worry there will be less fish if the farmers continue to use the same amount of water for their crops.

Scenario 3: Oil and Ethnicity
Sides: Bogians and Birdians

Augustus is a country split between a **Bogian** population in the North and a **Birdian** population in the South. The two populations have been fighting a civil war for many years over religious differences and competition for scarce farming land. Recently, a small reserve of oil was discovered in the middle of the country. Completely controlling the oil reserve would provide enough income for either side to win the civil war. Alternatively, the oil could also provide income to help rebuild the country if both sides could share, but there would need to be peace for this to happen. Many people on both sides believe that ending the war would mean admitting the other side had won. Finally, devoting land to drilling for oil will reduce the amount of already scarce farming land available to both Bogians and Birdians.

© 2006 FACING THE FUTURE: PEOPLE AND THE PLANET   www.facingthefuture.org

Lesson 35 Handout:
To Fight or Not to Fight? Conflict Resolution Worksheet

Group Member Names: _____

_____

Directions:
- In your group of 3, count off 1-3. Number 1 will mediate scenario 1, number 2 will mediate scenario 2, and number 3 will mediate scenario 3.
- The mediator will assign sides to the 2 other students.
- Each side will read, discuss, negotiate, and fill out 1 worksheet for each of the 3 scenarios. The mediator's job is to objectively help both sides reach a resolution through empathy and compromise – without giving up their vital interests.

1. Read your assigned scenario and write answers to the following questions:

I am (the **Side** you are representing): _____

My **Position** is (why you think you are right): _____

_____

My **Interests** are (what you want/need to get out of this negotiation): _____

_____

The **Interest(s)** I absolutely can't give up during negotiations are: _____

_____

I think the other side's **Interests** are (what you think the other side wants/needs):

_____

_____

2. Discuss the conflict. Tell the other side what your positions and interests are. The mediator should assist with the discussion, urging sides to practice empathy **(trying to understand the other side's position and interests) and** compromise **(giving up non-essential interests) to reach a resolution.**

_____

_____

_____

3. After your discussion and negotiation, briefly explain the resolution you reached (if any):

_____

_____

_____

Worldview Mingle

OVERVIEW

Students experience what it is like to stereotype and to be stereotyped based solely on brief identity descriptions (labels placed on students' backs) of people from particular backgrounds. The label identities are related to population, economic status, and the environment.

INQUIRY/CRITICAL THINKING QUESTIONS

- How do our own views of the world and cultural background affect how we view other people?
- How can we be aware of stereotyping people who are different from us?
- What are the disadvantages of stereotyping?
- What is "worldview" and how does it affect our actions?

OBJECTIVES

Students will:
- Experience what it is like to be labeled, judged, and stereotyped based solely on a brief description of their identity
- Consider how their own worldview shapes their perception of others
- Discuss and describe their experience of judging and being judged
- Discuss ways to be aware of and to shift their mental models and worldview

TIME REQUIRED: 30 minutes

KEY ISSUES/CONCEPTS

- **Cultural identity**
- **Stereotyping**
- **Worldview**

SUBJECT AREAS

- **Social Studies** (World Cultures, Geography, Global Studies, Contemporary World Problems)
- **Science** (Environmental)
- **Language Arts**

NATIONAL STANDARDS CONSISTENCY

- **NCSS: 1, 2, 3, 4, 5**
- **NSES: F**

GRADE LEVEL: 9–12

FTF Related Reading

- Intermediate: Chapter 9 from *Global Issues and Sustainable Solutions*
- Advanced: Unit 1, Chapter 3 and Unit 5, Chapter 4 from *It's All Connected*

Materials/Preparation

- Handout: *Worldview Mingle – Labels*, copy and cut so that you have 1 label for each student. (There are 21 labels so there may be more than 1 label with the same identity depending on the class size. If so, you can make up new labels.)
- Tape
- Because this activity explores the dynamics of cultural stereotyping, it can create some uncomfortable feelings for some students. Consider whether your students are mature enough to take part in the activity.

© 2006 FACING THE FUTURE: PEOPLE AND THE PLANET www.facingthefuture.org

Worldview Mingle

Activity

Steps

1. Tell students that they are going to have a mingling party, but before the party starts you will put an identification label on everybody's back. Tell them that they are not to look at their own label. During the party they are to walk around the room, read the label on a person's back, and talk to that person based on the label they read, focusing on their type of family (size, choices), their work and/or economic status, and their culture/place of origin. They should mingle and talk to as many people as they can.

2. The purpose is not to tell the other person his or her identity but, rather, to respond to each other's identity with questions, judgments, statements, etc. (You may want to model this for the students using one of the labels or one that you make up.)

3. Tape a label on the back of each student, making sure the student does not see what is written on his/ her own label.

4. Tell the students to start mingling. Encourage students to keep moving around the room and responding to each other's labels. You can also walk around the room, listen to the conversations, and participate in the activity.

5. After about 10 minutes, tell the students they can try to guess who they are based on the comments they have received. Encourage them to keep moving around the room responding to the labels and trying to figure out their own identities.

6. When you think most of the students have talked to everyone and/or figured out their own identity, have them sit in groups of 3-4. If there are students who have not yet figured out their identity, have the group tell them what it is.

7. Have students discuss in their group how it felt to be judged, and to judge, based solely on a label.

Worldview Mingle

8. Have the groups summarize their discussion to the whole class.
9. Conclude with the following reflection questions.

Assessment
Reflection Questions

For Intermediate and Advanced Students

- What surprised you about the responses you got and gave?
- Does this mirror the real world?
- Discuss the concept of "worldview" and how our own worldview influences the way we interact with others. Use the following ideas and questions to lead the discussion: "Worldview is to humans as water is to fish. It's the stuff we swim around in and don't even recognize. Think of fish in a bowl of water. They swim around and don't even think about the water around them. Worldview is our 'water', and many times we don't even realize we are surrounded by it until we step outside our own culture. Worldview is the lens through which we interpret the past and which helps determine our future. Worldview is what we believe is true about the world, but which other people in the world may not believe is true."
- Give students the following (or another personal) example of cultural worldview: "If you visited India, you might be shocked to see cows wandering around freely. That's because in the United States, cows are owned by farmers and ranchers and kept in pens. In India, however, cows are consider sacred and can roam freely. Before visiting India, you might have assumed that throughout the world cows are owned and kept contained – that would be your worldview. Here's another example of worldview: In the United States we have a strong focus on the 'individual' – your success is often based on what you have accomplished on your own. In some cultures your identity has more to do with your family or community, and therefore talking about what you have done or want to do may be considered rude."

© 2006 FACING THE FUTURE: PEOPLE AND THE PLANET   www.facingthefuture.org

Worldview Mingle

- Ask if any students have been somewhere (in or out of this country) where people had different ways of doing things that seemed strange or even wrong. What did they learn about themselves and others from the experience?

For Advanced Students

- How does our own worldview affect how we perceive others?
- How does understanding someone else's worldview help us understand him or her better?
- How do our actions reflect our own worldview?
- Does our worldview influence how we solve problems?
- How can we change our worldview if it no longer serves us well?
- What are some universal cultural characteristics that all humans have in common?

Lesson Extension

- Try this activity with other stereotype labels. For example, create labels focusing on a particular culture you are studying. Or create labels of common stereotypes in your school such as football player, surfer, cheerleader, punk, computer nerd, student member of gay/straight alliance, goth, etc.

Writing Connection

- Have students write a journal entry about their "different identity" experience. Or have them write a short story detailing the life of the person identified on their label, including enough details in the story to explain the person's worldview.

Technology Connection

- Have students do an Internet research project about people from a particular culture or nation, focusing on their views and beliefs about population, poverty, consumption, conflict, and environmental issues. Ideally, have students conduct an interview of someone from the culture or nation studied. Have them present their research findings and interview results to the class. Create a chart comparing the different views presented.

Action Projects

- Host a cultural fair at your school. Research the cultural history of your area through Internet research and interviews. Have students share their own stories or invite speakers into the classroom. Where did the people who live there come from? What new groups are arriving in your community? What cultures, traditions, and experience do they bring with them that help define your community? Identify organizations and resources in your community that work with immigrant and refugee populations and involve them in the fair.
- Visit **www.facingthefuture.org** and click on **Take Action** then **Fast Facts Quick Actions** for more information and action opportunities.

Additional Resources

Books

- *The Spirit Catches You and You Fall Down*, Anne Fadiman, Farrar, Straus and Giroux, 1998. This novel about the clash of 2 worldviews focuses on the story of a young Hmong girl with epilepsy and the conflict between the western doctors and the girl's family regarding her care.

© 2006 FACING THE FUTURE: PEOPLE AND THE PLANET   www.facingthefuture.org

© 2006 FACING THE FUTURE: PEOPLE AND THE PLANET   www.facingthefuture.org

Worldview Mingle Labels

U.S. married suburban mother of 3	CEO of Multinational Oil Company	U.S. single unemployed father of 2
Palestinian man from Gaza refugee camp	Married woman with no children	Immigrant farm worker in the U.S.
Iraq War veteran	U.S. unmarried teenage mother	Poor Pakistani mother with 6 children
Poor Ethiopian father of 5	U.S. homeless teenager	"Pro-life" activist
"Pro-choice" activist	Somalia woman with HIV/AIDS	Doctor who provides abortions
U.S. Real Estate Developer	Greenpeace (environmental) activist	Out-of-work logger
Yanomamo Indian from Brazil	Muslim exchange student in the U.S.	Guatemalan Rebel

Who Are the Nacirema?

OVERVIEW

Students read a short story about the body-related rituals of a cultural group called the Nacirema, and then use the same literary device employed in the original story to write their own short stories about rituals of the Nacirema. This writing exercise spurs a discussion on cultural awareness, assumptions, and worldviews.

INQUIRY/CRITICAL THINKING QUESTIONS

- How does our cultural worldview influence and inform our perception of people from other cultures?
- How can we be aware of and change our assumptions?
- How can we benefit from understanding our own cultural worldview and how it affects our relationships with other cultures?

OBJECTIVES

Students will:
- Identify and discuss a specific "cultural group" described in an anthropological study
- Write their own anthropological study on the same cultural group
- Discuss "cultural worldview" and how it informs different cultural perceptions and understanding between cultures

TIME REQUIRED: 1 hour

KEY ISSUES/CONCEPTS

- Cultural awareness and assumptions
- Worldview

SUBJECT AREAS

- **Social Studies** (World History, World Cultures, Geography, U.S. History, Global Studies)
- **Science** (Environmental)
- **Language Arts**

NATIONAL STANDARDS CONSISTENCY

- **NCSS: 1, 2, 3, 4, 5**
- **NSES: F**

GRADE LEVEL: 9–12

FTF Related Reading

- Intermediate: Chapter 9 from *Global Issues and Sustainable Solutions*
- Advanced: Unit 5, Chapter 4 from *It's All Connected*

Materials/Preparation

- Handout: *Body Ritual Among the Nacirema* by Horace Miner, 1 copy per student

Activity

Introduction

1. Choose a cultural group that the students will have some knowledge of and write it on the board or overhead. This could be a group of people they are currently studying, one that is in a piece of literature they are reading, or a cultural group that is currently in the news. Have the students brainstorm a list of what they know about this cultural group, focusing on specific cultural practices.

2. Tell the students that they are going to read an anthropological account of a cultural group.

Who Are the Nacirema?

Steps

1. Pass out the handout *Body Ritual Among the Nacirema* to each student and have them begin an aloud "read-around". Do not tell them that it is a fictional account.

2. After reading the first few paragraphs, stop and ask students if they are familiar with the cultural group described in the article. Ask those who are familiar to not reveal what they know about the Nacirema until the class has finished reading.

3. After reading, ask how many students now know who the Nacirema are. What made it hard to identify who they are? How does Minor's description of the Nacirema affect our ability to identify them? What are the techniques Minor uses to describe the Nacirema? (He uses a distinctly anthropological form of observation and writing called "ethnography", in which he merely reports what he observes without the benefit of understanding the culture he describes. It is as though he is from another planet)

4. Brainstorm other rituals of the Nacirema that might seem odd to someone from another culture or even from another planet (e.g. playing a particular sport, preparing and eating food, watching TV, shopping, going to a party, etc.)

5. Have the students write 1 or 2 paragraphs describing another "ritual of the Nacirema", either from the brainstorm list or one they think of on their own, using the same techniques Minor uses in his story.

© 2006 FACING THE FUTURE: PEOPLE AND THE PLANET   www.facingthefuture.org

Who Are the Nacirema?

6. Have students read their paragraphs to the class and have the class identify the ritual described.

7. Conclude with the reflection questions below.

Assessment
Reflection Questions

For Intermediate and Advanced Students

• Were you surprised when you figured out who the Nacirema were? (Americans)

• Explain why or why not.

• How does Body Ritual Among the Nacirema help us understand our own view of other cultures and how we are viewed by other cultures?

• Why do some of the practices and rituals of other cultures seem odd or foreign to us? How do our own cultural norms affect our understanding and perception of other cultures?

For Advanced Students

• What assumptions do we make about other cultures? What are some examples of practices in other cultures that we find odd and hard to understand? (e.g. arranged marriages, eating and preparing unusual foods, ritual body piercing, rites of passage)

• Go back to the brainstorm list created earlier about a specific cultural group. What are the assumptions in the list based upon? How does our own cultural worldview affect how we perceive this specific group?

• What techniques can we use to notice when we are making assumptions about others, and how can we avoid doing this?

Writing Connections

• Have students research a particular culture, focusing on the practices that might seem odd to someone from another culture, and exploring how assumptions drive our views and beliefs about that culture.

• Have students research and write about a particular practice or ritual from their own cultural background and present it to the class.

Action Projects

• Have the class write a play based on their paragraphs about the Nacirema and perform it for other classes.

• Work with the International Rescue Committee (or other similar organization in your area) to learn about resettled refugees in the U.S. Students can put together "welcome kits" for new refugees and orient them to the city. Invite refugee youth to your classroom to share their experience and culture.

• Visit **www.facingthefuture.org**, and click on **Take Action**, then **Fast Facts Quick Actions** for more information and action opportunities related to cultural diversity.

Additional Resources

Films

• *Koyaanisqatsi,* Godfrey Reggio, 1982, 87 minutes. The title is a Hopi Indian word meaning "life out of balance". The film is an apocalyptic vision of the collision of two different worlds – urban life and technology versus the environment.

Books

• *Zoom,* Istvan Banyai, Puffin Books, 1995. A wordless picture book that visually reveals different levels of perspective.

Websites

• **www.unesco.org** – United Nations Educational, Scientific and Cultural Organization (UNESCO). Click on Culture link for information and resources.

© 2006 FACING THE FUTURE: PEOPLE AND THE PLANET   www.facingthefuture.org

Body Ritual Among the Nacirema - Page 1

(Adapted from "Body Ritual Among the Nacirema" by Horace Miner, American Anthropologist Magazine 58(3), 1956, pp. 503–7)

The ritual of the Nacirema was first brought to the attention of anthropologists twenty years ago, but the culture of this people is still very poorly understood. They are a North American group living in the territory between the Canadian Cree, the Yaqui and Tarahumara of Mexico, and the Carib and Arawak of the Antilles. Little is known of their origin, although tradition states that they came from the east.

Nacirema culture is characterized by a highly developed market economy, which has evolved in a rich natural habitat. While much of the people's time is devoted to economic pursuits, a considerable portion of their day is spent in ritual activity. The focus of this activity is the human body, the appearance and health of which appear as a major concern in the people's belief. While such a concern is certainly not unusual, its ceremonial aspects and associated philosophy are unique.

The main belief underlying this ritual activity appears to be that the human body is ugly and that its natural tendency is to weakness and disease. Captive in such a body, man's only hope to avert these characteristics is through the use of ritual and ceremony. Every household has one or more shrines devoted to this purpose. The more powerful individuals in the society have several shrines in their houses and, in fact, the grandeur of a house is often referred to in terms of the number of such ritual centers it possesses.

The focal point of the shrine is a box or chest, which is built into the wall. In this chest are kept the many charms and magical potions without which no native believes he or she could live. These preparations are obtained from a variety of specialized practitioners. The most powerful of these are the medicine men, whose help must be rewarded with large gifts. However, the medicine men do not provide the potions for their clients, but decide what the ingredients should be and then write them down in an ancient and secret language. This writing is understood only by the medicine men and by the herbalists who, for another gift, provide the required charm.

Beneath the charm-box is a small font. Each day every member of the family enters the shrine room, bows his or her head before the charm-box, mingles different sorts of holy water in the font, and proceeds with a brief rite of cleansing. The holy waters are secured from the Water Temple of the community, where the priests conduct elaborate ceremonies to make the liquid ritually pure.

Body Ritual Among the Nacirema - Page 2

The medicine men have an imposing temple, or latipso, in every community of any size. The more elaborate ceremonies required to treat very sick patients can only be performed at this temple. These ceremonies involve not only the miracle-worker, but also a group of assistants who move quietly about the temple chambers in distinctive costume and head-dress. The latipso ceremonies are so harsh that a fair proportion of the really sick natives who enter the temple never recover. Despite this fact, sick adults are not only willing, but eager to undergo the long and drawn-out ritual purification, if they can afford to do so. No matter how ill or how grave the emergency, the guardians of many temples will not admit a client if he or she cannot offer a rich gift.

The Nacirema have an unrealistic horror of and fascination with the mouth, the condition of which is believed to have a supernatural influence on all social relationships. Were it not for the rituals of the mouth, they believe that their teeth would fall out, their gums bleed, their jaws shrink, and their friends desert them. They also believe that there is a strong relationship between oral and moral characteristics. For example, there is a ritual cleansing of the mouth for children, which is supposed to improve their moral character.

The daily body ritual includes a mouth-rite. This rite involves a practice which strikes the unfamiliar stranger as revolting. It was reported to me that the ritual consists of inserting a small bundle of hog hairs into the mouth, along with certain magical pastes, and then moving the bundle in a highly formalized series of gestures.

In addition to the private mouth-rite, the people seek out a holy-mouth-man once or twice a year. These practitioners have an impressive set of tools, consisting of a variety of augers, awls, probes, and prods. The use of these items in removing the evils of the mouth involves almost unbelievable ritual torture of the client. The holy-mouth-man opens the client's mouth and, using the abovementioned tools, enlarges any holes which decay may have created in the teeth. Magical materials are put into these holes. If there are no naturally occurring holes in the teeth, large sections of one or more teeth are gouged out so that the supernatural substance can be applied. In the Nacirema's view, the purpose of these religious functions is to arrest decay and to draw friends.

Our review of the ritual life of the Nacirema has certainly shown them to be a magic-ridden people. It is hard to understand how they have managed to exist so long under the burdens which they have imposed upon themselves.

Metaphors for the Future
(adapted from the lesson "Inventing the Future" by CPAWS Education, Alberta, Canada)

OVERVIEW
Students use metaphors describing different degrees of control we have over our future to explore how worldviews and mental models influence and shape our actions.

INQUIRY/CRITICAL THINKING QUESTIONS
- How do perception and worldview influence and shape our actions?
- How can we create the future that we want?

OBJECTIVES
Students will:
- Discuss and write about a pressing issue of the future from the perspective of a specific worldview
- Determine what metaphor best describes the student's view of the future
- Evaluate how different perspectives on our level of control over the future influence behavior and actions

TIME REQUIRED: 1 hour

KEY ISSUES/CONCEPTS
- **Metaphor**
- **Worldview**
- **Envisioning**

SUBJECT AREAS
- **Social Studies** (Geography, Civics/Government, Global Studies, Contemporary World Problems)
- **Science** (Environmental)
- **Language Arts**

NATIONAL STANDARDS CONSISTENCY
- **NCSS: 1, 2, 4, 6, 9, 10**
- **NSES: F, G**

GRADE LEVEL: 7–12

FTF Related Reading
- Intermediate: Chapter 9 from *Global Issues and Sustainable Solutions*
- Advanced: Unit 7 from *It's All Connected*

Materials/Preparation
- Handout: *Metaphors for the Future*
- The 4 metaphors of the future presented in this activity range from a perspective of pre-determinism to total self-determination. After analyzing a few critical issues from the perspective of 1 of these views of the future, students will have a chance to choose or create a metaphor that they feel best represents their own view of the future. One purpose of the activity is to allow students a chance to "see" the world through the eyes of someone else. Another purpose is to offer students a way to identify and form their own views of the future. Finally, students are encouraged to explore how different worldviews influence our actions and affect outcomes.

Activity
Introduction
1. Ask students to brainstorm some issues/problems/concerns that they feel humanity must address in the next 20 to 50 years (for example, the growing gap between the rich and poor, AIDS, or environmental degradation).
2. Tell students they are going to explore the future of some of these issues using several metaphors. You may need to define metaphor (i.e. a figure of speech in which one thing is described as if it were another, as in "Life is just a bowl of cherries.").

Metaphors for the Future

Steps

1. Arrange the class into at least 4 groups with no more than 5 students per group.

2. Assign each group 1 of the metaphors for the future from the handout, *Metaphors for the Future*. Do not have students share their view with the other groups.

3. In their groups, have the students read their metaphor together and then discuss and write a summary of how they would address 2 or 3 of the issues from the brainstorm list created in Step 1, as if they were a person who held the belief of their assigned metaphor. Have them discuss the positive and negative aspects of holding this view of the future. For example, the group with the metaphor that says "the future is a great roller coaster on a moonless night" might respond to the issue of AIDS by saying that there is nothing they can do about it and therefore they will choose to ignore this issue. A positive aspect of this view could be that they might not worry as much about this issue. The negative aspect of this view might be that the problem will persist and may eventually impact their lives even if they are not affected directly.

4. Have groups report to the class what their metaphor of the future is and describe their response to the issues.

5. After all of the metaphors and responses to the issues have been presented, have students choose which metaphor most closely represents their own view of the future and/or have students create a metaphor that describes their view of the future.

6. Have students share their chosen or newly created metaphor with a partner, and explain why they chose it.

7. Conclude with the following reflection questions.

Metaphors for the Future

Assessment
Reflection Questions

For Intermediate and Advanced Students

- Which metaphor was most popular? Which was least popular? Do you think this would hold true for most people? Which metaphor do you believe is most widely held by people in your family, school, community, and nation?

- Do you believe that people's actions are influenced by their views of the world and the future? Explain why or why not.

- Explain how you might act differently if you perceive that you have control over your future.

For Advanced Students

- Explain the underlying values and attitudes that led to your choice. For example, how do beliefs and values about fate (pre-determination) and freedom (self-determination) affect our perceptions?

- Which metaphor do you think someone would choose if he or she was a villager in India, a single mother in sub-Saharan Africa, a Palestinian refugee, a Chicago banker, or a homeless child in Brazil? What effect might their view of the world have on the way our future turns out?

- What will you need to implement your own metaphor or view of the future? For example, if you chose a ship on the ocean, what tools and information would you need to navigate the water?

Writing Connection

- Have students research a specific culture focusing on that culture's "worldview". Have them present and compare their findings.

Art Connection

- Have students make a collage display depicting the worldview and values of their culture.

Action Projects

- Adopt a school or classroom of younger students and do the Metaphors for the Future activity with them. Compare the differences between younger students' impressions of the future and older students'. Visit your adopted school or classroom once every month to do activities that address different global issues.

- Visit **www.facingthefuture.org** and click on **Take Action** for more information and action opportunities on a variety of global and local issues.

Additional Resources

Books

- *Ishmael (1992) and My Ishmael (1998)*, Daniel Quinn, Bantam/Turner. Ishmael, a gorilla rescued from a traveling show who has learned to reason and communicate, uses these skills to educate himself in human history and culture. Ishmael lays out a theory of what has gone wrong with human civilization and how to correct it – a theory based on the tenet that humanity belongs to the planet rather than vice versa. In the sequel, My Ishmael, Quinn focuses on the "Leavers" and "Takers", his terms for the two basic, warring elements of human sensibility.

© 2006 FACING THE FUTURE: PEOPLE AND THE PLANET   www.facingthefuture.org

Lesson 38 Handout:
Metaphors for the Future

1. The Future is a Great Roller Coaster on a Moonless Night.

It exists, twisting ahead of us in the dark, but we can only see the track that is just ahead. We are locked in our seats, and nothing we may know or do will change the course that is laid out for us. In other words, the future is predetermined and there is nothing we can do about it.

2. The Future is a Huge Game of Dice.

It is entirely random and subject only to chance. For example, a woman misses a plane by a few seconds and avoids dying when the plane crashes. Since everything is chance, all we can do is play the game, pray to the gods of fortune, and enjoy what luck comes our way. In other words, the future is totally random and we do not know how or if our actions make a difference.

3. The Future is a Great Ship on the Ocean.

We can travel freely upon it and there are many possible routes and destinations. There will always be some outside forces, such as currents, storms, and reefs, to be dealt with, but we still have the choice to sail our ship where we want to go. In other words, we can choose whatever future we want if we are willing to work with a purpose and within the knowledge and constraints of outside forces.

4. The Future is a Blank Sheet of Paper.

It is there for us to fill in with our actions and decisions in the present. If we choose the future we want and spend our daily lives trying to make it happen, it will probably materialize. If we leave it to the powers-that-be to decide upon and plan the future, we will have a very different kind of future—one dominated by the powerful. In other words, we have control over our future if we choose to act on it.

Deep Space 3000

OVERVIEW

Use this collaborative activity to help students envision and create a sustainable environment through the design of a "closed-system" spaceship that will be in outer space for 3,000 years, and then bring healthy and happy future generations back to Earth.

INQUIRY/CRITICAL THINKING QUESTIONS

- What is a "closed-system" and what are the ramifications of living in a closed versus open system?
- How can we create a sustainable environment capable of supporting everyone's physical, social, cultural, and political needs over an extended period of time?

OBJECTIVES

Students will:
- Identify the components necessary for human survival, how they are connected, and how to meet those needs in a closed environment
- Draw and list components of a sustainable "closed-system" spaceship that meets human needs
- Discuss the connection and application of their spaceship design to planet Earth
- Design and write about sustainable solutions

TIME REQUIRED: 2 hours

KEY ISSUES/CONCEPTS
- **Sustainable solutions**

SUBJECT AREAS
- **Social Studies** (Geography, Global Studies)
- **Science** (Environmental, Life, Physical)

NATIONAL STANDARDS CONSISTENCY
- **NCSS:** 2, 3, 5, 6, 7, 8, 9
- **NSES:** C, E, F

GRADE LEVEL: 7–10

FTF Related Reading
- Intermediate: Chapter 9 from *Global Issues and Sustainable Solutions*
- Advanced: Unit 7 from *It's All Connected*

Materials/Preparation
- Butcher paper, 1 sheet per group
- Marking pens, colored, 5–6 pens per group
- Handout, *Deep Space 3000*, 1 per student

Activity
Steps
1. Read the following scenario to the students: Your group is on a mission with the United Nations. The Earth's ecosystems have been severely damaged and are unable to support life. Your task is to outfit a spaceship that will be away for 3,000 years, and will bring future generations back to Earth alive, healthy, and happy. Assume that on its initial departure from Earth, the spaceship will have a crew of about 1,000 people. The ship will have an orbit around the sun similar to that of Earth's orbit. It will have big windows, and can be as large as you want it to be, within reason. You may bring items with you when your ship leaves Earth, but you may not get any more items once you leave. Once you depart, the ship is a "closed-system", which means that you

Deep Space 3000

cannot use anything from outside the ship – except for solar energy – nor can you remove anything from the ship except heat. You are allowed to use only today's technology, but should assume that the technical construction of the ship is already figured out.

2. Explain the following directions to the class:
   - You will need to address the following in your spaceship design: oxygen, food, fresh water, energy, waste disposal, governance, entertainment, and quality of life (Note: you may want to list these on the board or overhead).
   - Think about the kinds of products, services, and expertise you want to bring.
   - There are no wrong answers, but you will have to explain why you chose what you did, and how it meets the needs of the community. Remember, it is a 3,000-year voyage and you are responsible for your own well-being, and for that of hundreds of generations after you.

3. Arrange students in groups of 4 or 5, and give each group 1 handout, *Deep Space 3000*, 1 sheet of butcher paper, and a set of pens.

4. Using the handout, have each group begin by brainstorming and listing the material and nonmaterial needs of the crew, and what is necessary to meet those needs. Prompts: How do you ensure that you can grow food for 3,000 years? What are the difficulties in producing different products, such as vegetables, exotic fruits, meat, etc.? How will you provide fresh air and drinking water? What form of energy will produce the least waste and is both nontoxic and renewable? How are you handling waste? Is it possible to find ways to use "waste" for other purposes? How will you ensure the crew's physical and mental health? What

kinds of social interaction will you have? How will you entertain yourselves? What type of governance and community rules are necessary to maintain order and solve problems together?

5. After groups have completed their brainstorm and decided on the essential pieces, have them draw a picture of the spaceship, list the contents, show how the various parts relate to each other, and list any rules, community agreements, governance systems, and other nonmaterial aspects they decide on.

6. When the design process is complete, have each group report to the class on their spaceship. Ask them to explain what they identified as essential needs, how they designed the ship to meet those needs, and what issues they might encounter in the future (such as population growth, education, old age, etc.).

7. Conclude with the following reflection questions.

Assessment
Reflection Questions

For Intermediate and Advanced Students

- What did other groups provide for that your group neglected?
- What need was most difficult to meet?
- What characteristics of the Earth let us know that it is also a closed system, like the spaceship (e.g. finite amounts of land, water, and other resources, and a limited ability to absorb wastes)?
- How is the Earth different from your spaceship (e.g. Earth has more species diversity, it is larger, etc.)?
- How well did the group process work? How did you make decisions (majority-rule, consensus, etc.)? Were you able

Deep Space 3000

to come up with creative solutions? Did everyone participate? What can we learn about decision-making processes from this activity?

For Advanced Students

- Why do we sometimes act as though the Earth is not a closed system (such as dumping wastes into oceans, harvesting fish or forests faster than they can renew, and continuing exponential population growth)? What are the ultimate consequences of such actions in a closed system?

- What kinds of rules or government did you decide on? How did you deal with human rights? Would it be acceptable if half of the population did most of the work, but received less education and fewer resources? How would you address that inequity? How does this compare to human rights and women's rights on Earth?

Writing Connection

- Have students do a research project and report back on sustainable design features (such as solar energy, waste recycling, and water purification) included in their spaceship design. Students can then redesign their spaceship based on the research conducted. Have students include how these technologies and practices might be beneficial to address global issues on Earth. Students can send their final research papers (or a summary letter) to an elected official or person working in a relevant field.

Action Projects

- Do "Project Greenstar", a Service Learning project in which students conduct market research for communities in developing countries that are using solar technology to produce crafts. Students' research will help poor communities support themselves through the use of sustainable energy

sources. Visit **www.facingthefuture.org** and click on **Take Action**, and then **Service Learning Projects** for everything you need to get started on this project.

- Translate the spaceship analogy to your school by doing a comprehensive review of the sustainability of your school as a "closed system". How does your school use energy? What are the sources of energy used in the school? How much waste does the school produce? Does the school recycle? What type of food services are provided on campus and what are the impacts associated with that food? What policies does the school have for procurement of services and supplies? Based on students' research, have them make recommendations to the school board about how the school community could be more sustainable.

Additional Resources

Films

- *Cities* (from the "Reinventing the World" video series), directed by David Springbett and Heather MacAndrew, Bullfrog Films, 2000, 50 minutes. Focusing on large and diverse cities around the world, this documentary explores the question of how we can live sustainably, given human growth and resource scarcity.

Websites

- **www.bfi.org** – The concept of Spaceship Earth was first developed by the architect, engineer, mathematician, and poet, Buckminster Fuller. The Buckminster Fuller Institute serves a global network of design science innovators "to make the world work for 100% of humanity in the shortest possible time through spontaneous cooperation without ecological offense or the disadvantage of anyone."

© 2006 FACING THE FUTURE: PEOPLE AND THE PLANET   www.facingthefuture.org

Lesson 39 Handout:
Deep Space 3000

Name: _____

Human Needs	How You Will Address These Needs in Your Spaceship Design
Food	
Water	
Air/Oxygen	
Energy	
Waste Disposal	
Governance	
Community Rules	
Entertainment	
Quality of Life	
Other Needs	

Creating Our Future

OVERVIEW

How do we create a just and humane world for ourselves and for future generations? Help students identify and plan what they want their future to look like. Using an action-planning model, students visualize their desired future, identify objectives, develop a plan to address local and global issues, and implement their vision through action and service learning.

INQUIRY/CRITICAL THINKING QUESTIONS

- How do we envision and create a world we want for ourselves and for future generations?
- What unmet needs exist in our local and global communities?
- How do we identify structural solutions to global issues?
- How can we work together to plan a course of action?

OBJECTIVES

Students will:
- Visualize the future they desire
- Collaborate with their peers
- Identify issues they want to address, and identify and prioritize objectives
- Present their findings

TIME REQUIRED: 1.5 hours

1.5 hours for initial lesson; additional class time for implementing the action plan. Whereas the 1.5 hour lesson can be completed in isolation, ideally, students will have time to research their issues through community interviews, the Internet and books, develop their plans fully, and implement their projects.

KEY ISSUES/CONCEPTS

- **Creating a vision**
- **Identifying local and global issues**
- **Action/project planning**
- **Personal and structural solutions**

SUBJECT AREAS

- **Social Studies** (World History, World Cultures, Geography, U.S. History, Civics/Government, Economics, Global Studies, Contemporary World Problems)
- **Science** (Earth, Environmental, Life, Physical)

NATIONAL STANDARDS CONSISTENCY

- **NCSS: 2, 4, 5, 6, 10**
- **NSES: C, F, G**

GRADE LEVEL: 5–12

FTF Related Reading

- Intermediate: Chapters 1 and 9 from *Global Issues and Sustainable Solutions*
- Advanced: Unit 1, Chapter 1-3 and Unit 7, Chapter 1-3 from *It's All Connected*

Materials/Preparation

- Handout/Overhead: *Action Planning Worksheet*, 1 per group of 3-4 students, and make an overhead
- Butcher paper, 1 sheet per group
- Marking pens, colored, 1 set per group

© 2006 FACING THE FUTURE: PEOPLE AND THE PLANET   www.facingthefuture.org

Creating Our Future

Activity

Introduction

1. Ask students what they think the world will look like 20 years from now. Have 2 or 3 students briefly describe the future as if it were a picture (they may paint a picture of environmental, social, and economic destruction).

2. Now ask them what they want the world to look like in 20 years for themselves and for future generations (Note: you may need to define the difference between *think* and *want* for this part of the activity). Ask, "If this is the future we want, how do we make it happen?" Ask them to describe what they will see, hear, smell, taste, and touch. Explain that in order to create a world we want for ourselves and for future generations, we need to first envision what we want and then create a plan of action. This activity provides a model for doing just that.

Steps

1. Explain that, in order to help focus their vision of the future, it is helpful to think about specific quality-of-life issues that are important to them. Brainstorm and list quality-of-life issues (these may include all or some of the following):

Food	Transportation	Elder care
Water	Education	Child care
Housing	Environment	Recreation
Energy	Security	Spirituality/ Religion
Employment	Healthcare	Entertainment/ Art

2. (Optional) Have students do a 5-minute "free write" describing their vision of the world in 20 years, addressing some or all of the quality-of-life issues identified in the brainstorming exercise. Give them the prompt: "In my vision of the future..." Encourage students to focus on what they want the future to be like, not what they do not want it to be like. For example, rather than saying, "In the future, people will not use polluting fossil fuels," say, "In the future we will use clean, renewable energy sources." Tell them to provide as much detail as possible in describing their vision. Have students read aloud 1 or 2 sentences from their free writes or have them share in pairs.

3. Explain that they will develop an "action plan" to address 1 of the quality-of-life issues in the list (such as food, water, health care, the environment, etc.) using a model called an "Action Planning Sequence". Through this process, they will assess how the issue affects both local and global communities, and develop a plan to address the structural causes of the issue.

4. Give each student a copy of the handout, *Action Planning Worksheet*, and show the overhead of the same worksheet. Explain each step of the action planning process to the students, using the overhead as a guide.

5. Divide the class into groups of 3 or 4. Assign, or have each group choose, a topic from the list of issues. Give each group a piece of butcher paper and pens.

6. Give them about 20–30 minutes to follow the steps outlined in the handout. They should begin by discussing and agreeing upon a shared vision. Circulate the room and assist students as they are working.

7. After they complete the handout, have each group transfer the information to a piece of butcher paper. Encourage them to include pictures, graphs, quotes, etc.

8. Have each group present their displays to the class.

9. Bring the class back together for reflection questions.

Creating Our Future

Assessment
Reflection Questions

For Intermediate and Advanced Students

- Does describing what you want your future to look like help you realize it? How and why is this an important step in creating a world we want?
- Did the action sequence process work? How could the process be improved?
- How well did you work together in your groups? Did everyone participate? How did you make decisions?
- What will you do next to implement your plan?

For Advanced Students

- In what other circumstances could you use this action planning process?
- Once you have taken action on an issue, it changes the dynamics of the issue by producing unintended consequences or by revealing new solutions. What can you do next to address this issue and work toward your vision?

Creating Our Future

Writing Connection

- Have students write a letter to an influential entity (government agency, newspaper, etc.) and /or a family member or friend explaining their vision and outlining the steps to realizing it.

Art Connection

- Have students create a mural at the school (or as part of a local community development project) depicting their collective vision of the future.

Action Projects

- Have the class choose 1 topic, refine the action plan for that topic, implement it as a class project, and do a service learning project that addresses the issues.
- Show students your local community's comprehensive plan (available through the city or county planning department) and have the students compare it with their action plans.
- Have the class develop an action project database of local opportunities for youth by researching issues, identifying and contacting organizations, and publishing the information on a website, in the local media, through school networks, etc.
- Have each student commit to taking steps to make their vision of the future a reality by completing the **Facing the Future Pledge** on page 22.
- Visit **www.facingthefuture.org** and click on **Take Action** for more information and action opportunities on global and local issues.

Additional Resources

Films

- *Pay it Forward,* Mimi Leder, 2000, 123 minutes. Feature film about a young boy who attempts to make the world a better place.

Books

- *The Lemming Dilemma: Living with Purpose, Leading with Vision*, David Hutchens, Pegasus Communications, 2000. A charming story about a lemming's quest for meaning, aspiration, and value.

- *The Complete Guide to Service Learning,* Cathryn Berger Kaye, **www.freespirit.com**, 2004. A wealth of activities, ideas, and resources to encourage service learning in K-12 and higher education.

- *The Kid's Guide to Social Action,* Barbara A. Lewis, **www.greenfeet.com/kidguidtosoc.html**, This empowering book includes everything kids need to make a difference in the world: step-by-step directions for writing letters, doing interviews, raising funds, getting media coverage, and more.

Websites

- **www.facingthefuture.org** – For information, research, and website resources on service learning, and a framework for developing service learning projects in your classroom.

© 2006 FACING THE FUTURE: PEOPLE AND THE PLANET   www.facingthefuture.org

Lesson 40 Handout:
Creating Our Future
Action Planning Worksheet - Page 1

Group members:

_____

_____

Issue we are focusing on:

_____

_____

Scope of the Issue
Who or what is currently being affected by this issue?

_____

_____

How does this issue affect our local community?

_____

_____

How does this issue affect our global community?

_____

_____

_____

Visualize Desired Outcome
Brainstorm, discuss, and write a summary of the desired outcome for our specific issue:

_____

_____

_____

_____

Gather Companions
What is already being done to effect change on this issue? Brainstorm, discuss, and list the people and organizations that share a similar vision and can help us meet our vision:

_____

_____

_____

_____

© 2006 FACING THE FUTURE: PEOPLE AND THE PLANET   www.facingthefuture.org

Lesson 40 Handout:
Creating Our Future
Action Planning Worksheet - Page 2

Identify and Prioritize Objectives

What are the steps or parts that will lead to our vision? What does the vision look like? For example, if the vision is "full access to health care for all people," then the objectives might be more doctors per person, more clinics in poor neighborhoods, or more reproductive health care. Discuss, list, and prioritize 2 or 3 objectives that will lead to our vision.

_____

_____

_____

What are some specific things that will need to occur in order to realize our vision and to be sure that we are addressing structural solutions to the issue?

_____

_____

_____

Identify Obstacles

Discuss who or what might get in the way of realizing our vision. List a few obstacles and include ways we might address them:

_____

_____

_____

Identify Resources

What resources will we need to get our vision going? Is it information, money, time? How will we use these resources? Discuss and list information, resources, and other help we will need to realize our vision:

_____

_____

_____

Implement Action Plan and Follow Up

What steps will we take to start working on our vision? Who will be responsible for implementing each step? List the steps we will take to start implementing our vision:

_____

_____

_____

Keep the vision in mind and keep telling the story of the future you desire!

Photo Credits

© 2006 FACING THE FUTURE: PEOPLE AND THE PLANET   www.facingthefuture.org